Communication Technologies

Dennis O. Gehris, Ed.D.

Bloomsburg University
Bloomsburg, Pennsylvania

Linda F. Szul, Ed.D.

Indiana University of Pennsylvania
Indiana, Pennsylvania

Prentice
Hall

Upper Saddle River, New Jersey 07458

Library of Congress Cataloging-in-Publication Data

Gehris, Dennis.
    Communication technologies / Dennis O. Gehris.
        p. cm.
    Includes index.
    ISBN 0-13-040024-6
    1. Telecommunication.   2. Information technology.   I. Title.

TK5101 .G36 2002
621.382—dc21   2001021507

Executive Editor: Elizabeth Sugg
Production Editor: Linda Zuk, WordCrafters Editorial Services, Inc.
Production Liaison: Eileen O'Sullivan
Director of Manufacturing and Production: Bruce Johnson
Managing Editor: Mary Carnis
Manufacturing Buyer: Cathleeen Petersen
Art Director: Cheryl Asherman
Cover Design Coordinator: Miguel Ortiz
Cover Design: Joe Sengotta
Cover Illustration: Guy Crittenden, SIS/Images.com
Marketing Manager: Timothy Peyton
Editorial Assistant: Anita Rhodes
Composition: Publishers' Design and Production Services, Inc.
Printing and Binding: Von Hoffmann Press

Prentice-Hall International (UK) Limited, *London*
Prentice-Hall of Australia Pty. Limited, *Sydney*
Prentice-Hall Canada Inc., *Toronto*
Prentice-Hall Hispanoamericana, S.A., *Mexico*
Prentice-Hall of India Private Limited, *New Delhi*
Prentice-Hall of Japan, Inc., *Tokyo*
Prentice-Hall Pte. Ltd., Singapore
Editora Prentice-Hall do Brasil, Ltda., *Rio de Janeiro*

10 9 8 7 6 5 4 3 2 1
ISBN 0-13-040024-6

To my wife Deborah,
who provided loving support
during the writing and editing process.

D. G.

To my husband John and
my children Kristie and Mike,
who are my greatest supporters
in all of my endeavors.

L. F. S.

Brief Contents

Contents

Preface

Communication Technologies presents a thorough introduction to the fast-paced world of end-user communication technology and telecommunications. End users are those persons within organizations who represent the final or ultimate users of computer systems and use hardware and software after it has been fully developed and marketed. End users are unlike computer programmers and engineers, who utilize their high levels of technical expertise to develop and test computer systems. Communication technology is the area of end-user computing that affects everyone. No one can work in today's highly technical office environment without knowledge of the fundamentals of electronic mail, voice processing, teleconferencing, wireless communication, networking, and related technologies.

■ INTENDED AUDIENCE

Communication Technologies is intended for use as a college textbook for end-user communication technologies and telecommunications application courses usually found in the office information systems and computer information systems disciplines. Specific applicable courses might include those with such titles as Communication Technologies, Telecommunications, Communication Hardware, or Information Systems Hardware.

■ ORGANIZATION OF THE BOOK

The book consists of 15 chapters arranged as follows: Part One, Communication Technology: Introduction, History, and Future; Part Two, Communication Technology Applications; Part Three, The Internet and Intranets; and Part Four, Networking Fundamentals. Each chapter begins with a brief description of the chapter and a What You Will Learn section, which provides specifics of the chapter content. Each chapter ends with Questions, Projects and Problems, and Vocabulary. A glossary, which includes all the terms in the Vocabulary sections, is provided at the end of the book. Chapters are organized as follows:

- *Chapter 1: Introduction to Communication Technology.* An introduction to the concept of communication technology is presented and related terminology is defined.
- *Chapter 2: History and Future of Communication Technology.* A discussion of the major historical events in communication technologies is provided, which serves as a foundation for understanding the present state of communication technologies.
- *Chapter 3: Electronic Mail.* An introduction to electronic mail (e-mail) is presented as a major communication technology application.
- *Chapter 4: Teleconferencing.* A discussion of the evolution of teleconferencing; teleconferencing applications; types of teleconferencing systems; benefits and drawbacks of teleconferencing; and how to plan, conduct, and evaluate a teleconference is provided.
- *Chapter 5: Voice Processing and Facsimile.* The functions, applications, benefits, and drawbacks of voice-processing and facsimile technologies are presented.
- *Chapter 6: Wireless Communications.* Wireless communications as it pertains to pagers, cellular phones, global location/navigation systems, and handheld computers is discussed.
- *Chapter 7: Telecommuting and Electronic Data Interchange.* An introduction to telecommuting and electronic data interchange (EDI) as additional communication technology applications is provided.
- *Chapter 8: Introduction to the Internet and Intranets.* Various aspects relating to the Internet, including its history and uses, Internet addressing, connections, and protocols are covered. In addition, an explanation of intranets and how they are used, and what the future holds for the Internet and intranets are part of this chapter.
- *Chapter 9: Electronic Mail Discussion Groups and Newsgroups.* The use of electronic mail discussion groups and newsgroups is covered. Specifically, the chapter deals with finding, subscribing, unsubscribing, and communicating when using e-mail discussion groups, as well as how to use newsgroups.
- *Chapter 10: World Wide Web.* A description of the World Wide Web and a discussion of how information is accessed is provided. Also described are the features and types of Web browsers, how they are used, and how information is found.
- *Chapter 11: Creating Web Pages.* An examination of how Web browsers use hypertext markup language (HTML) to process information is provided. The basic HTML tags are presented, as well as instructions for using the FrontPage Express editor to create Web pages.
- *Chapter 12: Additional Internet Utilities.* The following Internet utilities are presented in this chapter: telnet, gopher, Archie and FTP search engines, and file transfer protocol. A definition is provided for each tool, as well as an explanation of how each tool is used.

- *Chapter 13: Introduction to Networks.* An introduction to networks and coverage of the following topics are included: types of networks, transmissions, and network media.
- *Chapter 14: Telecommunication Models and Network Connectivity.* Telecommunication models are discussed, as well as network topology, protocols, and methods for connecting networks.
- *Chapter 15: Telephony.* Voice communication technology, including a discussion of telephone circuits and the ways that computer and telephone technologies are being integrated, is presented.

■ OEIS CURRICULUM MODEL

The Organizational Systems Research Association (OSRA), formerly the Office Systems Research Association, "is a professional organization chartered for the purpose of pursuing research and education in the area of information technology and end-user information systems." OSRA provides a platform for dedicated professionals to meet and exchange ideas in the pursuit of excellence.

In 1996, a dedicated team of information systems academics and practitioners worked together to address the need for collegiate preparation of people who have skills related to the following: information systems developer, troubleshooter, change agent, trainer, systems evaluator, or savvy business person. This group developed a four-year model curriculum entitled Organizational and End-User Information Systems (OEIS).

The OEIS model curriculum underscores the notion that information systems at the desktop level are crucial to support organizational goals as well as to bolster and sustain employees' needs to do their jobs well and grow in their careers. It is intended to bring the impact of high-level talk about business reengineering to the practical level of implementation at the desktop, where it counts most. Increasingly, the end user, the person who actually uses systems in daily work activities, plays a variety of roles in systems needs assessment, design, implementation, and evaluation.

The curriculum model is designed to challenge students to understand their information systems role from an organizational viewpoint, the perspectives and needs of the people they support, and technologies used or accessed at the desktop. The curriculum is the result of group collaboration and its innovativeness has been acknowledged by the academic community, students, and the business communities. Following are the 11 courses in the OEIS model.

OEIS-1   Organizational and End-User Information Systems Concepts
OEIS-2   End-User Technology Solutions
OEIS-3   Organizational and End-User Information Systems Planning and Design
OEIS-4   Organizational and End-User Information Systems Implementation and Evaluation

OEIS-5   Designing and Managing Organizational Training
OEIS-6   Communications Technologies
OEIS-7   Cases in Organizational and End-User Information Systems
OEIS-8   Information and Media Management
OEIS-9   Special Topics
OEIS-10   Business Process Redesign
OEIS-11   Internship in Organizational and End-User Information Systems

Course OEIS-6 provides a technical overview of electronic communication systems, including a strong foundation in local area network (LAN) management, Internet resources, and telecommunications and video technologies. Upon completion of this course, students should be able to:

- Demonstrate an understanding of the vocabulary of telecommunications
- Select telecommunication solutions to address identified problems
- Demonstrate effective LAN management
- Demonstrate effective use of online telecommunication services
- Determine effective use of a wide range of telecommunication technologies
- Discuss effective application of emerging communication technologies

This book is designed to serve the specific needs of course OEIS-6 in the OEIS curriculum.

■ SUPPLEMENTARY AIDS

An instructor's CD-ROM contains lesson plans, solutions, and PowerPoint slides for each chapter. A test bank is also provided. A companion Web site is available at http://www.prenhall.com/gehris.

Acknowledgments

The authors wish to acknowledge those who contributed to the successful completion of this book. Thanks go to the technical reviewers: Marilyn R. Chalupa, Associate Professor, Business Education & Office Administration Department, College of Business, Ball State University, Muncie, Indiana; Tena B. Crews, Assistant Professor of Management/Business Systems, Richards College of Business, State University of Business, Carrollton, Georgia; Albert Fundaburk, Assistant Professor, Business Education & Office Information Systems Department, Bloomsburg University, Bloomsburg, Pennsylvania; and Walter H. Person, Jr., Instructor, Information Systems Technology, Central Carolina Community College, Sanford, North Carolina. All of them provided valuable suggestions on the content of the book.

Special thanks go to Brian McCarthy and Sheri Ashman, graduate assistants in the Department of Business Education and Office Information Systems at Bloomsburg University. Brian and Sheri assisted in the preparation of chapter questions, solutions, lesson plans, PowerPoint slides, test bank questions, and the companion Web site.

PART ONE

Communication Technology: Introduction, History, and Future

This part of the book provides an introduction to communication technology, a brief description of important events in the development of communication technology, as well as an analysis of predictions for the future.

Introduction to Communication Technology

I n this chapter you are introduced to the concepts of communication technology and telecommunications. The characteristics of effective communication are discussed, together with technology's role in communication, the benefits and drawbacks of using technology in communication, and careers in communication technologies.

WHAT YOU WILL LEARN

- Definitions of communication technology and telecommunications
- How the communications model operates
- Characteristics of effective communication: completeness, conciseness, consideration, clarity, courtesy, and correctness
- The role of technology in communications
- Benefits of using technology in communications
- Drawbacks of using technology in communications
- Career paths in communication technology

CHAPTER 1

■ DEFINITION OF TERMS

We live in an era that has been described as the *information age*, a time when great volumes of information are available to those who know how to access it. This time period could also be described as the *communication age* because we are learning new ways of communicating and sharing this information with one another. These new methods are described in detail in this book.

Communication is an integral part of every business today. Effective communication is not only expected, it is essential to any business's continued existence. There are several reasons for this. The most obvious is that without good communication, businesses would not be capable of competing successfully in today's business world. Because many businesses have downsized their workforce and adopted other cost-saving measures, effective communication is more important than ever. Employees are given more responsibilities and must complete their assigned tasks in less time. Effective communication helps them to accomplish this.

For purposes of discussion, two terms must be defined before we begin. As you will see, they are related and may be used interchangeably.

- *Communication technology.* **Communication technology** is the application and use of technology—computers, software, other electronic devices, and accompanying media and procedures—to make communication more effective than through using traditional means of communication that do not utilize technology. Computers are machines that can be programmed to perform complex and repetitive procedures quickly, precisely, and reliably and can quickly store and retrieve large amounts of data. Software represents the logical instructions executed by a computer, usually stored on a magnetic disk or on electronic devices that utilize electrical components such as transistors.
- *Telecommunications.* **Telecommunications** is defined as "communications via electronic, electromagnetic, or phontonic means over a distance" (Carr and Snyder, 1997, p. 6). The term *electromagnetic* refers to a rapidly varying (high-frequency) current used to carry telecommunication signals and *phontonic* refers to the use of light as a medium. The Greek *tele* means "at a distance." Therefore, literally, telecommunication is communication over a distance. However, modern telecommunications assumes that you are utilizing technology while communicating.

To gain an understanding of how data (information) moves over a telecommunication channel, one can view telecommunications in terms of conduit, context, and content. The *conduits* are the physical paths that telecommunications signals use to move from place to place and are sometimes referred to as *media*. The various types of conduits of data include twisted-wire pair, coaxial cable, microwave, fiber, satellite, and cellular. The *contexts* are the format that the telecommunication signals assume, depending on the type of message and the objectives of the communication. The various types of contexts include voice, data, images, pictures, audio, and video. Finally, the *content* is the end result of telecommunications; that is, what the receiver of the communication finds after the communication has completed its path from sender to receiver. Some possible contents include e-mail, hard-copy documents, maps, live radio, movie clips and recorded sound clips.

■ THE COMMUNICATIONS MODEL

To send data over a distance, you must have a *sender* (the *source*), a communications medium and telecommunications channel, and a *receiver* (the *destination*). This is often depicted as a **communications model** (see Figure 1-1).

In the case of voice communications, the sender, who has an idea or information that he or she wants to send, encodes it into speech and transmits it over the air, which serves as the channel. The receiver must receive the message from the air, decode (or interpret) the words, and receive the idea or information. While this process is occurring, there is the chance that *noise* (or *interference*) will be encountered. This could be external noise (such as traffic or construction noise) which may prevent the sender and/or receiver from encoding or decoding the idea or information accurately. Unrelated ideas or information (another type of noise) could cause the sender or receiver to fail to concentrate in a manner that is necessary for good communication.

In certain telecommunications systems in which technology is being used to accomplish the communications process, the medium might consist of wire, optical fibers, or radio waves. Noise often consists of some type of electrical interference (e.g., the "crackling" sound on a telephone line). Alterna-

The Communication Model

Figure 1-1
Communications Model

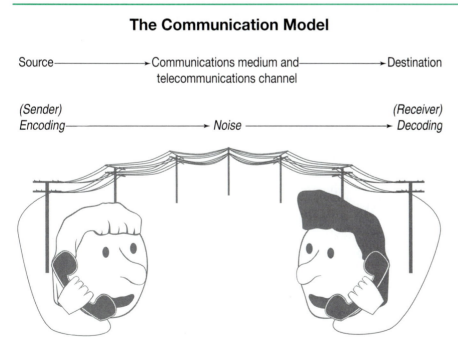

Source ————————→ Communications medium and ————————→ Destination
                        telecommunications channel

(Sender)   *(Receiver)*
Encoding ————————————→ *Noise* ————————————→ *Decoding*

tively, in data communications, where codes rather than words are sent and received, we are concerned that the proper characters are being sent and received in the correct sequence. Unlike voice communications, little concern is given to the intent of the message. It is important to understand the process of communications as it is applied to telecommunications so that we know how to use technology to solve business problems.

■ CHARACTERISTICS OF EFFECTIVE COMMUNICATION

To understand how technology improves communication and makes it more effective, it is wise to study the characteristics of effective communication as explained by Murphy, Hildebrandt, and Thomas (1997, pp. 31–61):

- **Completeness.** Completeness indicates that communication needs to provide all necessary information, answer all questions asked, and give something extra when desirable.
- **Conciseness.** Conciseness asks us to eliminate wordy expressions, include only relevant material, and avoid unnecessary repetition.
- **Consideration.** With consideration, we are to focus on "you" instead of "I" or "we," show audience benefit or interest in the receiver, and emphasize positive, pleasant facts.
- **Concreteness.** Concreteness means that the words and sentence structure used should be as brief as possible and free of as much elaboration and superfluous detail as possible.
- **Clarity.** Clarity indicates that we need to choose precise, concrete, and familiar words to construct effective sentences and paragraphs.
- **Courtesy.** Courtesy means that communications should be tactful, thoughtful, and appreciative. In addition, expressions that show respect should be used and nondiscriminatory expressions should be chosen.
- **Correctness.** Correctness asks us to use the right level of language, verify the accuracy of figures, facts, and words, and maintain acceptable writing mechanics.

■ TECHNOLOGY'S ROLE IN COMMUNICATIONS

Technology is all around us today—so much so that most people take it for granted. In fact, it's difficult to imagine life without it. If you used your videocassette recorder (VCR) to view your favorite movie, cooked dinner with your microwave oven, or prepared a letter using your personal computer, you have experienced technology in your home. Businesses also depend on technology to manufacture and market goods and services. All manufacturing entities utilize computerization to some degree. In fact, some firms apply robotics and other more advanced computerization techniques in their operations. Businesses utilize the electronic media—television, radio, and the Internet—to promote and sell products.

Technology plays a large role in communications today, both in the home and in today's business world. This is done largely through what can be called *communication technology devices*. In the home, these devices include, but are not limited to, devices that allow you to communicate with others. This includes the telephone, the newest version of which is the cellular telephone, which gives people the capability to place and receive telephone calls from practically anywhere. In addition, a personal computer with a dial-up modem allows us to connect to an Internet service provider, such as America Online®, via telephone lines to send and receive electronic mail (e-mail) messages and tap into the vast resources found on the World Wide Web.

Technology allows us to experience near-real-time reporting of events that occur all around the world (see Figure 1-2). Cable television has brought news into our homes, often as it is occurring. Television networks use satellite technology to report on such events as the Olympics and weather-related tragedies brought on by tornadoes, hurricanes, and floods. Weather conditions and other information are communicated to us by using computer-generated maps and other graphics.

Technology has also played a large role in the way that businesses communicate internally and externally with customers, clients, suppliers, creditors, banks, and other financial institutions. In addition to the telephone, which is one of the oldest communication technology devices, businesses also use e-mail to communicate. E-mail is made possible via the Internet and Intranets. The Internet allows businesses to engage in electronic commerce, not only to provide information about products, but also to provide a means

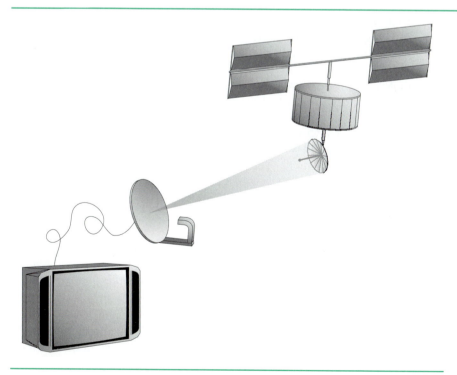

Figure 1-2
Technology Enables Us to Experience Real-Time Reporting of Events

by which customers can place orders. Networking computers also allow businesses to connect computers so that resources can be shared and to provide improved communications. Facsimile (fax) technology allows businesses, as well as individuals in their homes, to send almost any type of document to almost any business or person.

■ BENEFITS OF USING TECHNOLOGY IN COMMUNICATIONS

What are the specific reasons for using technology in communications? There are several benefits that we can list.

1. *Technology makes communication faster.* As mentioned previously, both individuals and businesses use e-mail extensively today. Messages that are sent via e-mail will be received within a matter of seconds. Similarly, the use of facsimile technology provides the time advantage of being able to get a copy of a document to its destination very quickly. The alternative to using e-mail and facsimile for visual communications is to use the U.S. Postal Service (sometimes called "snail mail") or other shipping companies, such as Federal Express and United Parcel Service, which are much slower than the technology applications discussed above.

2. *Technology makes people more productive and more efficient.* Because we can communicate faster, we are able to accomplish more in less time and can focus on more important, less monotonous work. This does not necessarily mean that fewer workers are needed. What it does mean is that workers often need higher-level skills, such as problem-solving and computer-related skills and expertise in using other communication technology devices.

3. *Technology helps to enhance communication.* The enhancement of communication comes about with the integration of multimedia and technology. *Multimedia* is the integration of at least two media, which may include text, photos, graphics, sound, music, animation, and full-motion video. *Multi* means more than one, and *media* means forms of communication. Businesses and some individuals use multimedia in communication when they use videoconferencing, a form of teleconferencing, which is discussed in detail later in the book. Videoconferencing combines sound and video to enhance communication. The use of presentation software, such as PowerPoint, enables people who are presenting ideas or details about projects to produce and use slides that may contain text, sound, graphics, and video, or animation.

■ DRAWBACKS OF USING TECHNOLOGY IN COMMUNICATIONS

What are the drawbacks of using technology in communications? There are several problems that we can list.

1. *Traditional communication methods may be better.* Some people assume that the most technically advanced methods must be used in all instances.

This may not be true. For example, if time is not important when sending a document, using regular mail may be preferable to faxing a document to someone when expensive telephone toll charges may be involved. For a legal document such as a contract, faxing the document (which is the equivalent of sending a copy of the document using traditional methods) may not be appropriate. In this case, traditional methods may be the only way to send it. In addition, there may be times when it is better to send a formal letter or document (e.g., a formal invitation or announcement) via regular mail or a courier service rather than sending an e-mail message. Remember that e-mail messages are usually very informal.

2. *Technology may be misused.* It is possible for people to misuse communication technology. An example of this is the temptation for employees to use e-mail to send and receive personal messages. Companies have the right to limit employees' e-mail use to business purposes only. A company can do this since it is paying for the e-mail system. In addition, sending personal messages may mean that employees are using company time for personal issues. One way that some businesses have curtailed this practice is to monitor e-mail messages and inform those who are breaking the "no personal e-mail messages" policy. Not only does this raise the question of whether this violates a person's personal rights, but it can create poor employee morale.

Another way that technology has been misused is in the area of **computer crime and fraud**. Computers can be used as a tool to gain access to valuable information and as a means to steal large amounts of money. Computer crime takes place when someone is able to gain access to a computer system by knowing, finding, or stealing a logon identification and password. For crimes of this nature to be carried out, the criminal must know how to manipulate the system after gaining access to it. A person who spends time learning and using computer systems is called a **hacker**, and a person who uses such knowledge to gain unauthorized or illegal access to these systems is often called a **cracker**. Recently, people have been caught developing and releasing illegal computer viruses, often through e-mail message attachments. A **computer virus** is a program that attaches itself to other programs. A **worm** is a type of virus that functions as an independent program, replicating its own program files until it interrupts the operation of networks and computer systems. Viruses have caused millions of dollars of damage to computer systems throughout the world.

Another way that computers can be the object of crimes is through software and Internet piracy. Most commercial software programs are copyrighted, similar to the way that movies and books are copyrighted. Copying copyrighted software is illegal and those who do it are engaging in **software piracy**. **Internet piracy** involves gaining illegal access to and using the Internet. Finally, some people who communicate with others on the Internet, especially through chat rooms, sometimes misrepresent themselves. Later face-to-face meetings have occasionally led to murder, rape, and other crimes. There have also been **computer-related scams** in which people have lost hundreds of thousands of dollars through the Internet when scam artists offer get-rich-quick schemes involving real estate, bank transactions, and lotteries.

3. *Technology may require training.* Some of the technology used for communication may require that some employees need training in its effective use. Using e-mail systems, facsimile systems, the Internet, network access, and other areas may necessitate training. Training is especially important for older employees, who are accustomed to using older methods of communication. Training can be accomplished in several ways. One way is to hold in-house seminars in which employees receive information and hands-on training. Some larger firms employ full-time workers to conduct ongoing training. Smaller firms may need to contract with external trainers to come onto the firm's premises to conduct training. Either method can be expensive, but essential.

An interesting prediction, made in the 1960s by Gordon Moore, former chairman of the board of Intel, the largest microprocessor chip maker, is now known as **Moore's law**. This hypothesis states that computer transistor densities on a single chip (part of a computer's microprocessor) will double every 18 months. This prediction has held up amazingly well over the years, as evidenced by the fact that computer hardware and software are upgraded at least every 12 to 18 months. As hardware and software change, more training is needed to provide workers with the ability to work with the new technology.

■ CAREERS IN COMMUNICATION TECHNOLOGY

Career opportunities in communication technology are expected to increase as companies continue to integrate technology with communications. People are needed to set up and maintain electronic mail, teleconferencing systems, and networks. These employees must be able to access the needs of the organization with regard to technology and plan, implement, and access ways to integrate technology with communications. They also need to be problem solvers, with the ability to assess when difficulties occur with present systems so that they can be accurately diagnosed and rectified. Table 1-1 lists some of the major job categories in the communication technology field.

Telecommunications Manager

A **telecommunications manager** is a person who manages the planning, installation, and day-to-day operation of telecommunications systems within an organization. This person may also supervise a staff of technicians.

Technician

A **technician** installs and maintains electronic equipment and provides technical user support for electronic mail, teleconferences, and other communication technology areas.

Job Title	Type of Job	Duties
Telecommunications manager	Managerial	Manages the planning, installation, and day-to-day operation of telecommunications systems within an organization
Technician	Technical	Installs and maintains electronic equipment and provides technical user support for electronic mail, teleconferences, and other communication technology areas
Communications manager	Managerial/technical	Supervises the day-to-day operation of all communication technology devices and systems, such as electronic mail, facsimile systems, and teleconferencing equipment
Network manager	Managerial/technical	Keeps the communication networks operational and reliable

Table 1-1
Communication

Communications Manager

A **communications manager**, sometimes called a *distribution services manager*, supervises the day-to-day operation of all communication technology devices and systems, such as electronic mail, facsimile systems, and teleconferencing equipment. One of this person's primary responsibilities is the coordination of all forms of telecommunications within an organization.

Network Manager

The **network manager** is concerned with keeping communication networks operational and reliable. There are day-to-day tasks that are required to keep a network's capacity up and running and to keep users satisfied. Responsibilities might include maintaining user workstations, modems, line concentrators, front-end processors, network operating systems, communications software, network management software, and all network hardware, including servers, hubs, routers, and bridges. Some people maintain a help desk where they receive and answer phone and e-mail inquiries. In other systems the network manager is alerted to problems through an alarm signal on the operator's terminal.

■ SUMMARY

We live in an era that has been described as the information age, a time when great volumes of information are available to those who know how to access it. This time period could also be described as the communication age, because we are learning new ways of sharing information with one another. Communication technology is the application and use of technology—computers, software, other electronic devices, and accompanying media and procedures—to make communication more effective than through using traditional means of communications that do not utilize technology.

Telecommunications is defined as "communications via electronic, electromagnetic, or phontonic means over a distance" (Carr and Snyder, 1997, p. 6) The term *electromagnetic* refers to rapidly varying (high-frequency) current used to carry telecommunication signals, and *phontonic* refers to the use of light as a medium. The Greek *tele* means "at a distance." Therefore, literally, telecommunication is communication over a distance. However, modern telecommunications assumes that you are utilizing technology while communicating.

To send data over a distance, you must have a sender (the source), a communications medium and telecommunications channel, and a receiver (the destination). This is often depicted as a communications model. To gain an understanding of what data (information) moves over a telecommunication channel, one can view telecommunications in terms of conduit, context, and content.

To understand how technology improves communication and makes it more effective, it would be wise to study the "seven C's of effective communication" of Murphy, Hildebrandt, and Thomas (1997, pp. 31–61): completeness, conciseness, consideration, completeness, clarity, courtesy, and correctness. Technology plays a large role in communications today both in the home and in the business world. This is largely through what can be called communication technology devices.

The benefits of using technology in communications include the following: technology makes communication faster, it makes people more productive and more efficient, and it helps to enhance communication. The drawbacks of using technology in communications include the fact that in some instances, traditional communication methods may be better, technology may be misused, and technology may require training. Career opportunities in communication technologies are expected to increase as companies continue to integrate technology with communications. Some of the available jobs include tecommunications manager, technician, communications manager, and network manager.

QUESTIONS

1. What is communication technology?

2. What is telecommunications?

3. Explain what is meant by *conduit*, *context*, and *content* in terms of telecommunications.

4. Explain how the communications model operates.

5. What are the characteristics of good communication? What is the meaning of each characteristic?

6. What is technology's role in communications? Provide several examples.

7. What are the benefits of using technology in communication? Explain each benefit.

8. What are the drawbacks of using technology in communication? Explain each drawback.

9. Explain career opportunities in communication technology.

10. Explain the nature and characteristics of each of the following jobs. What are the similarities and differences?
   (a) Telecommunications manager
   (b) Technician
   (c) Communications manager
   (d) Network manager

PROJECTS AND PROBLEMS

1. Identify five services that you use at least once a week which depend entirely on telecommunications.
   (a) Provide the name of the service or access device. Examples of these would be the Internet, cellular telephone service, and an automated teller machine (ATM).
   (b) Identify the name of the service provider.
   (c) Discuss why the service would be impractical without telecommunications.
   (d) If your service provider did not offer the service, would you drop it and find one that did provide the service?

2. Find an example of how telecommunications has significantly affected a local company or organization. Write a paragraph describing how the use of telecommunications has affected the way the company conducts business.

3. Interview someone who used telecommunications technology 10 to 15 years ago and is using it currently. Ask him or her what changes have taken place and what positive and negative effects, if any, these changes have made in the current work environment. Do any of these effects relate to the advantages and disadvantages that were cited in the chapter?

4. Do a job analysis at a firm that employs people in the following jobs: telecommunications manager, technician, communications manager, and network manager. Obtain the following information: required skills and education, job responsibilities and duties, and opportunities for advancement. Which job(s) do you think you would like to have? Why? Which job(s) do you think you would not like to have? Why?

5. Owners and managers of some small companies claim that they do not have the financial resources to adopt the latest technology related to telecommunications (e.g., e-mail, voice mail, use of the Internet). Assuming that these companies can somehow find the money to use up-to-date technology, what arguments can you provide that would encourage them to use it?

6. John Stevens, a friend of yours, can be described as a "technology skeptic." He has said: "Technology is overused and sometimes the old way of doing things is better." He gives as an example automobile accidents that have been caused when people use cell phones in their cars. How would you respond to him in support of the use of technology?

7. You have been hired as a telecommunications consultant for a medium-sized computer hardware manufacturer. The company wishes to establish a customer service operation for purchasers of its products. In addition to taking customer orders over the phone, sales representatives will answer consumer questions about how to use the products, where to take the products for repair, how to enhance performance, and so on. The company plans initially to train about 15 people to staff the customer service center. It has hired you to review its telecommunications solution.
   (a) How would you proceed?
   (b) What questions need to be asked?
   (c) What telecommunications equipment is needed?
   (d) What might be the annual cost for this operation?

Vocabulary

clarity	computer crime and fraud	correctness	software piracy
communication technology	computer virus	courtesy	technician
communications manager	computer-related scam	cracker	telecommunications
communications model	conciseness	hacker	telecommunications manager
completeness	concreteness	Internet piracy	worm
	consideration	Moore's law	
		network manager	

References

Carr, Houston H., and Charles A. Snyder, *The Management of Telecommunications: Business Solutions to Business Problems,* McGraw-Hill, New York, 1997.

Fruehling, Rosemary T., Constance K. Weaver, and Victoria R. Lyons, *Office Systems: People, Procedures, and Technology*, Paradigm Publishing, Brookline, MA, 1992.

Keen, Peter G. W., and J. Michael Cummins, *Networks in Action: Business Choices and Telecommunications Decisions*, Wadsworth Publishing, Belmont, CA, 1994.

Murphy, H. A., H. W. Hildebrandt, and J. P. Thomas, *Effective Business Communications*, 7th ed., McGraw-Hill, New York, 1997.

Rowe, Stanford H., II, *Telecommunications for Managers*, 4th ed., Prentice Hall, Upper Saddle River, NJ, 1999.

Stair, Ralph M., and George W. Reynolds, *Principles of Information Systems*, 4th ed., Course Technology, Cambridge, MA, 1999.

Tedesco, Eleanor Hollis, *Telecommunications for Business*, PWS-Kent, Boston, 1990.

CHAPTER

2

History and Future of Communication Technology

This chapter deals with a discussion of the major historical events in communication technologies. This will help you to better understand the present state of communication technologies. Because much of the terminology that is used today has its roots in telegraphy, terms related to telegraphy are presented. This chapter also deals with forecasts for communication technologies in the future.

WHAT YOU WILL LEARN

The invention and/or development of the following:
- Telegraph
- Telephone
- Wireless telegraph
- Microwave radio
- Satellites
- Computer communications
- Telecommunications networks
- Communication technology of the future

Table 2-1
History of Communication Technology

Technology	Inventor	Dates
Telegraph	Samuel Finley Breese Morse	1838
Telephone	Alexander Graham Bell	1876
Wireless telegraph	Guglielmo Marconi	1895
Microwave radio		1940s
Satellite communications		1960s
Computer communications		1950s
Telecommunication networks		1970s

■ HISTORY OF COMMUNICATION TECHNOLOGY

The history of communication technology is tied to the invention of several telecommunication devices and technologies: the telegraph, telephone, wireless telegraphy, microwave radio, satellites, computers, and telecommunication networks. Table 2-1 provides a summary of this history.

■ TELEGRAPH

The first major communication technology device to be invented was the telegraph. The word **telegraphy** comes from the Greek *tele*, distant, and *graphein*, to write. Putting these two root words together, **telegraphy** means "writing at a distance." With the telegraph it was possible to send news over a long distance by using a code consisting of dots and dashes, which became known as **Morse code** (see Figure 2-1).

The inventor of the first electric telegraph was Samuel Finley Breese Morse, an American inventor and painter (Figure 2-2). He developed the idea for the telegraph when he returned to the United States from Italy (Figure 2-3). In his studio at New York University, he needed about six years to finish this invention and received a patent for it in 1838. In 1851, Hiram Sibley, with a group of businesspeople, founded a company that built the first telegraph line in the midwest. In 1856 the company was registered as Western Union Telegraph & Company.

In 1860, while telegraph lines were spreading slowly throughout the country, a very spectacular express rider service, the pony express, came into existence. Six hundred horses, specially chosen for fleetness, toughness, and endurance, were purchased for this venture. On April 3, 1860, the first rider, Henry Wallace, left St. Joseph, Missouri and after 10 days and approximately 2000 miles, the last rider reached Sacremento, California. For this job they needed brave young men, preferably orphans, because it was a dangerous, adventurous life. They had to shoot very well, be excellent riders, and have no fear of Indian attacks. Each man had to ride 60 miles at top speed and

A .-	N -.	0 -----
B -...	O ---	1 .----
C -.-.	P .--.	2 ..---
D -..	Q --.-	3 ...--
E .	R .-.	4 ....-
F ..-.	S ...	5 .....
G --.	T -	6 -....
H	U ..-	7 --...
I ..	V ...-	8 ---..
J .---	W .--	9 ----.
K -.-	X -..-	Fullstop .-.-.-
L .-..	Y -.--	Comma --..--
M --	Z --..	Query ..--..

Figure 2-1
Morse Code

cover this distance in six hours with six different ponies. The pony express existed for only one and a half years. Its need came to an end upon completion of the transcontinental telegraph line between Missouri and California.

In 1866, twenty-two years after completion of the first telegraph line, between Washington, D.C. and Baltimore, Maryland, the first successful laying of an oceanic telegraph, the Atlantic cable, marked the beginning of a new era in telecommunications. By 1845 the first cables were laid across the Hudson River and New York harbor. However, these submarine cables lacked a

Figure 2-2
Samuel Finley Breese Morse

needed quality: physical durability. The only materials available to insulate wires at this time were asphalt, wax, and shellac. None of these lasted long even for short crossings, much less reaching 3000 miles across an ocean. The discovery in 1843 of a form of rubber led to a suitable insulation by 1847.

Global submarine cable telegraphy really began with a wealthy English merchant family named Brett, who financed a cable crossing the English Channel to France in 1850. That cable failed after only a few messages had been exchanged, and was finally replaced in September 1851 with an engineered design that could withstand the currents at the bottom of the channel. Also in the 1850–1851 period, former aerial crossings of the Mississippi and Ohio rivers that had been wrecked by floods were replaced with submarine telegraph cables. Development of that kind continued apace in Europe, where by 1852 cables were connecting England, Holland, Germany, Denmark, and Sweden, and another connected Italy with Corsica, Sardinia, and even across to Africa.

Meanwhile, some people in the United States and Europe had a vision of a telegraph cable across the Atlantic, connecting the two continents. Many scientists, including the French physicist Jacques Babinet, thought it would be impossible to lay a submarine cable over such a long distance. Even the Congress of the United States laughed at Samuel Morse when he proposed this idea. However, several people, including the British chief physicist Michael Faraday, supported plans for a transatlantic telegraph.

Cyrus W. Field, a wealthy New York paper merchant who had retired from active business at the age of 35, was enthusiastic about such an idea and decided to lay a submarine cable from the United States to England. In 1854 he and a number of wealthy New Yorkers joined to form a group called the New York Newfoundland and London Telegraph Company. After a failure in 1855, the company finished the first section of the transatlantic telegraph between New York and St. John's, Newfoundland in 1856. In the same year, Field went to England to get more partners. He founded the Atlantic Telegraph Company in London. This company tried to lay the cable across the ocean from England to Newfoundland.

After two failed attempts in 1857, the third trial on August 7, 1858 was successful. The cable was laid, and worked for four weeks, although never very well. Unfortunately, the insulation leaked, and on September 1, the telegraph broke down. This failure made it very difficult to start a new project and the Civil War delayed a new attempt. The British government appointed a commission to investigate the project. The commission sat for nearly two years and spent many thousands of British pounds in experiments. The result was a clear conviction that it was possible to lay a telegraph cable across the Atlantic.

In 1863, when the scientific and engineering problems were solved, Field began to prepare for a new attempt. On July 15, 1865, the cable was taken on board a giant ship, the *Great Eastern*, in England and a new trial began. After they had laid out nearly 1250 miles of cable and with only 560 miles to go, the cable broke and sank to the bottom of the sea. All trials to raise the cable failed, so a new attempt began on March 31, 1866. Just five months from the day that the new cable was manufactured, the first message was transmitted across the Atlantic Ocean. The first functional telegraph line between Europe and the United States was finished.

The following terms originated in the era of telegraphy. Many of these terms are still used.

- *Key* (or *transmitter*). In a telegraph network, the key is the device used to enter dots and dashes on the circuit.
- *Mark.* This is the state of the telegraph line when current is flowing.
- *Polling.* This is a method of calling stations and asking if they have traffic to send.
- *Receiver.* In a telegraph circuit, this is the device that sounds the dots and dashes as they reach the end of the circuit.
- *Sender.* In a telegraph circuit, the sender is the key that puts the message into the circuit as dots and dashes.
- *Sounder* (or *receiver*). In a telegraph circuit, the sounder is the device that converts electrical pulses back into audible dots and dashes.

TELEPHONE

The history of the **telephone** in the United States is tied to Alexander Graham Bell (see Figure 2-4). Bell was born on March 3, 1847 in Edinburgh, Scotland, the son of Alexander Melville Bell and Eliza Grace Symonds, daughter of a surgeon in the Royal Navy. His mother, who was a portrait painter and accomplished musician, began to lose her hearing when Graham (a name that was used by his family and close friends) was 12. His father had a worldwide reputation as a teacher and author of textbooks on proper speech and as the inventor of Melville's Visible Speech, a code of symbols that indicated the position and action of the throat, tongue, and lips in uttering various sounds. This system helped to guide the deaf in learning to speak, and Graham became an expert in its use for that purpose.

Graham and his two brothers assisted their father in public demonstrations in visible speech, beginning in 1862. At the same time he enrolled as a student–teacher at Weston House, a boys' school near Edinburgh, where he taught music and speech in exchange for being a student of other subjects. A year later, he became a full-time teacher at the University of Edinburgh while studying at the University of London.

In 1866, Graham carried out a series of experiments to determine how vowel sounds are produced. He combined the notes of electrically driven tuning forks to make vowel sounds, which gave him the idea of "telegraphing" speech. In 1870, both of his brothers died of tuberculosis and the family moved to Brantford, Ontario, Canada in an attempt to find a healthier climate. A year later Graham moved to Boston, where he opened a school for teachers of the deaf and in 1872 became a professor at Boston University.

Graham's interest in electricity continued and he attempted to send several telegraph messages over a single wire at one time. Lacking the time and skill to make the equipment for these experiments, he enlisted the help of Thomas A. Watson from a nearby electrical shop. The two became fast friends and worked together on the tedious experimentation to produce sounds over the "harmonic telegraph." It was on June 2, 1875, while Graham was at one end of the line and Watson worked on the reeds of the telegraph in another room, that he heard the sound of a plucked reed coming to him over the wire.

The next day, after much tinkering, the instrument transmitted the sound of Bell's voice to Watson. The instrument transmitted recognizable voice sound, not words. Bell and Watson experimented all summer and in September 1875, Bell began to write the specifications for his first telephone patent. The patent was issued on March 7, 1876. The telephone carried its first intelligible sentence three days later in the rented top floor of a Boston boardinghouse at 109 Court Street.

Elisha Gray (1835–1901) developed a telephone microphone at almost the same time as Bell. In fact, he patented his microphone system two hours after Bell received his patent. Gray used a metal bar that was connected to a membrane on one side and dipped into a liquid on the other end. Bell founded the Bell Telephone Company, which delivered and installed 50,000 telephones within the first three years and was soon the world's largest telephone company, eventually known as the American Telephone and Telegraph Company.

One year after the invention, five banks in Boston ordered one of Bell's telephone systems. This system revealed certain shortcomings, which included the fact that the microphone was not sensitive enough. This was improved by the invention in 1873 by David Edward Hughes (1831–1900) of the carbon microphone, which was more sensitive.

The telephone became very popular and common in all highly industrialized countries. The speed of this development slowed down only during wars or economic crises. In the following years, telephony became more and more technical. When somebody wanted to make a call, the person had to talk first to an operator, who made the connection manually on a connecting board. This took a long time because each telephone subscriber had to have his own socket, which had to be connected and disconnected by hand. This manual connection method was the only way of making telephone calls until 1889, when Almon B. Strowger invented a system that allowed each subscriber to establish his or her own telephone connections. It was at this point that a dialer was added to the telephone. This development made people more independent because they could dial themselves to establish their telephone connections. In 1892, Strowger founded the Strowger Automatic Telephone Exchange Company, which was the first telephone exchange without operators to establish connections.

■ WIRELESS TELEGRAPH

The discovery in 1888 of the electromagnetic wave by Friedrich Hertz opened up new ways of transmitting information. Hertz may not have envisioned how important his discovery would be in the following years and decades. In 1895, the Italian scientist Guglielmo Marconi (see Figure 2-5) experimented with **wireless telegraphy** and in 1899 was able to send messages across the English Channel between France and England. Only two years later, the first transatlantic signals were sent across the ocean from Europe to North America. Marconi's radio equipment was composed of a transmitting and a receiving unit. The transmitting unit was composed of a conductor that was connected to an antenna and to the ground. The receiver had an antenna, and like the transmitting unit, had a ground pole so that the signal transmitted could be received on the receiving side. Marconi knew how to make money out of his invention. He founded his own company in London, the Marconi Wireless Telegraph Company. Marconi produced his receiving and transmitting system and rented it to ship owners under the condition that only his personnel were allowed to operate the machines. He was thus able to keep a monopoly on his transmitting system. The first voice transmitting system with electromagnetic waves was built in the United States in 1906. In 1910 the

first song was transmitted by electromagnetic waves, sung by the famous singer Enrico Caruso of the Metropolitan Opera in New York.

■ MICROWAVE RADIO

The introduction of microwave carrier systems greatly increased the number of voice channels per circuit. **Microwave radio** relay links were introduced shortly after World War II (see Figure 2-6). Microwaves were transmitted through the air over a line-of-sight path from one station to another instead of using coaxial cable. Microwaves were used for both telephone communications and coast-to-coast communications.

■ COMPUTER COMMUNICATIONS

Telecommunications reached a new dimension when it became possible to connect computers over a telephone network. Today, this is accomplished with the use of a modulator/demodulator, or *modem*, which is a computer peripheral. The incompatibility between computer data and a network has been resolved by using a *transducer*, a translating device inserted between a computer and the telephone system at the origin of transmission.

■ SATELLITES

The transoceanic telephone network was made possible through the extension of cable and the advent of microwave radio. However, this system was far from ideal, and communications were often interrupted because of weather conditions. Satellites greatly improved worldwide telephone connections with far fewer problems. The first low-orbit nonsynchronous relation station was established with the launching of *Telstar* in 1962 by Bell Labs. *Syncom II*, a synchronous satellite positioned over the Atlantic Ocean in 1963, heralded the first regular commercial telephone service using satellite technology. A *nonsynchonous satellite* moves with respect to Earth's surface, whereas a *synchronous satellite* is one whose period of rotation is the same as that of Earth. If the satellite is positioned above the equator, it appears to be stationary. Additional U.S. satellites have been launched over the years, including *Syncom III* in 1964, which provided an active radio relay for intercontinental transmissions of television programs, and *Early Bird I*, another transatlantic telephone and television satellite.

■ TELECOMMUNICATIONS NETWORKS

The **telecommunications network** has evolved from manual to automatic, from mechanical to electronic, from wire to light beam (fiber optic), from voice only to voice, digital, and video. One problem had been the noisy telephone switching units. This was solved when they were replaced by microchips. Each new system improved on the one before, offering more capacity, greater speed, and more efficient services. These new services include information networks and mobile communications. New digital standards have been developed for global communications, including the integrated services digital network.

■ COMMUNICATION TECHNOLOGIES OF THE FUTURE

Global communications are becoming more and more intensified through electronic media, which facilitate trade contacts and international projects. The recent cooperation among many countries throughout the world shows clearly that it is now possible to think of the global implications of future technological advances. Our localized, national thinking regarding the communication technologies of the future must be deemphasized in an effort to realize and assume our joint, global responsibilities in this area. For example, a worldwide communications system that facilitates rapid information exchange is urgently required.

The key words for the future are *multimedia* and *mobile telecommunications*. Multimedia communications straddle the traditions of telecommunications and information technologies. As the technology evolves, it is becoming increasingly difficult to identify the boundary of networks. Computers, in the form of personal and portable devices, have broadly penetrated the marketplace. Further revolutionary changes in the way computers are used in connection with telephony are also anticipated. When a computer that contains a modem is connected to the telephone network, it becomes a valuable resource capable of performing a variety of telecommunication tasks. Some of these actions would include the following: electronic mail, data transfer, and videophone communications, as well as use of the telephone itself. Today, the trend is to communicate and conduct business away from the traditional office setting. The recent use of telecommuting, with workers working at least part of the workweek at home, is evidence of this trend. Currently, lack of transmission speed and bandwidth, especially in the current installed base of telephone networks, is hindering the growth of this phenomenon.

Industrialized nations are deploying the *integrated services digital network* (ISDN). This network technology offers speeds of more than a megabit per second using specialized copper and fiber optic cable. Researchers, consumer video services, and network element providers will collaborate to create a comprehensive platform for the interactive video services to be delivered to consumers' homes via standard television. These services will include movies on demand, **interactive television**, **teleshopping**, **telebanking**, databases, and **videophone**. A single cable to the home or one network for all is the target of this development. The origin of this concept was the Internet. The Internet can carry these real-time traffic types, to a limited degree today and to a larger degree tomorrow, and the new communications system will be able to contain all of these features.

In addition, researchers will need to solve the problems of connection between networks. Local area networks (LANs) and wide area networks (WANs) will need to be connected together. Network externalizations are essential, that is, the recruitment of end users, the compatibility of signal protocols and electrical interfaces, and the reliability and full-time availability of the infrastructure. If we want to build a worldwide network with the same coherence as the telephone network, we need international organizations for standardization of protocols similar to the International Telecommunications Union (ITU). Fault-tolerant software will be needed as well as the opportunity for customers to define services and manage them in a supportive environment. The network operator will manage each desktop component of customer equipment separately, offering transparent client and server computing through network services. The concept of self-provisioning will allow customers to buy network capacity in the same way they buy electricity.

The cable and satellite industries are the major players in the development of networks. These two components (terrestrial and satellite) must be as closely integrated as possible. Networks need transmission routes that enable fast transmission speed without loss in efficiency. The conduit (medium) of the future will be the fiber optic cable, which enables transmission speeds of 10 gigabits per second (Gb/s).

Mobile communications will also play a major role in the future. They will become less expensive and will be used by more people. The new mobile systems (e.g., using cellular telephones with notebook computers) provide a wide variety of services, possibly the same set of services as the fixed network and with the same quality. Communication will be possible from every point in the world.

However, we should not forget that these new communications technologies will not be without disadvantages. Networking may result in isolation of the user, and important social values such as tolerance, sense of community, responsibility, and personnel development could be more difficult to achieve. In the future we must build communication technologies that not only help us to communicate more effectively with one other but also ensure that users are able to interact in such a way that social and personal skills do not deteriorate.

■ SUMMARY

The first major communications technology device to be invented was the telegraph. The word *telegraphy* comes from the Greek *tele*, distant, and *graphein*, to write. Putting these two root words together, *telegraphy* means "writing at a distance." With the telegraph it was possible to send news over a long distance by using a code consisting of dots and dashes, which became known as Morse code. The inventor of the first electric telegraph was Samuel Finley Breese Morse, an American inventor and painter. The following terms originated in the era of telegraphy, but many of them are still in use.

- *Key* (or *transmitter*). In the telegraph network the key is the device used to enter dots and dashes on the circuit.
- *Mark*. This is the state of the telegraph line when current is flowing.
- *Polling*. This is a method of calling stations and asking if they have traffic to send.
- *Receiver*. In a telegraph circuit, this is the device that sounds the dots and dashes as they reach the end of the circuit.
- *Sender*. In a telegraph circuit, the sender is the key that puts the message into the circuit as dots and dashes.
- *Sounder* (or *receiver*). In a telegraph circuit, the sounder is the device that converts electrical pulses back into audible dots and dashes.

The history of the telephone in the United States is tied to Alexander Graham Bell. In September 1875, Bell began to write the specifications for his first telephone patent. The patent was issued on March 7, 1876. The telephone carried its first intelligible sentence three days later in the rented top floor of a Boston boarding house at 109 Court Street. Bell founded the Bell Telephone Company, which delivered and installed 50,000 telephones within the first three years and was soon the world's largest telephone company, eventually known as the American Telephone and Telegraph Company. The telephone became very popular and common in all highly industrialized countries. The speed of this development slowed down only during wars or economic crises. In the following years, telephony became more and more technical.

The discovery in 1888 of the electromagnetic wave by Friedrich Hertz opened up new ways of transmitting information. In 1895, the Italian scientist Guglielmo Marconi experimented with wireless telegraphy and in 1899 was able to send messages across the English Channel between France and England. Only two years later the first transatlantic signals were sent across the ocean from Europe to North America.

The introduction of microwave carrier systems greatly increased the number of voice channels per circuit. Microwave radio relay links were introduced shortly after World War II. The transoceanic telephone network was made possible through the extension of cable and the advent of microwave radio. However, this system was far from ideal, and communications were often interrupted because of weather conditions. Satellites greatly improved worldwide telephone connections with far fewer problems.

Telecommunications reached a new dimension when it became possible to connect computers over a telephone network. International Business Machines (IBM) introduced what they termed *teleprocessing*, which permitted data to be transmitted over the telephone network and reprocessed directly by computer. Today, this is accomplished with the use of a modulator/demodulator, or modem, which is a computer peripheral. The incompatibility between computer data and a network has been resolved by using a transducer, a translating device inserted between a computer and the telephone system at the origin of transmission.

The telecommunications network has evolved from manual to automatic, from mechanical to electronic, from wire to light beam (fiber optic), from voice only to voice, digital, and video. One problem had been the noisy telephone switching units. This was solved when they were replaced by microchips. Each new system improved from the one before, offering more capacity, greater speed, and more and more efficient services.

Global communication is becoming more and more intensified through electronic media, which facilitate trade contacts and international projects. The recent cooperation among many countries throughout the world shows clearly that it is now possible to think of the global implications of future technological advances.

1. Describe the history of the telegraph.

2. Who was Samuel F. B. Morse? Who was Hiram Sibley? Who was Cyrus W. Field? Why are they significant to the history of telecommunications?

3. Define each of the following terms as it relates to telegraphy.
   (a) Key (or transmitter)
   (b) Mark
   (c) Polling
   (d) Receiver
   (e) Sender
   (f) Sounder (or receiver)

4. Describe the history of the telephone. Who was Alexander Graham Bell? Who was Elisha Gray? Who was David Edward Hughes? Who was Almon B. Strowger? Why are they significant in the history of telecommunications?

5. Describe the history of wireless telegraphy. Who was Friedrich Hertz? Who was Guglielmo Marconi? Why are they significant in the history of telecommunications?

6. Describe the history of microwave radio.

7. Describe the history of satellites as they relate to communication.

8. Describe the development of computer communication.

9. Describe the development of telecommunications networks.

10. Describe the forecast for the future of each of the following:
    (a) Worldwide communication networks
    (b) Interactive video services
    (c) Connectivity of networks
    (d) Fault-tolerant software
    (e) Integration of cable and satellite technology
    (f) Mobile communication

PROJECTS AND PROBLEMS

1. Make a chart that outlines the history of important telecommunications technologies or devices. List the date (from earliest to latest) on which each invention was based, the name of the technology or device, the name(s) of the inventor(s), and the significance of this event. Use the following column heads:

   Date   Invention   Inventor(s)   Significance

2. Do you believe that encyclopedias on CD-ROM and the Internet will reduce or eliminate the need for reference sections in libraries? Why or why not?

3. Investigate the names of communication satellites currently in orbit and used by the United States. When was each satellite launched? What organizations or companies own and use each satellite? What is the expected life of each satellite?

4. Determine through research which of the following telegraphy terms are currently used in the telecommunications field: key (or transmitter), mark, polling, receiver, sender, sounder (or receiver).

Vocabulary

interactive television	polling	telecommunication network	teleshopping
key	receiver	telegraph	videophone
mark	sender	telegraphy	wireless telegraphy
microwave radio	sounder	telephone	
Morse code	telebanking		

References

Fachhochschule für Technik, Esslingen, Germany, "The FHTE Web History of Telecommunications," http://www-stall.rz.fht-esslingen.de/telehistory/welcome.html.

Rowe, Stanford H., II, *Telecommunications for Managers*, 4th ed., Prentice Hall, Upper Saddle River, NJ, 1999.

Tedesco, Eleanor Hollis, *Telecommunications for Business*, PWS-Kent, Boston, 1990.

The Telephone History Web site, http://www.atcaonline.com/phone.

Communication Technology Applications

In Part Two we provide a
description of major
communication applications,
including electronic mail,
teleconferencing, voice processing,
facsimile, wireless communications,
and other applications.

3

Electronic Mail

This chapter serves as an introduction to electronic mail (e-mail) as a major communication technology application. Electronic mail is defined and the benefits and drawbacks listed. In addition, e-mail addressing, finding e-mail addresses, using e-mail, and implementing e-mail systems are discussed.

WHAT YOU WILL LEARN

- ■ Definition of e-mail
- ■ Benefits of e-mail
- ■ Drawbacks of e-mail
- ■ How to address e-mail
- ■ How to find e-mail addresses
- ■ How e-mail is used
- ■ How e-mail systems can be implemented

◼ ELECTRONIC MAIL DEFINED

Electronic mail has become one of the most commonly used communication technology applications. **Electronic mail (e-mail)** is defined as electronic messaging that permits those who have an Internet or intranet connection and have been assigned a user identification (e.g., jsmith@psu.edu) to send electronic messages to others connected to the Internet or an intranet. As we will learn in a later chapter, the **Internet** is a network of computer systems that are interconnected in approximately 130 countries. An **intranet** represents a local area network within an organization that may or may not be connected to the Internet but which has some similar functions. Today, almost every business and many individuals use e-mail. For those who use this application, it is often difficult to envision life without it. Before the advent of e-mail, people relied on internal mail systems, courier services, private delivery companies such as United Parcel Service and Federal Express, or the U.S. Postal Service (often called "snail mail") to send hard copies of correspondence to others within and outside organizations.

Users can send e-mail messages to one or more persons. Additionally, a **distribution list**, which is prepared to send messages to a number of e-mail addresses, may be used. In either case, messages are sent by keying them on a microcomputer or computer terminal and are received by reading them on a computer screen, or they can be printed out and read as hard copy. With e-mail it is relatively easy for users to receive and respond to messages in order of priority, and messages can be stored electronically in subject folders for subsequent retrieval. E-mail is a **store-and-retrieve system** which means that each character is transmitted individually using stop bits, and the mail message is stored on a server until it is retrieved. A very important advantage is that sender and receiver do not have to communicate with each other at the same time but the message gets delivered immediately. Because it is a text-based medium, e-mail is more suited to the exchange of short, factual, numerical communications than to longer, subjective communications.

◼ BENEFITS OF ELECTRONIC MAIL

Electronic mail possesses a number of advantages:

1. E-mail may increase the productivity of organizations by making communication more effective and efficient.
2. E-mail users do not need to be at the same place at the same time. This means that you do not have to pick up the phone to leave a message, nor do you need to be at your desk to receive a message. E-mail transcends space and time.
3. E-mail is usually very fast, providing rapid transmission and reply. As a result, it supports collaborative work on text. This is a clear advantage over other media when transporting text, although direct connection between two personal computers using file transfer protocol to transport files is faster.

4. E-mail can be sent one to one, one to many, or many to many. This is computer conferencing, which is discussed later in the text. Information can be spread more easily throughout an organization. People will be able to receive and send much more information to/from others within and outside an organization.

5. E-mail can be stored in external memory for future retrieval, searching, editing, and forwarding to others. E-mail is a digital medium: The message is already stored in a digital version and can easily be manipulated by the receiver.

6. E-mail may actually encourage people to engage in more face-to-face communication to discuss the content of e-mail messages related to a particular project. In work groups, this can be a big advantage over other media.

7. Research has proven that the use of e-mail decreases the power distance inside an organization. This means that lower-level employees can address higher-level employees more easily. The reason for this in unclear, but it could have something to do with the information nature of many e-mail messages.

8. An e-mail system makes it possible for everybody in an organization to send and receive information. The result is that information becomes very easily accessible to everybody in an organization.

9. There is the possibility of attaching other documents to e-mail messages. This means that in addition to sending a message, entire documents— pictures, sounds, text, or programs—can be sent. This is an advantage over using facsimile or U.S. Postal Service–mailed letters, because the receiving parties can use the document directly on their computer.

▪ DRAWBACKS OF ELECTRONIC MAIL

Although electronic mail offers a number of advantages, it also possesses some disadvantages.

1. There may be uncertainty concerning when an e-mail message was received and read by the recipient. This may make it difficult to interact with someone when you don't know whether he or she has read your e-mail message. Although some e-mail systems are capable of sending an acknowledgment that a message has been received or opened, this feature does not usually work with e-mail sent outside an organization.

2. At the present time, e-mail is primarily text based. This is a disadvantage because it is sometimes difficult to interpret a message that is totally text based. Text contains very few cues to assist us in determining what the reader intended in comparison with other media. In an organization, one solution to this problem is to train employees to compose messages that are clear, concise, and easily understood. Another solution is to encourage the use of what are called **emoticons** or **smileys**. These are icons that are used to express various types of emotion in an e-mail message by keying keyboard symbols that are viewed from the side [e.g., :-) :-(>:( ].

3. E-mail inboxes can become cluttered with messages that were not requested. When information is on paper, people tend to be more careful to

send information only to the people who really need it. Due to the relative ease of sending e-mail messages, the possibility of information overload is a very real concern. The sending and receiving of unwanted, unsolicited e-mail is called **spamming**.

4. E-mail can be monitored and used for surveillance purposes. Some organizations are concerned that employees may be using e-mail to send personal messages or to conduct personal business. Almost every organization appoints at least one person to be responsible for monitoring e-mail messages. In addition, management may use surveillance to check exactly what is being keyed into a person's computer at any point in time, to verify the propriety of e-mail use. Although there may be legitimate reasons for doing these things, an organization must be aware of the effect that they may have on employee morale.

5. When e-mail becomes a substitute for person-to-person interaction, it may have an adverse effect on an organization because of the difficulties that can arise in interpreting an e-mail message.

■ ADDRESSING E-MAIL

Before you can send an e-mail message, you must know the e-mail address of the person to whom you are sending the message. In the next section we show you how you can find the e-mail address of a person who has an Internet or intranet connection. However, first let's examine the parts of an e-mail address.

An e-mail address consists of two parts. The first part is the *user name* of the person with whom you wish to communicate. User names are commonly up to eight characters long and are often derived from a person's real name. For example, the author uses *dgehris*, which is derived from Dennis Gehris. In some cases, users use only their first names (such as joe), their first name plus a last initial (such as *jimp*), or names that don't relate to their real names at all (such as *chief* or *master*).

The second part of an e-mail address is the domain name of the mail server (a computer) where the person's electronic mailbox is located. When you put the user and domain names together, you have a unique e-mail address for a specific person. An "at" symbol (@) is always placed between the user name and the domain name of the mail server. E-mail addresses are not case sensitive; that is, capitalization doesn't matter, but they're usually keyed as all lowercase. Also, e-mail addresses cannot contain spaces. An e-mail address uses the following format:

username@domain-name

Here are some examples of e-mail addresses:

listserv@netcom.com

stanleyt@.earth.ptu.edu

johnr@epix.net

The various extensions that are used at the end of e-mail addresses are as follows: .edu, .com, .gov, .mil, .net, and .org. Each describes the type of organization where the message originated. The .edu extension denotes an education institution; .com, a commercial organization; and .gov, a governmental body. The .mil extension means that the address originated with the military, .net denotes a network, and .org represents an organization.

FINDING ELECTRONIC ADDRESSES

To send someone an e-mail message, you must know the unique e-mail address of that particular person. This is similar to sending mail through the U.S. Postal Service, in that you must know the address of the person (street, city, state, zip code) to place on the outside of the envelope. If you don't place the entire correct address on the outside of the envelope (e.g., if you omit the zip code), the post office will sometimes be able to deliver it anyway. E-mail delivery on the Internet is less forgiving. If you omit just one part of the e-mail address or have an incorrect letter or word, the message will not be delivered.

The obvious method of finding an e-mail address for someone is to ask the person. An increasing number of businesses are placing e-mail addresses on business cards of their employees. Businesses are also placing e-mail addresses on Web pages and business stationery.

Another way to determine someone's e-mail address is to consult an e-mail directory that maintains a database of thousands of e-mail addresses. This is similar to consulting a local telephone book. Popular e-mail directories are *WhoWhere?*, *Four11*, and *Switchboard*.

USING ELECTRONIC MAIL

There are several terms associated with sending and receiving e-mail messages that are common regardless of the e-mail system that is being used.

The **header** contains the name and address of the recipient, the name and address of anyone who is being copied, and the subject of the message. Some e-mail programs also display the sender's name and address and the date of the message. The **body** contains the message itself. As discussed above, if you use the wrong address or mistype it, your message will be bounced back to you and you will receive a "Return to Sender" or " Address Unknown" message. When you receive an e-mail message, the header tells you where it came from, how it was sent, and when. It's like an electronic postmark.

Most e-mail programs let you insert what is known as a **signature** at the bottom of the message. This can be anything from a clever quote to additional information about you, such as your name, company name, title, phone number, and fax number. If you're creative, you can create a design using the characters on your keyboard and include it in your signature.

Here are some suggestions for using electronic mail.

1. Choose the subject heading carefully. The subject should identify the content of the message concisely and accurately. E-mail users frequently look only at the subject heading before deciding whether to read or delete a message.
2. Be careful with spelling and punctuation. Errors in an e-mail message reflect poorly on the sender. This is true whether the recipient is located within or outside an organization. Many e-mail programs contain spell check programs and some also contain grammar check programs. These tools should be used before sending a message.
3. Make your message as concise as possible, but don't make it cryptic and unclear. Both extremes should be avoided so that the message communicates effectively.
4. Include parts of the original message when you are writing a reply. This suggestion is made because the readers of a message may have forgotten the content of their original message. Many e-mail programs provide the capability to include the original message in the reply automatically.
5. Check the address when you compose or reply to a message. The reason for this is obvious: It is a waste of time if you have to resend the message.
6. Be careful when using humor and sarcasm. This sends a negative impression to many people and should be avoided. Humor and sarcasm are often misunderstood in a text-based document.
7. Don't assume that e-mail is private. It can easily be intercepted by e-mail administrators or others, and could be forwarded to unintended recipients. In the past, e-mail has been gathered to help convict people accused of committing crimes.
8. Take some time to consider what you will write. E-mail should be treated no differently than other forms of communication, which require planning before writing. Outlining is a good technique to use before composing an e-mail message.
9. Include a signature with your e-mail. As mentioned earlier, a signature is a good way to identify yourself to the reader of the message, as well as providing alternative ways for the recipient to contact you (phone, fax, physical address).

■ IMPLEMENTING ELECTRONIC MAIL

When an organization decides to implement an e-mail system, this does not mean that the system will automatically be successful. The success of an e-mail system depends on a variety of factors. This section deals with factors that need to be considered when implementing an e-mail system, and we discuss the strategies of implementation and acceptance. It will become clear that there is no single right way to implement e-mail, but that the right way depends on a variety of factors.

Four general conditions determine the success of e-mail. "Success" can be defined as the efficient use of e-mail through an entire organization. The first condition is the **geographical spreading** of the parts of the organization. It has been found that e-mail is used relatively infrequently in organizations that are located in one building. The importance of e-mail increases when an organization is more dispersed. In organizations with a wide geographic spread, e-mail can provide significant savings, which can change the entire organizational process.

Another condition is the **mutual dependency** of organizational parts. The various parts must have a need for communication and coordination; otherwise, a system like e-mail isn't really needed. E-mail provides an opportunity to increase an organization's integrity, but only if the system is widely accepted throughout the organization.

The third aspect that is important for the implementation of e-mail is the **critical mass**. To make the use of e-mail attractive, there must be a minimum number of users. A potential user must always compare the investment of time and effort needed to learn how to use the new system with the benefits that will ultimately be derived from its use. The benefits increase when the number of users is larger. The theory of the critical mass claims that a certain number of users can make the system accepted by the other employees. However, there are a few situations in which this theory doesn't stand up. One is effective use of e-mail between the only two employees of a company.

It can be concluded that the chance for acceptance increases with the number of users, but this is not a necessary or sufficient condition. If one really wants to make e-mail a success, the policy of the organization needs to be directed toward providing the entire organization with e-mail in a very short time. The policy should also encourage the use of e-mail whenever possible. The fourth condition is the **coupling** of e-mail systems of different types.

Frequently, work groups choose their own computer system, and different computer systems utilize different e-mail systems. A lack of integration between these systems causes a loss of functionality. An e-mail policy should consider the possibility that in the future, coupling to other systems may be needed. Another reason for having an e-mail policy is the growing exchange of e-mail messages between organizations. Therefore, selection of an organization-wide e-mail system is an important goal.

In theory, an organization can choose from three different strategies for the implementation of e-mail. In practice, these strategies are not totally separated, and organizations will use them in combination. The first is the strategy of **laissez-faire**. This is actually not a real strategy, in that the e-mail system is implemented in one department of the organization and then management waits for other departments to express an interest in having e-mail. This occurs until the entire organization is provided with e-mail. The second strategy can be called **controlled growing**. This approach often starts with selecting a department to initiate a pilot test, after which new groups of users are added systematically. These new users are first trained and then get their own e-mail accounts. The availability of training capacity determines the speed of growth.

The third strategy is **fast implementation**, whereby the users get access to the new system as quickly as possible. After an entity has decided to offer e-mail, it is implemented as quickly as possible. One potential problem with this strategy is that people who have not had a chance to receive training may become frustrated with trying to learn the system on their own.

Several recommendations can be made for the implementation of an e-mail system. First, it is important to create a sufficient mass of users quickly. Despite the criticism of the theory of the critical mass, it is true that risk of the loss of early users is larger if they can communicate with only a few other colleagues. It is important to discover which groups of employees communicate a great deal with each other and then connect these groups to the e-mail system.

Second, it is recommended that training be made broader and more flexible. Training should emphasize the ways in which e-mail can be used: for example, in which situations is it an appropriate medium, and in which situations might another medium be better? A user must learn to determine which medium is most appropriate for a specific purpose.

Third, managers must be involved in the process of implementation and acceptance. Often, it is difficult to convince managers of the benefits of the new medium, especially if they do not know how to use it themselves. However, acceptance by management seems to lead to the success of a system.

■ SUMMARY

Electronic mail (e-mail), which has become one of the most used communication technologies applications, is defined as electronic messaging that permits those who have an Internet or Intranet connection and have been assigned a user identification (e.g., jsmith@psu.edu) to send electronic messages to others connected to the Internet or an intranet.

Electronic mail possesses a number of advantages. E-mail may increase the productivity of organizations by making communication more effective and efficient. E-mail users do not need to be at the same place at the same time. E-mail is usually very fast, which provides rapid transmission and reply. E-mail can be sent one to one, one to many, or many to many. E-mail can be stored in external memory for future retrieval, searching, editing, and forwarding to others. The message is already stored in a digital version and can easily be manipulated by the receiver. E-mail may encourage people to engage in more face-to-face communication to discuss the contents of e-mail messages related to a particular project. Research has proven that the use of e-mail decreases the power distance inside an organization. Finally, there is the possibility of attaching other documents to e-mail messages.

Although electronic mail offers a number of advantages, it also possesses some disadvantages. These include the fact that there may be uncertainty concerning when an e-mail message was received and how to react to someone you don't know. E-mail at the present time is text based. This is a disadvantage because it is sometimes difficult to interpret a completely text-based message. E-mail inboxes can become cluttered with messages that were not requested. E-mail can be monitored and used for surveillance purposes.

When e-mail becomes a substitute for person-to-person interaction, it may have an adverse effect on an organization because of the difficulties that can arise interpreting an e-mail message.

An e-mail address consists of two parts. The first part is the user name of the person with whom you wish to communicate. User names are commonly up to eight characters long and are often derived from a person's real name. The second part of an e-mail address is the domain name of the mail server (a computer) where the person's electronic mailbox is located. When you put the user and domain names together, you have a unique e-mail address for a specific person. An "at" symbol (@) is always placed between the user name and the domain name of the mail server.

To send someone an e-mail message, you must know the unique e-mail address of that particular person. The obvious method of finding an e-mail address for someone is to ask the person. An increasing number of businesses are placing e-mail addresses on business cards, Web pages, and business stationery. Another way to determine someone's e-mail address is to consult an e-mail directory that maintains a database of thousands of e-mail addresses.

There are several terms associated with sending and receiving e-mail messages that are common regardless of which e-mail system is being used. These include the header, the body, and the signature. Some suggestions for using electronic mail include: choose the subject heading carefully; be careful with spelling and punctuation; make your message as concise as possible, but don't make it cryptic or unclear; include parts of the original message when you are writing a reply; be careful when using humor and sarcasm; don't assume that e-mail is private; take some time to consider what you will write; and include a signature with your e-mail.

When an organization decides to implement an e-mail system, this does not mean that the system will automatically be successful. Obviously, there is no one right way to implement e-mail. The success of an e-mail system depends on a variety of factors.

QUESTIONS

1. Define electronic mail (e-mail).

2. List and describe the benefits of using e-mail.

3. List and describe the drawbacks of using e-mail.

4. What are emoticons or smileys? What is their purpose?

5. How is e-mail addressed? What are the parts of an e-mail address?

6. How are e-mail addresses found?

7. Define the following terms associated with e-mail:
   (a) Header
   (b) Body
   (c) Signature

8. List five suggestions regarding the use of e-mail.

9. List and describe the four general conditions that determine the success of e-mail.

10. List and describe three strategies that can be used for the implementation of e-mail in an organization.

PROJECTS AND PROBLEMS

1. Talk to someone in a company or organization that had previously not used e-mail and is now using it, and determine the following:
   (a) Whether the use of e-mail has reduced the number of written memorandums within the organization. To what extent?
   (b) Whether the use of e-mail has reduced the number of letters and other correspondence to customers, clients, vendors, and others outside the organization. To what extent?
   (c) Whether there has been a decrease in the number of pieces of correspondence that the organization has received from individuals or companies outside the organization. To what extent?

2. Take a survey of businesses in your city or region to determine the brand of e-mail program that is being used. Which program is being used the most?

3. Compose five new smileys (emoticons) for use in e-mail messages to denote various emotions or thoughts that might not be easily conveyed through text only.

4. Which of the following e-mail addresses are acceptable? Which are not acceptable? Why not?
   (a) smith@byo.com
   (b) dsmith@main.byo.com
   (c) david smith @ byo.com
   (d) david_smith@byo.com
   (e) dave-smith%byo.com

5. An alternative for those who do not have an Internet service provider at home or when they are away from home are the free, advertisement-based e-mail providers. These are very popular among students. This e-mail can be accessed over the World Wide Web at any one of many e-mail providers. Advertising pays for this type of service and no special software is required. Some of the better known e-mail providers are Yahoo (http://www.yahoo.com), Hotmail (http://www.hotmail.com), and Bigfoot (http://www.bigfoot.com). How do these services work? How can they provide e-mail accounts without charging for them?

6. Assume that you are a telecommunications coordinator and your company has decided to utilize e-mail for the first time.
   (a) Explain the procedures that you would take to help the firm decide which e-mail system to adopt.

   (b) What would you do to ensure that an e-mail system is widely accepted and used properly?

7. Several fictitious e-mail messages have been sent to people telling them of pending legislation that would supposedly authorize the U.S. Postal Service to charge e-mail users "alternate postage fees." One of the messages indicated that there would be a five-cent surcharge on every e-mail delivered, which would be done by billing Internet service providers. Consumers would be billed in turn by their service providers. The messages go on to indicate that the U.S. Postal Service is claiming that lost revenue due to the proliferation of e-mail is costing nearly $230,000,000 in revenue per year. Since the average citizen received about 10 pieces of e-mail per day in 1998, the cost to the typical person would be an additional 50 cents per day, or over $180 dollars per year, above and beyond their regular Internet costs. It was noted that this would be money paid directly to the U.S. Postal Service for a service they do not even provide.
   (a) Comment on the reason you think this type of fictitious e-mail message was written.
   (b) Do think that the U.S. Postal Service might be concerned with increased use of e-mail?
   (c) Do you think that there will ever be a charge for sending e-mail messages as described? Why or why not?

8. Although John Eschbach was new to the Internet, he was quickly turning into a fanatic. He had been using the Net for about two months and everywhere he looked he saw opportunities for his business, Eschbach's Software Training. John had grown his company into the largest training firm in Kutztown in the short space of four years. He could see that the Internet might be an easy way to expand, even beyond the borders of the town. One day in a local bookshop John found a book that described the potential of using mass e-mail to reach possible clients. It seemed to him he would be a fool not to follow the authors' advice! As John saw it, World Wide Web pages are fine, but e-mail was the better way to reach customers. More people use e-mail than use the Web, and in addition, you have to wait until people happen to arrive at your Web site. With e-mail, your message goes to them directly. In addition, the cost of sending e-mail to 100,000 people is not much more than sending it to 1000 people. John got in contact with a group that could send e-mail to over 200,000 online consumers. The price was unbelievably

low compared with that of direct mail. John could hardly believe the opportunity.

(a) Would John's proposed use of e-mail be an example of spamming?

(b) Does spamming hurt its recipients? How might this be measured?

(c) Are people who engage in spamming under any legal or contractual obligation not to engage in unsolicited mass e-mailings? Is any dishonesty apparent or possible in the sending of spammed e-mail?

(d) If John were to send the spammed e-mail, might at least some of the recipients find it a bargain and get to take advantage of training that they might not have the opportunity for otherwise? Could one argue that since John has this opportunity, he has a duty to send this e-mail?

Vocabulary

body
controlled growing
coupling
critical mass
distribution list
electronic mail (e-mail)
fast implementation
geographical spreading
header
Internet
intranet
laissez-faire
mutual dependency
signature
emoticon
smiley
spamming
store-and-retrieve system

References

"Advantages and Disadvantages of E-Mail in Organizations," http://www.pscw.uva.nl/is/js/mail/5adv.htm.

Gehris, Dennis O., *Microsoft Internet Explorer 5.0*, South-Western Educational Publishing, Cincinnati, OH, 2000.

Gehris, Dennis O., *Using Multimedia Tools and Applications on the Internet*, Wadsworth Publishing, Belmont, CA, 1998.

"Learn the Net," http://www.learnthenet.com/english/index.html.

Rowe, Stanford H., II, *Telecommunications for Managers* 4th ed., Prentice Hall, Upper Saddle River, NJ, 1999.

Teleconferencing

In this chapter we provide a definition of teleconferencing and discuss the evolution of teleconferencing, teleconferencing applications, types of teleconferencing systems, benefits and drawbacks of teleconferencing, and how to plan, conduct, and evaluate a teleconference.

WHAT YOU WILL LEARN

- Definition of teleconferencing
- Evolution of teleconferencing
- Teleconferencing applications
- Types of teleconferencing systems
- Benefits of teleconferencing
- Drawbacks of teleconferencing
- How to plan, conduct, and evaluate a teleconference

■ EVOLUTION OF TELECONFERENCING

Since the 1970s, organizations have been using audio conferencing because it is inexpensive, can be accessed on demand, and the equipment required is already available. The world was introduced to AT&T's Picturephone at the 1964 New York World's Fair. The Picturephone was the first videoconferencing system to be developed. However, because of the excessive cost of videoconferencing equipment and transmission, it did not enjoy widespread use, except in a few industries, such as the aerospace industry. The lower cost for equipment and transmission in the early 1980s, however, made videoconferencing more attractive to an increasing number of organizations. Today, with the use of the Internet and intranets within organizations, the use of videoconferencing is at an all-time high. This use, and that of other types of teleconferencing, are predicted to continue in the future.

■ TELECONFERENCING DEFINED

A *conversation* involves people communicating with one another on a one-to-one basis, whereas a *conference* implies that more than two people are involved. A conference is seen as a more efficient way of communicating because it brings people together by reducing the number of face-to-face meetings. **Teleconferencing** is defined as the use of a telecommunications system for communicating with two or more groups or with three or more people at separate locations. It offers an alternative to the traditional meeting, which is one of the basic activities of business; at the same time, it changes how people communicate.

Teleconferencing can be either synchronous or asynchronous. Synchronous conferences are real-time conferences in which all participants are present simultaneously, regardless of the location or time zone. Most teleconferences are conducted in real time. In **store-and-forward conferences**, on the other hand, participants check in and respond at will, with each person deciding when he or she desires to participate.

■ TELECONFERENCING APPLICATIONS

The ways in which teleconferencing can be used in business, education, and for personal use are almost unlimited. The discussion here touches on only a few possible applications for this exciting technology.

Business

Larger businesses are already using teleconferencing, and smaller businesses are beginning to realize the benefits that it provides. Businesses typically use teleconferencing to exchange information; solve problems; introduce a new product, service, or procedure; conduct seminars for employees, customers, or clients; access experts; view documents/blueprints with others at different locations; train employees; hold a one-time event for employees at all locations to view simultaneously; or respond to emergency meetings.

Education

The term **distance learning** is often used in education to denote the use of teleconferencing in the classroom. The concept of distance learning is to use technology to link several classrooms containing students or a group of students together with a single instructor or lecturer. Some school districts envision the use of distance learning to broaden course offerings. If, for example, enrollment does not warrant the employment of French teachers for each of three high schools and junior high schools in a district, one teacher could be hired to use teleconferencing with links to each school. Some schools have also experimented with the use of distance learning as a supplement to home instruction. In this way, students who are unable to travel to school for health reasons, distance, or parental preference can hear and participate in classes from their own homes.

Colleges and universities are now using technology to broadcast what are commonly referred to as **telecourses**. Telecourses allow a student to view a series of videotaped lectures over a local television cable system or broadcast. After completing other requirements, such as taking tests and submitting research papers, a student receives the usual course credit. Some of the larger universities have been experimenting with supplementing or replacing telecourses with live broadcasts of lectures and seminars, so that the telecourses become a type of distance learning component.

Bill Gates, chairman and CEO of Microsoft Corporation, envisions schools installing in classrooms what he refers to as **digital whiteboards**. The whiteboards would be used to project images from the information highway. Whiteboards could be used for teleconferencing, making it unnecessary to install large video screens or other projection devices.

Personal Use

There are also many potential personal-use applications for teleconferencing. It could be used to bring together friends who, because of distance, aren't able to get together as frequently as they would like. Children or adults could use it to play video games or to research a topic by teleconferencing with a person who possesses expertise in a subject area. Internet-based teleconferencing is already in use. In the future it is likely to take the form of interactive television, in which a person would be able to express opinions relating to an issue or question being discussed by pressing a button via a handheld device.

■ TYPES OF TELECONFERENCING SYSTEMS

There are many different teleconferencing configurations that can be used, ranging from the very simple, in which the teleconference utilizes a simple speakerphone, to an expensive two-way video conference, in which people can see and hear each other and exchange graphics and documents. The investment in teleconferencing can range from as little as $100 to over $1 million.

The four types of teleconferencing that organizations can choose to use are listed and described briefly below. Each type can operate independently or can be combined with another.

1. **Audio conferencing.** This is the simplest and least costly of the four systems. It consists of an audio-only configuration in which two or more groups or three or more individuals at separate locations exchange verbal information with each other using either conference calls and/or amplified telephone speaker devices (speakerphones). Because this is an audio-only system, participants can hear and be heard but cannot see or be seen. In a variation of this system, the audio-only system is supplemented by a fax machine, so that sites can send photographs, documents, graphics, and the like, transmitting them as the audio conference is progressing. This variation is sometimes referred to as *enhanced audio conferencing* or as an *audiographic system.*
2. **Videoconferencing.** This is the most complex and most costly of the four teleconferencing systems but offers the most multimedia capability. It provides two or more sites with interactive two-way video, audio, and graphics capabilities.
3. **Business television.** This system transmits live television one way from a central site to one or more sites. Such a system is usually complemented by two-way audio transmission (usually via a telephone), so that viewers may enter into a discussion with speakers.
4. **Computer conferencing.** This is an electronic means of sending, viewing, and sharing real-time communications in areas of common interest by using a computer keyboard.

Next, we examine each type of teleconferencing in greater detail.

Audio Conferencing

Audio conferencing permits voice interaction among a number of participants, usually over standard telephone lines. One way to accomplish this is to make a standard **conference call**, in which the telephone company assists in linking three or more people so that each person can communicate with each of the others using standard telephones and one telephone connection. Audio conferencing is an indispensable tool for any business on the go, including telecommuters and anyone who works from a virtual office. It's an easy, effective, and affordable way to get things done: to update projects, brainstorm, make announcements, and share information. AT&T believes that audio conferencing can help employees to expedite decisions, optimize productivity, react more quickly to events in the marketplace, conduct meetings, and coordinate activities when traveling away from the office. AT&T audio conferencing is available 24 hours a day, seven days a week.

There are three options that organizations can choose: operator-dialed, dial-in, or host-dialed services. With operator-dialed service, AT&T makes audio conference arrangements for you. The dial-in option provides flexibility by enabling participants to call into the audio conference from virtually any telephone, including hotel phones and public pay phones. The host-dialed service is designed for spur-of-the-moment interactive audio conferences and for conferences you want to set up yourself.

Another way to conduct audio conferencing is to use only two sites with multiple participants at each site while making one telephone connection. Each site is equipped with a speakerphone, which is placed in a conference room. All participants at both sites are told when to meet in the conference room.

AT&T offers the following suggestions when using audio conferencing.

Before the call:

- Plan ahead!
- Advise participants of the teleconference date, time, and expected duration.
- Provide all printed materials to participants in advance.
- Let people know that you will start promptly.
- Remember: Equipment makes a difference. Speakerphones should be of the highest quality available.
- Be aware that air-to-ground and cellular phones may adversely affect sound quality and plan accordingly.

During the call:

- Call the roll.
- Begin with the agenda and ground rules for the meeting.
- Direct questions and comments to specific persons or locations.
- Encourage participation and keep things moving.
- Choose a date and time for your next teleconference while everyone is still on the line.

Ask participants to:

- Speak naturally.
- Identify themselves when speaking.
- Pause for others to comment.
- Spell out unusual terms, names, and numbers.
- Mute the speakerphone microphone when not speaking.
- Seat key participants closest to the speakerphone or use a handset if possible.
- Avoid putting phones on hold—phone systems with music-on-hold will disrupt the teleconference.

After the call:

- Follow up.
- Call to reserve your next teleconference.

It is also possible to conduct an audio conference using a private branch exchange (PBX) or other telephone system conference bridge. A **conference bridge** is an electronic device that connects three or more sites via the participant's telephone lines in order to reduce the amount of signal loss and background noise. It permits calls to be made at lower cost and makes it possible to use **WATS telephone service**. These bridges are usually limited to six lines and cannot amplify weak connections. To ensure reasonable quality without amplification, PBX bridges usually restrict audio conferencing to the use of only two or six outside lines.

Equipment Needed

- *Telephone.* The simplest audio conferencing terminal is the telephone. However, the telephone can be awkward to use when taking notes and can be tiring for long conferences. A solution to these problems when using a standard telephone is to use a headset that allows hands-free conversations.

- *Speakerphone.* A **speakerphone** is a simple modular audio terminal that consists of a microphone, an on–off switch, volume control, an indicator light, and a loudspeaker. Some speakerphones are peripherals into which standard telephones are plugged. Other speakerphones have all of these components built into a standard telephone, which makes it possible to switch from using standard telephone headset to speakerphone components and back again. One of the complaints of using speakerphones is that they sometimes generate a barrel effect, a slight echo from the speaker's voice. This can be overcome by using a meetingroom that has better acoustics and by reducing the distance between the speaker and the microphone. Meetingrooms should contain materials that absorb sound, such as carpeted floors, drapes, and acoustic tile ceilings.

- *Facsimile.* **Facsimile machines** (described in Chapter 5) provide audio-conferenced meetings with immediate copies of documents, including charts, graphics, or any other necessary information. Faxed documents must be timed carefully to keep the discussion flowing smoothly.

- *Electronic whiteboard.* An **electronic whiteboard** (sometimes called a *telewriter*) is an electromechanical device that allows participants to write or draw their contributions as they talk. Every mark, line, or dot that is drawn or written on the whiteboard is translated immediately into signals that are communicated through the telephone network. Some Web-based computer conferencing and videoconferencing programs use whiteboards. At the receiving end, the information is displayed on a video monitor, exactly as it is drawn on the board. Some whiteboards have the capability of recording the entire discussion, including graphics, on a magnetic medium such as cassette tape.

Audio Conferencing Applications.   Audio conferences lend themselves more easily to certain types of applications than to others. Audio conferencing is a quick way to conduct a meeting when little time is allotted for planning before initiating a conference. For example, if an expert were brought in for a presentation on short notice, an audio conference would be a good way for more employees to participate in the discussion. Organizations have also used audio conferences to conduct screening sessions for job applicants, and to conduct seminars.

Videoconferencing

Videoconferencing is a sophisticated type of teleconferencing that has recently gained much interest for use in business and in education, defined as a full-motion two-way video/audio system that permits two or more people in different locations to communicate with each other. This is in contrast to what has been referred to as **business television** or *point-to-multipoint videoconferencing*, in which all participating sites receive video images but only one site is able to transmit them. Two-way videoconferencing is often used for large groups and by colleges and universities that offer video courses.

Organizations have experienced several barriers to using videoconferencing. One problem has been that the cost of equipment, as well as transmission costs for running a videoconferencing system, have been very high. Consequently, only a few very large organizations have been able to afford to install videoconferencing systems. Today, the costs associated with this technology have decreased greatly, allowing smaller organizations the opportunity to enjoy the benefits of videoconferencing. However, a problem that continues is the lack of a national broadband network that makes it possible to send multiple applications over telephone lines simultaneously. Until a broadband network is operational, use of the integrated services digital network (ISDN) or digital simultaneous voice data (DSVD) technology are the best alternatives.

There are various facility configurations that allow for videoconferencing. One configuration, which is used by larger organizations, consists of built-in or permanent videoconference rooms that contain cameras and other video equipment, but otherwise resemble a regular conference room. Another configuration is the mobile or portable conference system that is contained in a unit that can be moved from one room to another. The third configuration is the desktop system, in which a personal computer is combined with a camera, microphone, and network connection. Special computer software is also needed to make a desktop videoconferencing system complete.

Conducting a Successful Videoconference.   There are certain things to consider when conducting a videoconference:

- *Lighting.* When preparing for a videoconference, you should not rely on overhead lights, especially fluorescent lights, and you should make sure that a window is not directly behind the speaker, as he or she will appear as a dark shadow. You should try to avoid squeezing more than two or three people into your video window, as it is important to be able to see a speaker's facial expressions as he or she talks. You should also avoid the use of a portable light that shines on the speaker in "spotlight" fashion.

■ *Cue cards/eye contact.* Speakers' notes should be printed on posterboard in very large type to make cue cards. This will prevent the audience from viewing the speaker's forehead instead of his or her eyes, as would occur if the speaker were using traditional cue cards. The speaker should look directly into the camera as he or she is speaking. It is suggested that the person holding the cue cards stand behind the camera so that the speaker appears to be looking into the camera when accessing notes.

■ *Audio.* To overcome poor audio transmission over the network, you should pause video transmission frequently and remind participants to speak loudly, distinctly, and at a slow rate. Speakers should also vary the tone of their voices and use inflection in their speech.

■ *Photos and props.* It is recommended that speakers use photos and props to enhance presentations. In this capacity, the speaker should consider himself or herself as a storyteller. A simple way of accomplishing this is to hold a photo or prop in front of the camera and cause the picture to pause. After resuming, the speaker tells the story that goes with the picture. This approach is much more effective than watching a "talking head."

■ *Interactivity.* It is recommended that you stop at least every 10 minutes to allow for interaction, as the main reason for using "live" video is so that the viewers can interact with the speakers.

■ *Appearance and attention.* Because it is very distracting to see viewers fidgeting, yawning, or talking among themselves, these gestures should be avoided. If participants feel that they must engage in these actions, the video transmission should be suspended temporarily. Some clothing appears better on video transmissions than other attire. Those conducting a videoconference should experiment before the event to see what fabric colors and patterns look best.

■ *Moderator.* The use of a moderator for a videoconference is highly recommended, and he or she should play a major part in the conference. The moderator should make the welcoming comments, cue each participant when it is his or her turn to speak, keep the pace of the conference moving along, and end the conference as planned.

■ *Video clips.* Very short video clips (less than 2 minutes) can be used to enhance the videoconference. One should keep in mind that the video clip may appear to viewers to be progressing much more slowly than it may to you.

■ *Rehearsals.* Rehearsals are a very good idea, especially when dealing with inexperienced presenters. Participants should practice in front of the camera and critique one another several times before the actual videoconference.

CU-SeeMe Videoconferencing.   Currently, a very popular two-way videoconferencing software that is being used over the Internet is **CU-SeeMe** (pronounced "see you, see me"), which was developed and distributed free of charge by Cornell University in Ithaca, New York. The first network-capable version of CU-SeeMe, called WatchTim, was created in August 1992. CU-SeeMe developers at Cornell were asked to assist in setting up an Internet videoconference sponsored by the National Science Foundation in 1993. The developers have also had a relationship with the Global Schoolhouse, which is a project that links schools with businesses and government throughout the United States. White Pine Software teamed up with Cornell University to further develop the CU-SeeMe software. Currently, First Virtual Communications is marketing an enhanced color version of CU-SeeMe. For more information on this version, visit their home page at http://www.fvc.com.

Currently, software is available that will work with both Macintosh and Windows (PC-compatible) computers. CU-SeeMe users can connect to one another point to point, so that the connection operates somewhat like a videophone. To use CU-SeeMe point to point, two people must be connected to the Internet and using CU-SeeMe software simultaneously. Each person will see a video window of the other person and should be able to speak to the other person with the use of a microphone. One user must know the numeric IP (Internet protocol) address of the other person. Internet service providers assign IP addresses to users dynamically. Therefore, a different address is assigned each time one connects. Thus, there must be a means of determining the IP address before the meeting.

CU-SeeMe can also be used for group conferencing, which necessitates the use of a reflector. In this way, several video windows appear on the screen, one for each person connected to the reflector. A reflector is a computer that uses the UNIX operating system, which runs special software. The reflector redistributes video and audio streams to another, which connects to it. Because of the amount of bandwidth required for a group conference, a regular phone connection (using a modem) may not yield good results. A direct Internet connection is much more effective when using CU-SeeMe for group conferencing.

CU-SeeMe can also be used for one-way broadcast sessions. For example, the National Aeronautics and Space Administration broadcasts NASA television, which is carried on several CU-SeeMe reflectors. The broadcasts show ongoing NASA operations, including press conferences, launches, and landings. Some of these broadcasts are live; others are videotaped.

The special hardware that is required for CU-SeeMe falls into two categories: video and audio. Video equipment is needed to send video images to others who are participating in a videoconference. Although CU-SeeMe will work without video equipment, its effectiveness will be greatly diminished. The audio equipment may be necessary for you to hear others talk and for you to participate in the conversations.

Video Equipment. The most desirable basic piece of video equipment is some type of video camera. Video cameras can be classified into two categories: dedicated desktop cameras and general-purpose analog cameras. Dedicated cameras are designed specifically for desktop applications but are generally more expensive than general-purpose cameras. To use a general-purpose camera (and some dedicated cameras) with a PC-compatible computer, you will also need a video capture card. Not all video capture cards will work with CU-SeeMe. Check the CU-SeeMe documentation for a list of compatible cards.

One desktop camera that will work with CU-SeeMe is the Quickcam by Logitech. This is an inexpensive, color image camera that is currently available for both the Macintosh and Windows (PC-compatible) computers. The camera is a golf-ball-size camera that does not require a video capture card. On the Macintosh it works with QuickTime software and connects to the computer via a serial cable to a printer or modem port. On a PC-compatible computer, it uses Video for Windows software and connects via the printer or USB ports. The QuickCam Pro camera provides images up to 640 by 480 pixels with 8 bits/color output and operates at up to 30 frames per second. It has an onboard microphone, a field of view of about 65 degrees, and a fixed focus. Although the microphone is functional, it competes for bandwidth with the video signal. For that reason, you may want to consider a separate microphone, discussed in the next section.

Audio Equipment.   The following audio options are available for use with a Macintosh computer: the external microphone or the PlainTalk microphone appropriate to the machine; the built-in microphone, third-party microphones, and general-purpose desktop video camera microphones. Using an add-on microphone with CU-SeeMe will work if the Macintosh has a built-in audio input jack.

Audio support for CU-SeeMe for Windows is a recent addition to the software. Any PC-compatible computer with built-in sound capabilities or an added sound card should work. However, the card needs to be full-duplex, which means that it must accept input and output audio at the same time. SoundBlaster, which is the most popular sound card for PCs, is only half-duplex at the time of writing this book. Although a half-duplex card will work, the audio signals will be interrupted by other signals being transmitted at the same time. Future SoundBlaster products that will become available while this book is in use may be full-duplex. An add-on microphone will connect to a jack on the sound card or to a jack somewhere on the computer if the sound is built in.

Business Television

Some people confuse videoconferencing with business television. As we've seen, videoconferencing involves two-way video and sound transmission that can also be called point-to-point conferencing. Although business television uses video, it is instead **point-to-multipoint conferencing,** since all sites receive images, but only one site can transmit them. That is, business television allows a company to broadcast audio and video messages simultaneously to all or any of its geographical offices. Although the receiving sites cannot transmit video, their audio component may be bidirectional, allowing them to participate in a discussion with the sending site.

Organizations that want to use business television need to have a television studio, which is usually located on the organization's premises, although some companies use public or commercial production facilities. The programs are either broadcast live or taped and then rebroadcast from television studios. Viewers at the receiving locations gather around the television set and watch the program.

Live business television broadcasts usually have a telephone available that allows viewers to call in and ask questions of the people who are speaking. Viewers may telephone a number flashed on the screen or may give a written question to a designated person for telephoning to the transmuting station.

Business television programs are often encrypted before transmission to prevent unauthorized people from viewing them. Television signals are sent via receiving sites by microwave, local area networks, or satellite networks.

Business television can be used for occasional events, such as new product introductions, special employee meetings, or press conferences. It can also be used for ongoing activities such as routine meetings and employee training. Educational programs are available that schools and colleges can often utilize, such as lectures by world-renowned economists or panel discussions conducted by professional associations.

Computer Conferencing

Unlike e-mail, computer conferencing allows you to communicate or "chat" via your computer with people who share the network connection in real time. That is, you are able to carry on "live" conversations with these people on any topic that you choose. As you key your message, the other persons connected see your message on their computer screens. Some computer conferencing systems allow you to include links to graphics and audio files.

In business firms, computer conferencing augments or replaces face-to-face conferences. It combines the back-and-forth discussion of a meeting with the capability of retrieving research reports and other documents stored on the network. The online conference gives all employees an opportunity to add suggestions and comments to the discussion. The person at an organization who is responsible for managing a conference is called a *moderator*. This person is responsible for establishing the conference, specifying the rules of membership, conducting the conference, and terminating the conference. Computer conferences can be private or public. Private conferences are restricted to a particular group of people, whereas public conferences are open to anyone.

There are two main types of computer conference application programs: UNIX- and Web-based programs. UNIX-based programs are text-based programs that operate with a server that operates under the UNIX operating system. The most popular UNIX-based computer conferencing program is called Internet Relay Chat. The Web-based programs are multimedia programs that can use text, graphics, and audio. These programs operate with a Web browser such as Internet Explorer or Netscape.

UNIX-Based Programs.   There are several text-based computer conferencing programs that have been available for use on the Internet for some time. These cannot be considered multimedia applications because they are UNIX-based and do not necessitate the use of a Web browser. Examining how these programs work will help you to better understand multimedia-based programs. Ask your network administrator which of the following text-based programs are available for your use. You may have already used these programs, as most local networks have one or both of these programs available.

Talk.   The simplest of these programs is called Talk. To use Talk, it must be installed on your host computer. Both parties must be logged on for a Talk session to occur. One person initiates the session and the other person accepts or rejects it. As an example, to initiate a session, the initiator would key "talk jsmith@grantu.edu" at the UNIX prompt. If the person is logged on, his or her terminal will beep and the following message will appear on the screen, asking him if he wants to talk: "talk: connection requested by ssmith@pluto.henry.edu". If he or she wants to talk, the person will enter "talk@pluto.henry.edu" and the screen will split in two halves. The top of the screen displays what you key, and the bottom half of the screen displays what the other person keys.

Internet Relay Chat. **Internet Relay Chat (IRC) is** the most used text-based computer conferencing program. IRC is either installed on your host computer or you can telnet to another site that has made IRC available. If IRC has been installed on your local network, keying "irc" (lowercase) at the UNIX prompt usually initiates the program. With IRC all participants assign themselves nicknames or "handles," and conversations are conducted on channels, where people discuss various topics. A similar system is used on the multimedia computer conferencing systems discussed below.

After assigning yourself a nickname and logging on to initiate an IRC session, you key "/list" to see the names of the active channels, numbers of current participants, and the channel topics. After finding a channel that you'd like to join, you key "/join #channelname", where channelname is the actual name of the channel. You can key your message, which should appear on the screen, along with the messages from other people who have joined the channel. For some channels you must have an invitation to join, in which case you key "/who #channelname" to see a list of the participants. You then pick a name of the person with "@" next to the name and send the person a message (e.g., "/msg name I'd like to join #channelname).

Some IRC channels maintain Web pages. The "IRC Channels Lists" page (http://www.irchelp.org/irchelp/chanlist) provides an index to the Web pages of over 200 IRC channels, including such channels as #comics, #romance, and #windows95. The typical page has an FAQ for users of the channel, a directory of frequent channel users (often with photos), and a collection of links to related sites. Next we look at some of the most common Web-based computer conferencing programs. Many of these programs possess multimedia features.

Web-Based Programs. There are several multimedia computer conferencing programs available that are Web-based for use with the Internet. One of these programs is **Go Chat**, which is a very popular, real-time fully multimedia computer conferencing application for the Web. Go Chat allows visitors at Web sites to engage in live conversation, similar to IRC. The difference between Go Chat and IRC is that users can quickly incorporate images, video and audio clips, and "hotlinks" into their chat. Go Chat server software is available that runs as an add-on to most Web servers. However, you can use Go Chat with any standard browser and no special software needs to be downloaded to begin chatting immediately. The URL to access Go Chat is http://www.go.com/Community/Chat. Figure 4-1 shows the Go Chat network screen.

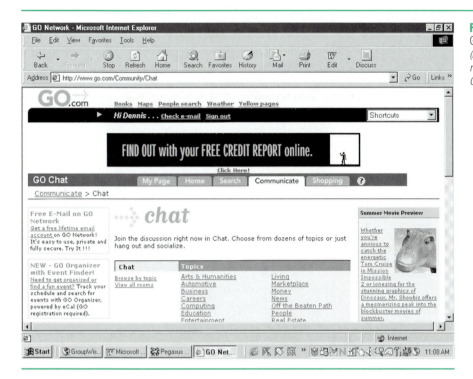

Figure 4-1
Go Chat Network Screen.
(Microsoft Internet Explorer™ screen shot reprinted by permission from Microsoft Corporation)

■ BENEFITS OF TELECONFERENCING

There are some distinct benefits associated with business use of teleconferencing:

1. *It improves productivity.* By eliminating the need to travel to another place for a meeting, more time is made available to concentrate on other activities.
2. *It controls travel costs and time.* Traditionally, meetings have been held off-site at remote locations. The costs of holding meetings off-site include the cost of transportation, lodging, and meals, mailing expenses, as well as nonproductive employee time. Even though some face-to-face meetings may be necessary, organizations that utilize teleconferencing can greatly reduce the costs mentioned previously.
3. *It solves problems quickly and efficiently.* There are times when an organization must solve a problem in a short time. Problem solving is expedited by quickly arranging for a teleconference instead of trying to coordinate the schedules of people involved in a traditional meeting.
4. *It provides access to experts.* Teleconferencing can help organizations make experts available to employees when key individuals do not have time to travel to meetings or lectures. In particular, videoconferencing and business television provide an excellent way to tap into the advice that is available from experts.

5. *It provides a good opportunity to exchange information.* Teleconferencing allows for the rapid exchange of verbal information, as well as graphics and other documents. Although e-mail is a good vehicle for the exchange of information, teleconferencing is better for this purpose, because of the chance for participants to interact with one another more thoroughly.

6. *It facilitates employee training and cuts training costs.* Training can be a very expensive cost, especially when trainers or trainees need to be moved to another location. Teleconferencing can provide an excellent way of cutting these costs while providing consistent training to all employees throughout an organization.

7. *It provides tighter control of meetings.* Because of the fact that participants are aware of the costs incurred related to transmission charges associated with a teleconference, it is likely that teleconferenced meetings will be more structured and shorter then traditional meetings.

8. *It allows customers and employees who are dispersed over a wide geographical area the opportunity to exchange ideas more frequently.* Because of the loss of time and related travel costs needed to bring people together, some meetings are held infrequently or not at all. Teleconferencing provides the opportunity for meetings that might never have taken place with traditional face-to-face conferencing.

9. *It provides an alternative method to announce new products and services.* Teleconferencing can be used as a promotional medium to make customers, company salespeople, and other employees aware of the existence of new products, product lines, and services in a short period of time.

■ DRAWBACKS OF TELECONFERENCING

There are some drawbacks of teleconferencing for business that should be noted:

1. *It may decrease interpersonal contact and morale.* Humans are social beings and human interaction among employees provides greater motivation and increases morale. Although teleconferencing brings people together, it is often not a good substitute for face-to-face interaction.

2. *Teleconferencing depends on technology that can malfunction.* Technology cannot always be relied on to provide flawless service without some downtime. Unfortunately, this downtime cannot always be predicted. For example, weather conditions may affect a satellite link and disrupt service. Since teleconferencing will not work without technology, there may be times when electronic meetings cannot take place when planned because of a malfunction. It is also possible for people to sabotage equipment and transmissions so that they will not work when planned.

3. *It can increase nonproductive time spent in meetings.* Because some organizations feel that they need to increase the number of electronic meetings in order to justify costs, there may be an increase in the number of meetings. If this happens, time may be wasted that could have been spent on more productive job activities.

4. *It can encourage narrowness and overspecialization.* As mentioned above, organizations may feel that they need to increase the number of meetings when using teleconferencing methods. The additional meetings that are scheduled may result in topics that are unnecessarily narrow in scope.

5. *It can decrease managerial freedom of operation in local* divisions and departments. Field managers may feel that their managerial prerogative is being usurped when teleconferenced meetings are held at a central location rather than locally. Although this may be a false perception, it can cause managers to feel that central management is exerting too much control.

■ PLANNING, CONDUCTING, AND EVALUATING A TELECONFERENCE

Successful teleconferences do not just happen. They are a result of careful planning, monitoring, and evaluation, involving much time and effort to ensure that they provide maximum benefits for an organization. A well-planned teleconference involves four steps: conducting a needs assessment, planning the teleconference, conducting the teleconference, and evaluating the teleconference.

Step 1. Conduct a Needs Assessment.   A needs assessment first involves identification of the work groups that can benefit from teleconferencing. Once this has been decided, the type of teleconference, equipment, and facilities are determined. The process involves an analysis of the types of meetings that are currently being conducted, the travel costs of these meetings, and a determination of the unproductive costs and outcome. Here is a list of questions that should be answered in the needs assessment:

- What types of meetings is the department or organization conducting?
- What are the purposes of these meetings?
- Who attends these meetings?
- Where are the meeting participants located?
- How is information currently being exchanged (i.e., through discussion, demonstration, and/or lecture)?
- How often are meetings held?
- How are meetings scheduled?
- What are the travel expenditures to and from meetings?
- What would be the cost to utilize teleconferencing for these meetings?
- Is there a cost savings by using various types of teleconferencing? If yes, how much and over what period of time?

Step 2. Plan the Teleconference.   If the results of the needs assessment show that a cost savings would result by utilizing teleconferencing, the next step is to decide which type of teleconference to implement and to complete the steps that will be necessary to conduct the first teleconference. Figure 4-2 is a form that will assist in planning a teleconference. Some of the items may need to be adjusted, depending on the type of conference.

Figure 4-2
Teleconferencing Planning Form

TELECONFERENCING PLANNING FORM

Subject of Teleconferencing Meeting _____

The teleconference will be held on _____

☐ Facilities have been reserved   ☐ Equipment has been reserved

Purpose of the Meeting _____

MEETING AGENDA:

Agenda Item	Amount of Time
#1 _____	_____
#2 _____	_____

(add more lines if there are additional agenda items)

PARTICIPANTS:

Name	Notified on	Notified by
_____	_____	☐ Telephone ☐ E-Mail ☐ Interoffice
Memo		
_____	_____	☐ Postal Mail
Memo		
_____	_____	☐ Telephone ☐ E-Mail ☐ Interoffice
Memo		

(add additional lines if there are additional participants)

SUPPORTING MATERIALS:
(including list of attendees and their telephone numbers)   ☐ Postal Mail

Description   ☐ Telephone ☐ E-Mail ☐ Interoffice

_____

_____   ☐ Postal Mail

When prepared _____When mailed/e-mailed _____

IMPLEMENTING AGENDA ITEMS:

How will each agenda item be presented (i.e., interview, report, lecture)?

#1 _____

#2 _____

(add additional lines if necessary)

How will information for each agenda item be exchanged (i.e., round-table discussion, brainstorming, and/or case study)?

#1 _____

#2 _____

(add additional lines if necessary)

CHECKLIST FOR CONDUCTING A TELECONFERENCE

_____ Conference started on time

_____ Attendance taken

_____ Objectives, agenda, and meeting rules reviewed

_____ Participants asked to identify themselves when they speak

_____ Everyone encouraged to participate

_____ Questions asked to stimulate discussion

_____ Agenda followed

_____ Paused occasionally to allow others to comment

_____ Key points summarized

_____ Follow-up action activities assigned

_____ Next meeting scheduled and planned

_____ Decisions summarized

_____ Meeting adjourned

Figure 4-3
Checklist for Conducting a Teleconference

Step 3. Conduct the Teleconference. By planning your teleconferenced meeting carefully, you will ensure that it will be successful. Figure 4-3 is a checklist for conducting a teleconference. Some of the items may need to be changed, depending on the type of teleconference.

Step 4. Evaluate the Teleconference. On completion of the teleconference, it is a good idea to distribute a questionnaire to participants to ask them how effective they felt the meeting was and to solicit suggestions for future meetings. The results of the questionnaires should be analyzed to determine how future teleconferences might be improved. Periodically, additional questionnaires should be distributed to everyone who participated in a teleconference to assess whether teleconferencing is meeting its objectives. Examples of such objectives would include improving decision making, cutting costs, or improving revenues.

■ SUMMARY

Since the 1970s, organizations have been using audio conferencing because it is inexpensive, can be accessed on demand, and the equipment required is already available. A conversation involves people communicating with one another on a one-to-one basis, whereas a conference implies that more than two people are involved. A conference is seen as a more efficient way of communicating because it brings people together by reducing the number of face-to-face meetings.

Teleconferencing is defined as the use of a telecommunications system for communicating with two or more groups or with three or more people at separate locations. It offers an alternative to the traditional meeting, which is one of the basic activities of business; at the same time, it changes how people communicate.

The ways in which teleconferencing can be used in business, education, and for personal use are almost unlimited. There are many different teleconferencing configurations that can be used, ranging from the very simple, in which the teleconference utilizes a simple speakerphone, to an expensive two-way video conference, in which people can see and hear each other and exchange graphics and documents. The investment in teleconferencing can range from as little as $100 to over $1 million.

The four types of teleconferencing that organizations can choose to use are audio conferencing, videoconferencing, business television, and computer conferencing. The benefits of business use of teleconferencing include increased productivity, control of travel costs and time, problems solved quickly and efficiently, access to experts provided, employee training facilitated and training costs cut, tighter control of meetings, brings together customers and employees dispersed over a wide geographical area, and provides a good way to announce new products and services.

There are also some drawbacks of teleconferencing that should be noted. It may decrease interpersonal contact and morale, it depends on technology that can malfunction, it can increase nonproductive time spent in meetings, it can encourage narrowness and overspecialization, and it can decrease managerial freedom of operation in local divisions and departments.

Successful teleconferences do not just happen. They are a result of careful planning, monitoring, and evaluation involving much time and effort to ensure that they provide maximum benefits for an organization. A well-planned teleconference involves four steps: conducting a needs assessment, planning the teleconference, conducting the teleconference, and evaluating the teleconference.

QUESTIONS

1. What is teleconferencing?

2. How has teleconferencing evolved from the 1970s to the present?

3. How is teleconferencing used in business, education, and for personal use?

4. What are the four types of teleconferencing? How is each defined?

5. What are three options for the use of audio conferencing?

6. How are conference bridges used with audio conferencing?

7. What equipment is needed for audio conferencing? Explain each type.

8. Provide examples of how audio conferencing can be used.

9. What are barriers to the use of videoconferencing?

10. What are various facility configurations for videoconferencing?

11. What should be considered when conducting a successful videoconference related to the following: lighting, cue cards/eye contact, audio, photos and props, interactivity, appearance and attention, moderator, video clips, and rehearsals?

12. What is CU-SeeMe videoconferencing? What is a reflector?

13. What special hardware is required for CU-SeeMe?

14. How does business television differ from videoconferencing? How is it similar?

15. What is required for using business television?

16. How is computer conferencing defined? How does it differ from e-mail?

17. What are the two main types of computer conferencing programs?

18. What is Internet Relay Chat (IRC)?

19. What is Go Chat?

20. What are the advantages of computer conferencing over e-mail?

21. What are the benefits of business use of teleconferencing?

22. What are the drawbacks of business use of teleconferencing?

23. Explain how to plan a teleconference.

24. Explain how to conduct a teleconference.

25. Explain how to evaluate a teleconference.

PROJECTS AND PROBLEMS

1. Prepare a chart that lists the types of teleconferencing and the advantages and disadvantages of each type. Use the following column heads:

   Type of Teleconferencing   Advantages   Disadvantages

2. Recommend a type of teleconferencing for each of the following situations. State the reasons for your choice.
   (a) A transportation company is screening applicants for a middle-management position and wants to determine which applicants to invite in for a formal interview.
   (b) A software training firm wants to deliver training for a word processing program to a group of office managers.
   (c) A snack food manufacturer wants to introduce a new product to its sales force.
   (d) An automobile manufacturer wants to inform dealers of the new models and the status of delivery availability.

3. To install a videoconferencing system for use in training employees, a company must make a significant investment in monitors, cameras, and other equipment. In determining how this expenditure can be justified, what costs associated with "traditional" training in which a trainer is employed to train employees at each of six sites would be reduced?

4. The Thurman Company trains field salespersons in sales techniques and new products using the "traditional" method. During the 10 years of operation, the company has assembled all salespersons at a central location within each of the six regions. You have been hired as a consultant to select a teleconferencing system that would take the place of traditional training. Recommend one of the types of teleconferencing for the Thurman Company. State the reasons for your recommendation.

5. Assuming that you have the necessary hardware, download and install the shareware or demonstration version of a teleconferencing program. You can also search for a teleconferencing program on the Tucows Network (http://www.tucows.com) or Strouds CWSApps (http://www.cws.internet.com). Use the software and report back your experiences while using it.

6. Access and use Internet Relay Chat (IRC) or one of the Web-based computer conferencing programs, such as Go.com (http://www.go.com/chat) or ICQ (http://www.icq.com/community/chat.html). Report on your experiences while using these.

7. A computer hardware company has just developed a new combination facsimile/color laser printer, which is to be introduced into the market at the end of the current month. Since the printer is significantly different from previous laser printers, it will be necessary to train the sales staff on how to use the product and how to sell it. The company estimates that the training will require 5 hours. The company usually

conducts its training by sending a product engineer to each of its three regional sales locations. The company is currently considering the possibility of conducting training from its main engineering facility using videoconferencing. A facsimile machine would also be available for the transmission of training documents during the teleconference. The approximate costs of sending the engineer to travel to each site with one overnight stay are as follows: airfare ($300), lodging ($125), and per day payment to the engineer ($100). Costs of a videoconference include videoconferencing equipment for each site ($5000). Costs of the long-distance telephone charges for facsimile transmission are $35 per hour, and ISDN connection service for the videoconference costs $25 per hour.

(a) What are the costs of each training approach ("traditional" training method and videoconference for all three sites)?

(b) Which approach do you recommend?

(c) What are the benefits and drawbacks of your recommendation?

Vocabulary

audio conferencing

business television

computer conferencing

conference bridge

conference call

CU-SeeMe

digital whiteboard

distance learning

electronic whiteboard

facsimile machine

Go Chat

Internet Relay Chat

point-to-multipoint conferencing

speakerphone

store-and-forward conference

teleconferencing

telecourse

videoconferencing

WATS telephone service

References

AT&T, "AT&T Audio Conferencing," http://www.att.com/conferencing/general.html.

AT&T, "Tips and Techniques for Audio Conference Calls," http://www.att.com/conferencing/tipstech.html.

Gates, Bill, *The Road Ahead*, Penguin Books, New York, 1995.

Gehris, Dennis, *Using Multimedia Tools and Applications on the Internet*, Wadsworth Publishing, Belmont, CA, 1998.

Global Schoolhouse, http://www.k12.cnidr.org/gsh/gshwelcome.html.

Rowe, Stanford H., II, *Telecommunications for Managers*, 4th ed., Prentice Hall, Upper Saddle River, NJ, 1999.

Tedesco, Eleanor Hollis, *Telecommunications for Business*. PWS-Kent, Boston, 1990.

CHAPTER

5

Voice Processing and Facsimile

I n this chapter we provide a definition of voice processing terminology and discuss voice processing technologies, functions, applications, benefits, and drawbacks. The chapter also covers facsimile hardware, applications, benefits, and drawbacks.

■ VOICE PROCESSING TERMINOLOGY DEFINED

Voice processing is another important communication technology application that deals with computerized speech, reacting to human speech, and storing and understanding the human voice. Through computerized voice functions, people can access information bases and services. We are all accustomed to entering data via computer keyboards, but voice processing permits input either through a touch-tone telephone or with the human voice itself. In this way anyone with either a telephone or a computer linked to the Internet or an intranet and the necessary software and hardware can request and receive information, simply by speaking into a microphone or headset or by punching the buttons on a phone. **Voice processing** is an umbrella term for the various voice functions that permit use of the voice to input data.

■ VOICE PROCESSING TECHNOLOGIES DEFINED

There are a few technologies that make voice processing possible. These include digitized speech, speech synthesis, and voice recognition. **Digitized speech** uses a computer to convert human speech into digital signals for storage on a computer disk and then reconverts the signals to human speech for someone to hear on command. Digitized speech can be heard when a voice has been recorded on a CD-ROM disk on an educational program or game. It most closely imitates the human voice and is very similar to recording a voice using other magnetic media, such as a cassette tape.

The components of a digitized speech system include a computer, specialized computer software that controls the system's operation, a **codec device** that converts analog voice signals into digital form and then reconverts them, and disk storage that stores the digitized voice message. The speech can be input via a microphone or with a two-way telephone and/or tie lines that connect the digitized speech system to the telephone network or to a company's internal telephone system.

In a **text-to-speech system**, a computer reads text and creates **synthesized speech** from the text. Synthesized speech allows a caller with a telephone or a computer with a sound card and speakers to access an electronic mail message or word processing document without having to read it from a computer screen or hard-copy printout. The computer reads the message or document over the telephone or through the user's computer. Speech synthesis can also be used as an output method with weather reports, inventory, telephone directories, and other database applications.

Text-to-speech conversion is accomplished by configuring a computer to convert textual information stored in ASCII code into a computer-generated voice that synthesizes human speech. This is done with the use of phonemes that represent the basic units of sound that make up words (usually, vowels, consonants, and diphthongs). The computer is programmed to construct phonemes based on letter combinations. The phonemes are then analyzed phonetically by separating each word into a series of individual phonemes and then generating the phonemes in the proper sequence to speak words and sentences. This process produces text that sounds computer-generated and mechanical rather than human. The robot Hal from the movie *2001: A Space Odyssey* used this type of speech.

The opposite of text-to-speech systems are **voice-to-text speech systems** which are commonly called **voice recognition** or *speech recognition systems*. Voice recognition uses the computer to convert the wavelengths of the human voice into computer text. The obvious advantage is that someone does not need to transcribe and edit material that has been written by someone else, thus increasing productivity and efficiency.

There are two types of voice recognition systems: discrete speech systems and continuous speech systems. **Discrete speech systems** require that the speaker speak slowly and distinctly and separate each word with a short pause, usually between $\frac{1}{10}$ and $\frac{2}{10}$ second between words. **A continuous speech system** allows the originator to speak naturally without pauses between the words. Most systems are speaker dependent, usually necessitating an enrollment (training) period of 15 to 60 minutes in order to understand a new speaker. Some systems are speaker independent, which means that an enrollment period is not needed to begin recognition. Thus, such a system will comprehend any person who speaks into the system as soon as the person starts speaking.

Voice recognition technology utilizes software that incorporates **a speech engine**, which is the key to speech recognition. This mechanism translates sounds into words and sentences. The speech engine receives the audio input, or speech, from a microphone via a personal computer with a standard sound card such as the Creative Labs Sound Blaster. **The acoustic processor** filters out background noise and converts the captured audio into a series of sounds that correspond to the phonemes—units of speech—making up the language selected, such as American English. The speech engine attempts to match the sounds to the most likely words in two basic ways. **Acoustical analysis** is used to build a list of possible words that contain similar sounds. **Language modeling** (the likelihood that a given word would appear between those coming before and after it) is then used to narrow the list and come up with the best candidates. The **decoder** selects the most likely word based on the rankings assigned during word matching and assembles the words in the most likely sentence combinations. The results sometimes appear in the application and are saved as an application file. Dragon Systems' Dragon NaturallySpeaking and IBM's ViaVoice include their own word processors. Results are saved in rich-text format or pasted into another application.

■ VOICE PROCESSING APPLICATIONS

There are numerous voice processing applications in business. These applications include the following: voice mail, call routing, telephone answering, transaction processing, and information providing. Each offers distinct advantages of voice technologies to enhance communications more efficiently than do traditional communication or other technologies. That is not to say that some of these applications do not have drawbacks. However, any businesses find that the advantages far outweigh the disadvantages if the applications are well-planned and used in an efficient manner.

Voice Mail

Voice mail, sometimes referred to as *Interactive Messaging*, provides "non-simultaneous" conversations that allow subscribers to send messages to one or more subscribers or groups of subscribers and the ability to reply to voice messages. Some PBX telephone systems have voice mail as a part of the system or as an option that can be added to the system after initial installation. In addition, some regional telephone companies, such as Pacific Bell, offer customers a voice mail service. Each of these options provides employees with a private voice mailbox that only the employee can access via a password. With the use of voice mail, a manager could inform the eight employees in his or her department that a meeting has been scheduled for the next day without having to place individual calls. The voice processing system will dial a list of telephone numbers automatically and deliver the manager's spoken message to each one. When each employee enters his or her office, either a light on the telephone will appear to blink or a distinctive dial tone will inform the person that a voice message is waiting.

Call Routing

Call routing, sometimes called a *call tree*, acts like an automated phone attendant whereby a recorded message gives instructions for using a touch-tone phone to access menu items. Callers hear a recorded message that presents them with a menu of options. For example, they might be told to press 1 for the sales department, 2 for the technical support department, or 3 for the shipping department. After pressing 1, 2, or 3, a phone in one of these departments would ring or another set of choices would be provided. In our example, if this is a computer sales company, pressing 1 for the sales department might provide the following options: "Press 1 for business computer systems; 2 for home computer systems; 3 for computer peripherals." Some systems allow callers to key an employee's telephone extension or name to route their calls automatically. It is recommended that the caller be offered a menu of no more than six choices at a time, with three choices being the optimal number. With too many choices, the caller might not be able to remember all of the options available. Often, a caller tends to remember only the first and last choices, but not those in between.

Telephone Answering

Telephone answering allows subscribers and nonsubscribers to leave messages for subscribers as they would on an ordinary telephone answering machine. As with voice mail, telephone answering systems are either built in to a company's PBX telephone system or are provided by a regional telephone company. The system will play a recorded greeting to a caller and record the caller's message. Once the system receives a message, the called party can retrieve this message from any remote location. What sets a telephone answering machine apart from a telephone answering system is that voice processing systems record messages in computer memory rather than on magnetic tape. Because of this, hundreds of hours of storage time can be provided for many more users.

Transaction Processing

Transaction processing, or *voice response*, consists of a telephone interface with an external computer for access to its database or other information. One application of transaction processing is order entry. Either a customer or a field salesperson can dial a number and enter information regarding an order by pressing buttons on the telephone keypad when prompted. Examples of information that might be entered would be customer number, merchandise stock numbers, and quantities. Many banks use transaction processing to permit their customers to use an 800 number to access their account information from the bank. After entering a password and account number, they can find information about their accounts, such as balances, deposits, credit card payments, and whether certain checks have cleared the bank. Some systems of this type also allow people to transfer deposits between bank accounts. Some banks even provide bill-paying service which can be initiated through voice response. In all cases, the user is prompted to enter data after hearing a synthesized voice.

Information Providing

Information providing, sometimes called *audiotex*, consists of a type of voice bulletin board in a "listen-only" mode. After dialing a publicized number, the caller is directed to hear prerecorded voice files containing messages that the caller seeks. There are two types: public bulletin boards and subscriber bulletin boards, which are password driven. Examples of public bulletin boards are those used by companies to provide instructions for product availability and those used by airlines to provide arrival and departure information and flight schedules. Examples of subscriber bulletin boards are the voice bulletin boards of the latest financial and stock news provided by investment companies to subscribers and those that physicians use to obtain information on drugs and medications.

■ BENEFITS OF VOICE PROCESSING

The following are specific benefits realized when using all or some voice processing functions:

1. *Capability of integrating voice processing with other electronic systems.* Voice processing can be used in combination with other communication technologies, such as electronic mail systems, PBX, and centrex telephone

systems. Integration saves time, as separate systems employees may not require retraining to use these new integrated systems. There may also be a cost savings since less hardware and software may be needed.

2. *Convenient one-way communication.* Voice processing technology makes it easy for people located within and outside an organization to communicate with each other. Some systems provide the capability of retrieving stored messages from any location and the ability to send messages to other voice subscribers. Easy access to these systems is made possible through the use of a touch-tone telephone.

3. *Reduction in "telephone tag."* Voice processing, particularly voice mail, helps to solve the common problem of telephone tag, which takes place when people fail to reach one another over the phone because they are busy or are away from their desks and therefore not able to talk. Since voice mail does not require that the recipient of a message be present to receive a message, he or she retrieves the message at his or her convenience. Since less time is spent trying to make contact with people, productivity increases.

4. *No unanswered calls.* As a result of using voice processing systems in an efficient manner, no telephone call should be placed on hold when an extension is busy, nor should any caller be forced to hang up because no one answers a phone.

5. *Privacy.* When using voice mail, privacy is increased because each person is assigned a voice mailbox with a password. Thus, only the employee is capable of retrieving his or her messages. Privacy is a concern when paper messages are left for people.

6. *Reduced number of interoffice memos.* Along with other communication technologies, voice processing helps to reduce the number of hard-copy interoffice memos that are necessary. This provides more communication efficiency and reduces paper and printing costs.

7. *Relative ease of use by those not keyboard oriented.* Some managers and other executives are not proficient in using the computer keyboard to key electronic mail messages and hard-copy memos. Voice processing makes it easier for these people to communicate using voice mail and other voice processing technologies.

8. *Shorter calls.* Studies have shown that the average telephone call in business today is between 4 and 5 minutes. The use of voice processing usually reduces these calls to 1 minute or less. In business, time is money. Providing more time to employees allows for possible increases in productivity.

DRAWBACKS OF VOICE PROCESSING

Some people do not like voice processing because it does not permit them to speak with a real person. This is frustrating for those who feel that nothing can be accomplished without human interaction. Although voice processing can be one of the major ways to increase productivity, there are some drawbacks associated with its use. The following are specific drawbacks when using all or some voice processing functions:

1. *High cost of voice processing systems.* Although the costs of voice processing systems have been decreasing, the costs may still be higher than those of other forms of electronic communication.
2. *No common terminology and standards.* Unfortunately, the manufacturers of some voice processing systems in the past tended to be inconsistent in the terminology that they assigned to the various voice processing technologies and functions. For example, some manufacturers use the term *speech recognition*; others use *voice recognition*. *Call processing* is the term that some vendors associate with all voice processing functions; others use the term *telephone answering*. There has also been inconsistency in the way that manufacturers standardize voice processing hardware. This makes it difficult to use the hardware components of one manufacturer with another vendor's equipment.
3. *No written records.* One of the major complaints that people have when using voice processing is that it often does not provide a written record of the messages left by callers. Organizations rarely assign someone the task of transcribing messages or use voice recognition systems to document messages.
4. *User resistance.* As mentioned in the introduction to this section, some people feel that human interaction is essential and refuse to leave voice messages. Although there are probably fewer and fewer people who resist using voice processing, this may be a major problem when a new voice mail or telephone messaging system is installed, as people gradually become accustomed to using the technology.
5. *Misuse.* Some people use voice processing as an expensive answering machine. It is important to have an effective greeting recorded, and training may be necessary to teach users how to personalize greetings.

■ FACSIMILE DEFINED

The use of facsimile has become very commonplace in today's business office. In fact, it is quite unusual to find a company that does not have this capability. Many people also have facsimile machines in their homes and encourage friends and relatives to send them faxed messages. **Facsimile (fax)** is defined as a transmission that sends and/or receives an exact replica of the original document from one location to another using communication lines. Figure 5-1 is a picture of a Canon facsimile machine.

The steps involved in using facsimile are as follows:

1. Prepare your fax machine for sending and receiving documents.
2. Connect your fax machine to a telephone line, the network over which the fax machine communicates to another fax machine.
3. Connect your fax machine to a telephone instrument.

Figure 5-1
Canon LC3170 Facsimile
Machine. *(Courtesy of Canon USA.)*

4. Plug your fax unit into an electrical outlet to obtain power.
5. Ensure that the fax machine contains paper—sometimes roll paper—to print any document that it receives.
6. Send your document.
   (a) Insert your original document into the document feeder of the fax machine.
   (b) Dial the number of the fax machine that is to receive the copy.
   (c) Once the connection is made, press the "transmit" key on your fax machine and a replica of your document will be transmitted.
7. Receive a document. Turn on your fax machine (or keep your machine on throughout business hours). You do not have to be present to receive a document.

■ TYPES OF FACSIMILE HARDWARE

Facsimile system components consist of the following: transmitter, receiver, modem, and transmission facility. The **transmitter** is a document scanner that scans the original document and converts images to electronic signals. The transmitter scans the original document and dissects it into small picture elements called pixels. **Pixels** are tiny dots that form letters, numbers, symbols, and pictures. Analog processing methods can transmit at speeds ranging from 2 to 6 minutes, while systems using the digital processing method can transmit at speeds under 1 minute. There are two facsimile processing methods: analog and digital.

The **analog processing method** consists of group 1 and 2 faxes. This method scans every part of an original (characters, spaces, margins). The **digital processing method** represents the newer group 3 and 4 faxes. This method analyzes the document's actual picture elements and converts these elements into binary codes (1's and 0's). Most facsimile machines that use the analog processing method (group 1 and 2 faxes) have been retired. Today, most facsimile machines are digital (group 3 and 4 faxes) and adhere to the standards developed by the International Telecommunication Union (ITU) and other organizations.

The **receiver** is a recorder or printer, which reproduces data usually on paper. Faxes using the analog processing method use paper that is either coated so that it is electrolyte- and electrosensitive or, when electrostatic and dielectric techniques are used, plain paper. Digital faxes use thermal printing, ink jet, or laser printing.

The **modem** changes electronic signals into audible signals. The transmission facility consists of the existing telephone network, which connects the sending and receiving stations and transmits data to the receiving unit. It is recommended that businesses that use facsimile extensively to send and receive communications have a telephone line or extension that is dedicated to the fax machine. Although most fax machines can differentiate between the receipt of a voice call and a fax transmission, having a dedicated fax line assures that the chances of the sender of a fax receiving a busy signal are reduced. At least one additional line should then be devoted to voice communications.

There are five types of facsimile equipment: stand-alone units, multi-functional and integrated units, computer fax boards, and Internet-enabled network faxing. **Stand-alone fax units** perform only fax functions. **Multi-functional fax units** combine fax functions with other office technologies. The **fax copier** serves as a low-volume copier to preview fax transmissions. The **faxphone** is fax with a telephone in one unit. **Videofax** combines a fax with a 16-millimeter camera, display screen, and telephone interface. Integrated fax units are compatible with other office equipment. The **FS-232-C interface** makes it possible to communicate with computers and word processors. **Computer fax boards** are usually a combination modem and fax board. This will allow anything on a computer monitor to be faxed with the proper software.

Whereas a traditional fax sends a transmission entirely over the telephone network, an Internet-enabled network fax infrastructure makes it possible to send a fax end to end from sender to recipient over the Internet. Instead of paying expensive international voice rates, companies send fax documents by making a local telephone call at either end and using the Internet to handle the transport. As an example, one system allows documents to be sent from a fax machine or a personal computer (PC) desktop. After dialing a fax number, the system forwards the fax to the closest local point of presence (POP) on the user's ISP. The fax servers then take over and route the fax to the closest off-ramp POP, where there is a receiving server. Then the server makes a local phone call to deliver the document to the receiving fax machine or a PC. Fax machine vendors have developed Internet-enabled

(Internet protocol) fax machines to replace traditional analog machines. This equipment enables companies to utilize Ethernet connections and route faxes to certain destinations over an Internet network rather than using traditional phone lines. The IP fax machine has analog and Internet network connections, enabling companies to send and receive faxes via either connection. Companies that use IP fax machines at both ends of a fax transmission receive the added benefit of internal (intracompany) faxing for free. This is a great benefit for large companies with more than one location.

■ FACSIMILE APPLICATIONS

The following are examples of applications for using the facsimile in the office environment:

- Home offices use the fax to transmit interoffice memos and letters for decision-making purposes.
- Corporate offices use the fax to exchange documents with their branches.
- Sales representatives speed the processing and delivery of orders by faxing them.
- Sales departments send customers the following via fax: notices of order actions, delivery schedules, product specifications, proposals, drawings, and price quotes.

In addition, there are many other ways that the fax can be used in specific applications and industries:

- Hospitals fax x-rays and laboratory reports to doctors' offices or to other hospitals for faster, more accurate diagnosis of patients' illnesses.
- Legal offices fax copies of legal documents such as depositions, wills, settlements, and agreements to their clients and copies of deeds, briefs, transcripts, and so on, to courts.
- Banks fax documents such as daily reports and loan applications to their branches and fax money transfers to other financial institutions. In addition, banks can fax a notice of an approved loan application to real estate agents and automobile dealers, allowing people to purchase items more quickly.

■ BENEFITS OF FACSIMILE

The facsimile offers the following benefits over other forms of communication:

1. *There is immediate receipt of a copy of a document.* When comparing use of the facsimile to other standard methods of sending a document, which include the U.S. Postal Service (USPS), United Parcel Service (UPS), and Federal Express (Fedex), the primary benefit is that an exact copy of a document can be received immediately. This helps to reduce both time

and money, which are frequently lost, while people are waiting for a document. Although there may be long-distance telephone charges with a fax, the cost can usually be justified because of the time saving. People who use next-day or overnight services offered by the USPS, UPS, and Fedex must pay premium fees for this type of delivery.

2. *Equipment installation is easy.* A fax machine is easily installed at any location that has access to a telephone line and electrical power.

3. *Minimal training to operate is required.* See the steps for operating a facsimile in the "Facsimile Defined" section. The steps illustrate how easy a fax machine is to operate compared with some other pieces of office equipment.

4. *No rekeying or scanning is necessary.* Compared with sending a text-intensive document via e-mail and/or other methods, the document does not need to be rekeyed or scanned using a document scanner and/or optical character recognition software.

5. *Various types of documents can be transmitted: handwritten, typed, text, charts, graphs, photos.* It is easy to transmit various types of documents using a fax. Although it is possible to attach files containing these documents to an e-mail message, people who receive the files sometimes have difficulty in viewing the files when they do not have the appropriate programs (word processing, spreadsheet, graphics, etc.).

DRAWBACKS OF FACSIMILE

Although the facsimile has a number of advantages, it also has some disadvantages compared with other communication methods:

1. *A faxed copy may be unacceptable if an original is required.* This problem usually is associated with sending a legal document, such as a contract. The question that must be asked is: Is a faxed copy a legal document? Usually, the answer to this question is "no," although a faxed legal document is often accepted on the condition that a hard copy of the original document is sent later.

2. *Color usually cannot be transmitted.* Although color transmission has improved with newer fax machines, most fax machines receive only in black or red. This presents a problem today, as many documents, especially charts, graphs, and photographs, are prepared in color.

3. *Other delivery methods may be less expensive* (e.g., U.S. mail, express mail, courier services). Usually, each fax transmission includes a cover sheet, which increases the cost of faxing. The cover sheet usually includes the following: the sender's and receiver's names, company telephone number, fax number, and the total number of pages being sent. If speed is not an important factor when sending a document, other, more traditional methods may be better, due to the costs associated with faxing. This is especially true of a document that contains multiple pages.

4. *The system is open to receiving junk faxes.* Many fax numbers are published on company letterhead, business cards, or in company advertising.

Directories are also published that list fax numbers. Since people are able to access fax numbers easily, some companies receive "junk" faxes containing advertising. Some states have proposed legislation that bans and restricts unsolicited fax advertising. Obviously, this helps to alleviate the problem. Some organizations have dealt with the problem by installing systems that require passwords to send a fax to a dedicated fax number.

5. *Reproduction of photos is sometimes poor.* The newer fax machines do a better job in reproducing photographs than do older machines. However, many faxed photos still result in poor reproductions on the receiver's machine.

6. *The sender must know the fax number.* As mentioned, fax directories have been printed which make the process of finding fax numbers easier. This has led to the problem of receiving "junk" faxes. However, certain people who need to know the fax number, such as customers and clients, must be provided with it. Without knowledge of the number, no fax transmission can occur.

7. *The sender's and receiver's equipment must be compatible.* Although compatibility of fax machines is less of a problem today than in the past because of the adoption of industry standards, some fax machines continue to be incompatible. This is especially true when individuals and organizations utilize older fax equipment (i.e., group 1 and 2 faxes rather than group 3 and 4 faxes).

■ SUMMARY

Voice processing is another important communication technology application that deals with computerized speech, reacting to human speech, and storing and understanding the human voice. Through computerized voice functions, people can access information bases and services.

There are a few technologies that make some of the voice functions possible. These include digitized speech, speech synthesis, and voice recognition. Digitized speech uses a computer to convert human speech into digital signals for storage on a computer disk and then reconverts the signals to human speech for someone to hear on command. Synthesized speech allows a caller with a telephone or a computer with a sound card and speakers to access an electronic mail message or word processing document without having to read it from a computer screen or hard-copy printout. Text-to-speech conversion is accomplished by configuring a computer to convert textual information stored in ASCII code into a computer-generated voice that synthesizes human speech.

There are two types of voice recognition systems: discrete speech systems and continuous speech systems. Discrete speech systems require that the speaker speak slowly and distinctly and separate each word with a short pause, usually between $\frac{1}{10}$ and $\frac{2}{10}$ second between words. A continuous speech system allows the originator to speak naturally without pauses between words.

There are numerous voice processing applications in business. These applications include the following: voice mail, call routing, telephone answering, transaction processing, and information providing. Each offers distinct advantages of voice technologies to enhance communications more efficiently than do traditional communication or other technologies.

The following are specific benefits realized when using all or some voice processing functions: capability to integrate voice processing with other electronic systems, convenient one-way communication, reduction in "telephone tag," no unanswered calls, privacy, reduced number of interoffice memos, relative ease of use by those not keyboard oriented, and shorter calls.

Although the advantages of using voice processing are numerous, some people don't like voice processing because it may not permit them to speak with a real person. This is frustrating for those who believe that nothing can be accomplished without human interaction. Although voice processing can be one of the major ways to increase productivity, there are some drawbacks associated with using it: the high cost of voice processing systems, no common terminology and standards, no written records, and user resistance.

The use of facsimile has become very commonplace in today's business office. In fact, it is quite unusual to find a company that does not have this capability. Many people also have facsimile machines in their homes and encourage friends and relatives to send them faxed messages. Facsimile (fax) is defined as a transmission that sends and/or receives an exact replica of the original document from one location to another using communication lines. Facsimile system components consist of the following: transmitter, receiver, modem, and transmission facility.

The following are examples of applications for using the facsimile in the office environment: home offices use the fax to transmit interoffice memos and letters for decision-making purposes; corporate offices use the fax to exchange documents with their branches; sales representatives speed the processing and delivery of orders by faxing them; sales departments send customers the following via fax: notices of order actions, delivery schedules, product specifications, proposals, drawings, and price quotes.

In addition, there are many more ways that the fax can be used in specific applications and industries: hospitals fax x-rays and laboratory reports to doctors' offices or to other hospitals for faster, more accurate diagnosis of patients' illnesses; legal offices fax copies of legal documents such as depositions, wills, settlements, and agreements to their clients and copies of deeds, briefs, transcripts, and so on, to courts; banks fax documents such as daily reports and loan applications to their branches and fax money transfers to other financial institutions. In addition, banks can fax a notice of an approved loan application to real estate agents and automobile dealers, allowing people to purchase items more quickly.

The facsimile offers the following benefits over other forms of communication: immediate receipt of a copy of a document, easy installation of equipment, minimal training to operate, no rekeying or scanning necessary, and ability to transmit a variety of documents.

Although the facsimile has a number of advantages, it also has some disadvantages compared with other communication methods: A faxed copy may be unacceptable if an original is required, color usually cannot be transmitted, other delivery methods may be less expensive (e.g., U.S. mail, express mail, courier services), receiving junk faxes may be a problem, reproduction of photos is sometimes poor, the sender must know the telephone number, and the sender's and receiver's equipment must be compatible.

QUESTIONS

1. Define *voice processing*.

2. Define *voice processing technologies*.

3. Identify the technologies that make some of the voice functions possible.

4. Identify five voice processing applications.

5. Identify eight benefits of voice processing.

6. Identify four drawbacks of voice processing.

7. How is facsimile defined?

8. Identify the steps involved in using facsimile.

9. Identify the types of facsimile hardware.

10. Identify facsimile applications.

11. Identify five benefits of using facsimile.

12. Identify eight drawbacks of using facsimile.

PROJECTS AND PROBLEMS

1. Visit a local company that uses voice processing technologies. Report back on which of the following technologies are used by the firm: voice mail, call routing, telephone answering, transaction processing, and information providing, as defined in the chapter. How are these technologies used? Who uses them?

2. Assuming that you have sound capabilities on your computer (sound card, speakers, or headset), access the Bell Labs Web site at http://www.bell-labs.com/project/tts/voices.html and practice voice synthesis using the various settings and types of voices available. Report on what you find.

3. Use the Internet and a search engine to do a Web search on the topic "speech recognition program." Determine the speech or voice recognition programs that are available, their capabilities, the type of speech recognition program that they represent, whether they involve discrete or continuous speech, whether they are speaker-dependent or non-speaker-dependent, costs, and other information.

4. Treadwell Company would like to utilize voice processing technologies. Suggest a specific voice processing function or application for each of the following situations or problems. Make sure that you define the function or application before you describe how it might apply in each situation.

    (a) Visually handicapped workers are needed to assist in taking inventories.

    (b) Paper messages distributed to several people within the company are often lost.

    (c) Hundreds of orders that field salespeople generate each day result in a massive paper-handling and order-entry operation. Many employees are required to open the mail and process the day's orders.

5. Use the Internet and a search engine to do a Web search to determine the types and costs of facsimile machines that are on the market today. Report on the following:

    (a) What is the brand name?

    (b) What features does the facsimile machine possess? Are any of these features new or unique?

    (c) Is the facsimile machine integrated with any other office technology?

    (d) What transmission speed is possible with a regular (analog) telephone line?

    (e) What type of toner, if any, is required? How many pages can be printed before the toner needs to be replaced?

(f) What type of paper is required?

(g) What is the cost of the facsimile machine?

6. Ullinger Company, which is located in New York City, frequently needs to make decisions on whether to utilize their facsimile machine to send documents to their customers, vendors, lawyers, bank, or others outside the firm, or utilize the U.S. mail or a courier service such as United Parcel Service or Federal Express. For each of these situations, decide whether they should utilize the facsimile machine or utilize one of the other methods. State the rationale for your answer.

(a) The company needs to send a price quotation to a customer who must have the information to make a purchase decision today.

(b) The company's bank needs to examine a copy of its financial records, consisting of nearly 100 pages, to determine if it is eligible for a loan.

(c) The company needs to send a good-quality color photograph of a new product to a printing firm that has been contracted to print a company product brochure.

(d) The company needs to send a signed contract to its lawyers.

(e) The company wants to send product literature consisting of three pages to a potential customer who has requested it.

7. Over 750 field salespeople are on the road taking orders from retailers and wholesalers. A large volume of paper handing and order entry results from the hundreds of orders that these salespeople generate each day. Fifteen employees at the main office are required to open mail and process the day's orders. Order-entry error rates run close to $7\frac{1}{2}$%, and the manual operation costs average \$3.50 per order. The average order takes two days from the time the salesperson is in the store to the time that the order is loaded for processing on the company's computer. Confirmation of an order is mailed soon thereafter.

(a) How could a voice processing system help this company?

(b) Suggest how the company could use one or more of the voice functions to reduce the time needed to process an order.

Vocabulary

acoustic processor	decoder	information providing	telephone answering
acoustical analysis	digital processing method	language modeling	text-to-speech system
analog processing method	digitized speech	modem	transaction processing
call routing	discrete speech system	multifunctional fax unit	transmitter
codec device	facsimile (fax)	pixel	videofax
computer fax board	fax copier	receiver	voice mail
continuous speech system	faxphone	speech engine	voice processing
	FS-232-C interface	stand-alone fax unit	voice recognition system
		synthesized speech	voice-to-text system

References

Bouchard, Thaddeus. "New Networking Faxing Solutions Deliver Hard-Dollar Savings," *Communication News*, June 1999, p. 86.

Gerwig, Kate, "Net Faxing Finds Industry Niche," *Communications Week*, June 9, 1997, p. 23.

Tedesco, Eleanor Hollis, *Telecommunications for Business*, PWS-Kent, Boston, 1990.

CHAPTER

6

Wireless Communications

I n this chapter we discuss wireless communications as it pertains to pagers, cellular phones, global location/navigation systems, and handheld computers.

WHAT YOU WILL LEARN

- Definition of wireless communications
- The history of pagers
- Types of pagers
- Benefits of using pagers
- Definition of cellular phones
- The history of cellular phones
- How cellular phones are billed
- Types of cellular phones
- Benefits of cellular phones
- Drawbacks of cellular phones
- Definitions of global location/navigation systems
- How global location/navigation systems are used
- Definition of handheld computers
- Types of handheld computers
- How to use a handheld computer for communications

■ WIRELESS COMMUNICATION DEFINED

Traditionally, communication technology has used wires (i.e., twisted pair, coaxial, fiber optic) as the media to connect a sender and receiver together to transmit a message. A **wireless communication** is, very simply, a communication without wires. The purpose of the first radio telephone service was to provide links where wires ordinarily could not be used, primarily across bodies of water.

Two-way radio, such as the dispatch systems used by taxi and ambulance services, uses two-way communications for short messages. In addition, **citizens' band (CB) radio**, a system of two-way radio communication for short distances, provides a large number of broadcasters with a party line. In addition, **air/ground services** provide two-way communication between airborne telephones and the public switched telephone network. **Marine radio telephone** services include very high frequency (VHF) maritime service, coastal-harbor services, and high-seas maritime radio telephone service. **High-speed train service** provides telephone service between a passenger train and the public switched telephone network.

The focus of this chapter is on land communication, in which wireless communication is accomplished with the use of devices that include pagers, cellular telephones, and global location/navigation systems. Businesses are using these devices increasingly to provide communications links for employees who are away from their offices or need to find their destination when traveling by automobile.

■ PAGERS

A **pager** is a wireless communication device that offers one- or two-way communication. The mobile user carries a small, pocket radio receiver, a pager or *beeper*. In a paging system, the paging terminal, after accepting an incoming page and validating it, encodes the pager address and message into the appropriate paging signaling protocol. The signaling protocol allows individual pagers to be identified/alerted uniquely and to be provided with an additional voice message or display message, if desired. Pagers come in a variety of sizes, types, and features. These types and features are discussed in the next section.

The beginning of the paging industry can be traced back as far as 1921, when the Detroit Police Department pioneered the first land-mobile radio system. This effectively introduced the concept of one-way information broadcasting. The 1930s saw widespread use of radio paging in the United States by government agencies, police departments, and the armed forces. Radio paging used powerful transmitters to broadcast voice messages from a stationary location (base station) to a mobile unit. From a voice-broadcast service, paging evolved into a digital service with addressing, by which messages could be addressed to specific pagers.

Earlier models of radio pagers, such as Motorola's Pageboy I introduced in 1974, had no display screen nor message buffering. Display pagers were introduced in the early 1980s. As tone, numeric, and alphanumeric paging services evolved, paging codes also became standardized. To some extent, the steady growth of the paging industry could be attributed to the internationally accepted standard radio paging code, the Post Office Code Standardization Advisory Group (POCSAG) code, which was developed in 1976 by an international group of engineers. Two other codes, the GSC and 5/6-tone codes, are still being used in some markets, although to a smaller extent. FLEX, Motorola's next-generation paging protocol, has been designed to allow for major new growth in the industry. Technologically more advanced than existing protocols, FLEX offers paging operators significantly faster messaging speed, greater capacity, and higher reliability.

Paging systems have also undergone dramatic development. Radio transmission technology has advanced to the extent that multiple transmitter systems using simulcast techniques can now broadcast the same information from multiple transmitters on the same frequency at the same time. The computer hardware and software used in radio paging systems has also evolved from simple operator-assisted systems to terminals that are fully computerized. These systems include such features as message handling, future delivery, user-friendly prompts to guide callers to a variety of functions, and automatic reception of messages that are input through touch-tone phones.

Early paging systems were nonselective and operator assisted. Operators at central control received voice input messages which were taped as they came in. After an interval of time (e.g., 15 minutes), these messages were then broadcast and received by all of the paging system subscribers. This meant that subscribers had to tune in at appointed times and listen to all messages broadcast to see if there were any messages for them. Not only did it waste air time, the system was inconvenient, labor intensive, and offered no privacy.

The inconvenience and lack of privacy associated with nonselective paging was overcome with the use of address encoders at the central control station and associated decoders in the pagers. Each pager was given an address code. The address of the recipient was entered followed by the message. In this way, only the party addressed was alerted to switch on his or her pager for the intended message. With selective paging, tone-only alert paging became possible. The called party was alerted by a beep tone to call the operator or a prearranged number (e.g., home or office telephone number) to have the message read to him or her.

Up to this point, an operator was always employed either to send the paging signal or to playback or relay messages meant for the called party. With automatic paging, a telephone number is assigned to each pager. The paging terminal signals automatically for voice input, if any, from the calling party, after which it will automatically page the called party with the address code and relay the input voice message. One-way pagers signal people over a paging network. Two-way pagers can be as simple as receipt of page confirmation (page acknowledgment) or as complex as full two-way capability in sending and receiving data. All pagers use formats that fall into one of the two basic coding techniques: tone coding format or binary coding format. Tone coding uses an analog transmission technique; binary coding uses a digital transmission technique to transfer information to pagers. In digital transmission, the signal to be transmitted is first digitized, that is, converted into a form that is represented by a series of ones and zeros. Digital transmission has many advantages over analog transmission, the most important being its superior performance in the presence of noise.

Types of Pagers

There are four different types of pagers: tone only, tone and voice, numeric pager display, and alphanumeric display. **Tone-only pagers** alert the user with a tone or pulse and do not possess a display for showing information about the reason for the page or who is paging the person. Some tone-only pagers use different types of audible signals that allow the user to distinguish between people and locations. For example, one type of tone can be used for routine calls and another for emergency calls. Another option would be that one type of tone could identify calls from a person's home, while another would identify pages from the office.

Tone and voice pagers provide the additional capability of relaying a voice message, which allows the user to hear the voice of the person who is paging him or her. **Numeric pager display** has the ability to show the user a message such as a telephone number on a visual display. Since these pagers provide a silent alert, messages can be read privately. Most pagers provide the capability of message storage so that the message may be viewed at a later time. Also, there is less chance of a garbled message, as may be the case with a voice pager. This reduces doubt as to the content of the message, thereby eliminating error and confusion. Most numeric pager display pagers offer large channel capacities.

Alphanumeric display pagers display alphabetic or numeric messages that are entered by the calling party on the telephone or by using a computer with a modem. The advantage of these pagers over numeric pagers is that users receive complete and thorough messages. These pagers eliminate the need to make a phone call in order to get the message. Obviously, this reduces the incidence of phone tag. In addition, users can screen messages and can make better action decisions. Figure 6-1 shows the Motorola Express-xtra FLX Pager.

■ CELLULAR PHONES

A **cellular phone** is a type of wireless communication that is most familiar to mobile phone users. It is called *cellular* because the system uses many base stations to divide a service area into multiple *cells*. Cellular calls are transferred from base station to base station as a user travels from cell to cell. Cellular phones send radio signals to low-power transmitters located within cells 5 to 12 miles in radius. As you travel from cell to cell, the signal carrying your voice is transferred to the nearest transmitter. Cellular phone calls are usually not intercepted by electronic devices such as radios and baby monitors. However, cellular phone conversations can be received by radio scanners.

Figure 6-1
The Motorola Express-xtra FLX Pager.
(Courtesy of Motorola, Inc.)

The basic concept of cellular phones began in 1947 when researchers looked at crude mobile car phones and realized that by using small cells with frequency reuse, traffic capacity could be increased substantially. The "cells" that they envisioned would represent a range of service areas. However, the problem was that the technology to do it was nonexistent. Any form of broadcasting and/or sending of a radio or television message out over the airwaves is subject to Federal Communications Commission (FCC) regulations. These regulations specify that a cell phone is actually a type of two-way radio. In 1947, AT&T proposed that the FCC allocate a large number of radio spectrum frequencies so that widespread mobile telephone service could become feasible. This would provide AT&T with an incentive to research the new technology. We can partially blame the FCC for the gap between the concept of cellular service and its availability to the public. Because of the FCC decision to limit the frequencies in 1947, only 23 phone conversations could occur simultaneously in the same service area. Clearly, this was not a market incentive to foster extensive research.

In 1968 the FCC reconsidered its position and concluded that "if the technology to build a better mobile service works, we will increase the frequencies allocation, freeing the airwaves for more mobile phones." AT&T's Bell Labs proposed a cellular system to the FCC consisting of many small, low-powered broadcast towers, each covering a cell a few miles in radius, collectively covering a larger area. Each tower would use only a few of the total frequencies allocated to the system, and as cars moved across the area, their calls would be passed from tower to tower.

By 1977, Bell Labs constructed and operated a prototype cellular system. A year later, public trials of the new system were started in Chicago, Illinois, with over 2000 trial customers. In 1979, the first commercial cellular telephone system began operation in Tokyo, Japan, and in 1981, Motorola and American Radio Telephone started a second U.S. cellular radio-telephone system test in the Washington–Baltimore area. By 1982, the slow-moving FCC finally authorized commercial cellular service for the United States. A year later, the first American commercial for analog cellular service or AMPS (advanced mobile phone service) was offered in Chicago by Ameritech. Despite the incredible demand, it took cellular phone service 37 years to become commercially feasible in the United States.

Consumer demand quickly outstripped the system's 1982 capabilities, and by 1987, cellular telephone subscribers exceeded 1 million. The airways were crowded. There were three options to improve service. The first was to increase the frequency allocation. Another way was to split existing cells. The third alternative was to improve the technology. The FCC did not want to hand out any more bandwidth. In addition, the building and splitting of cells would have been expensive and would add considerable bulk to the network. In 1987, to stimulate the growth of new technology, the FCC declared that cellular licensees may employ alternative cellular technologies in the 800-megahertz band. The cellular industry began to research new transmission technology as an alternative.

Cellular Phone Billing

Whether you are trying to buy the perfect plan with just the right number of minutes, or you are trying to manage your connect time more effectively, it pays to understand how your carrier handles per-minute charges. Most wireless carriers round up air time to the nearest minute. For example, a 1-minute 20-second conversation on your watch is going to tally as a 2-minute conversation by most carriers when it comes to billing. Most wireless carriers use what's called *send-to-end billing*. With this type of billing, the charges start the instant you press the Send key on your phone. The billing clock ticks while the call is connecting and the phone is ringing. A few carriers, such as Omnipoint, Powertel, and Houston Cellular, don't start the billing clock until your call is answered. The billing clock stops when you press the End key. Some carriers, including AirTouch, AT&T, and Bell Atlantic Mobile, continue charging until the network computer disconnects your call physically, which can occur a few seconds after you press the End key.

Aerial and Nextel are the only carriers that bill by the second, but Nextel waits until the conversation has gone past a minute before it begins its per-second billing—anything under a minute is rounded up to a full minute. Most wireless carriers do not charge for busy signals or unanswered calls. However, some carriers will charge the user for connect time if you let the phone ring longer than a specific time or if you stay on the phone for more than half a minute after receiving a busy signal. Cellular One in Boston, for example, charges you a minute of connect time if you let the phone ring longer than 30 seconds. Comcast Cellular charges a minute of connect time if you stay on the phone longer than 45 seconds after receiving a busy signal.

When phoning outside your home calling area, which is called *roaming*, your carrier's billing rules no longer apply. The carrier whose network you actually use while traveling sets the rules. Your home carrier sends you a monthly statement itemizing roaming charges, but it has no control over how the roaming carrier measures your connect time. If your carrier rounds up to the next whole minute, you'll maximize your connect time use if you keep your calls in near-minute increments. You'll need to shorten your calls by a few seconds if your carrier starts the meter running as soon as you hit the Send button or if your carrier doesn't stop the connect time clock until you are disconnected from the network. Be sure to hang up immediately if your carrier charges for staying on the line during a busy signal. Additionally, if the party you are trying to reach does not answer, hang up after a few rings, as your carrier may charge after a certain number of attempts. Now that you know the different ways that carriers handle billing, you'll want to examine Table 6-1 to find out how various carriers treat per-minute charges.

Table 6-1   Comparison of Wireless Billing*

Features	Nextel (Direct Connect 500 Plus)	AT&T Wireless Services (AT&T Local Enhanced Prepaid Wireless)	Qwest Wireless (Standard 60)	Sprint PCS (Free and Clear 20)	VoiceStream Wireless
Monthly access charge	$39.99	N/A	$24.99	$19.99	N/A
Minutes Included					
Anytime minutes	100	0	60	20	0
Peak minutes	N/A	N/A	N/A	N/A	N/A
Off-peak minutes	N/A	N/A	N/A	N/A	N/A
Weekend minutes	N/A	N/A	60	N/A	N/A
Evening minutes	N/A	N/A	N/A	N/A	N/A
Nextel Direct Connect	500	N/A	N/A	N/A	N/A
Off-peak minute package	$10 for unlimited off-peak minutes	None	None	$10 for 200 off-peak minutes	None
Peak period	7 A.M.–8 P.M. M–F	None	None	7 A.M.–8 P.M. M–F	None
Off-peak period	8 P.M.–7 A.M. M–F; Sat.–Sun.	None	None	8 P.M.–7 A.M. M–F; Sat.–Sun.	None
Contract	1 yr	None	1 yr	Monthly or 1 yr	None
Activation fee	$25/1; $50/2 or more plans	None	$25	$34.99	None
Cancellation fee	$200	None	$200	None/monthly; $150/1-yr contract	None
Rate per minute of additional airtime	$0.35 anytime	N/A	$0.45 anytime	$0.40 anytime	N/A
Roaming charges per minute	$0.00 w/in Nextel network	$0.85 anytime	$0.00 within Qwest wireless network, $0.60 outside	$0.00–0.69	N/A
Long-distance charges per minute	$0.15 anytime	None	$0.15 anytime	$0.15 anytime	$0.20 anytime
Incremental billing	1 sec, after first minute	1 min	1 min	1 min	1 min
Free first minute on incoming calls	No	No	Included	No	No
Directory assistance	$0.99/call	$0.99/call	$0.85/call	$0.99/call	$0.75/call
Air interface technology	Digital cellular (iDEN 800 MHz)	TDMA 1900 MHz (PCS)	Digital PCS (CDMA 1900 MHz)	Digital PCS CDMA (1900 MHz)	Digital PCS (GSM 1900 MHz)

Source: Copyright Point.com, Inc. All rights reserved.

*Comparisons shown for Baltimore, Maryland.

Types of Cellular Phones

There are three types of cellular phones: handheld, transportable, and installed phones These phones are available with a wide variety of features and options. Many of these options, such as call forwarding and call waiting, are similar to the features available with wired phones. However, unlike the installed phone, the cellular phone is fully transportable. All operating components are contained in a carrying case or within the instrument itself. The **handheld phone** is the most portable and lightweight of the cellular phones, usually weighing less than 1 pound. The battery provides over eight hours of normal operation between charges. A drawback is its low power, resulting in a transmitting range smaller than that of other types of cellular phones. The **transportable/car phone** is usually larger than a handheld phone and can be used in a car or other mode of transportation, such as an airplane or train. Figure 6-2 shows the Nokia 5120 cellular phone. The **installed phone** is similar to the transportable/car phone, but it is permanently installed in a car, airplane, or train.

Benefits of Cellular Phones

Cellular phones offer the following benefits:

1. *Falling prices.* Between 1995 and 1999, wireless rates have dropped 60 percent. In many parts of the country this has resulted in wireless costs being level with those of wired phones. Recently, the advent of flat-rate plans has also made going completely wireless more attractive for some people. These plans provide unlimited roaming and long distance, either regionally or across the entire United States for one monthly charge. This provides an ideal situation for those who make a lot of long-distance calls. Prior to the availability of flat-rate plans, the additional cost of long-distance charges and roaming fees led some wireless owners to use their phones only for short calls within their home service area.

Figure 6-2
Nokia 5120 Cellular Phone. *(Courtesy of Nokia Corporate Communications.)*

2. *Eases living with others.* People with roommates, or those living in a home with older children who use a single phone line, have probably experienced the tedious ritual of scrutinizing the monthly phone bill to determine who made each of the calls on the phone bill. With cellular phones this is no longer a problem because each person receives a separate bill.

3. *Keeping a single phone number.* Another advantage to a wireless-only lifestyle is that it is easier to keep one phone number when moving within a city, especially if you live in a large metropolis with multiple area codes. However, if you move a long distance from your previous area code, you'll probably have to change your number to match the area code in your new location.

Drawbacks of Cellular Phones

The use of cellular phones has the following drawbacks:

1. *Interpreting charges.* One of the problems already discussed is that cellular phone carriers calculate billing charges differently and these charges may be difficult to interpret .

2. *Sharing a phone.* All the benefits discussed above might not matter if relying solely on a cellular phone becomes a major inconvenience. One person might be less than pleased when he or she needs to use the phone and another employee has left it in another office. According to Larry Swasey, vice-president of media research for Allied Business Intelligence, a New York–based consulting firm, the main reason why more people haven't gone completely wireless is the simple fact that it is difficult to share a mobile phone.

3. *Problems using cellular phones to access the Internet.* If you enjoy surfing the Internet and you go completely wireless, consider that you'll use up connect time while you're logged on. In addition, it will take nearly six times longer to download information compared to a standard phone line connection because of the way that data are transmitted when using a cell phone.

■ GLOBAL POSITIONING SYSTEMS

Global positioning systems (GPSs) are at present the only systems capable of showing your exact position on Earth anytime, in any weather, anywhere. Two dozen satellites orbit at 11,000 nautical miles above Earth. They are monitored continuously by ground stations located worldwide. The satellites transmit signals that can be detected by anyone with a GPS receiver. Figure 6-3 shows the GPS satellite system.

Using the receiver, you can determine your location with great precision. GPS is one of history's most exciting and revolutionary developments. New uses of this technology are constantly being discovered. Before we learn more about GPS, it is important to understand a bit more about navigation.

Since prehistoric times, people have been trying to figure out a reliable way to tell where they are, to help guide them to where they are going, and

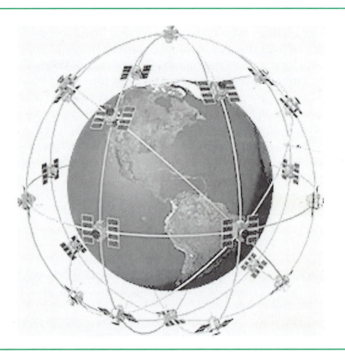

to get them back home again. Humans living in caves probably used stones and twigs to mark a trail when they set out hunting for food. The earliest mariners followed the coast closely to keep from getting lost. When navigators first sailed into the open ocean, they discovered they could chart their course by following the stars. The ancient Phoenicians used the North Star to journey from Egypt and Crete. According to Homer, the goddess Athena told Odysseus to "keep the Great Bear on his left" during his travels from Calypso's Island. Unfortunately for Odysseus and all the other mariners, the stars are visible only at night—and only on clear nights.

The next major developments in the quest for the perfect method of navigation were the magnetic compass and the sextant. The needle of a compass always points north, so it is always possible to know in what direction you are going. The sextant uses adjustable mirrors to measure the exact angle of the stars, moon, and sun above the horizon. However, in the early days of its use, it was only possible to determine latitude (the location on Earth measured north or south from the equator) from the sextant observations. Sailors were still unable to determine their longitude (the location on Earth measured east or west). This was such a serious problem that in the seventeenth century, the British formed a special Board of Longitude, consisting of well-known scientists. This group offered £20,000, equal to about 1 million of today's dollars, to anybody who could find a way to determine a ship's longitude within 30 nautical miles. The generous offer paid off. In 1761, a cabinetmaker named John Harrison developed a shipboard timepiece called a *chronometer*, which lost or gained only about 1 second a day, incredibly accurate for the time. For the next two centuries, sextants and chronometers were used in combination to provide latitude and longitude information. In the early twentieth century, several radio-based navigation systems were developed, which were used widely during World War II. Both allied and enemy ships and airplanes used ground-based radio-navigation systems as the technology advanced.

A few ground-based radio-navigation systems are still in use today. One drawback of using radio waves generated on the ground is that you must choose between a system that is very accurate but does not cover a wide area, or one that covers a wide area but is not very accurate. High-frequency radio waves (e.g., ultrahigh-frequency television) can provide accurate position location but can only be picked up in a small, localized area. Lower-frequency radio waves (e.g., AM radio) can cover a larger area but are not a good yardstick to tell you exactly where you are.

Scientists therefore decided that the only way to provide coverage for the entire world was to place high-frequency radio transmitters in space. A transmitter positioned high above Earth sending a high-frequency radio wave with a special coded signal can cover a large area and still overcome much of the "noise" encountered on the way to the ground. This is one of the main principles behind the GPS system.

GPS has three parts: the space segment, user segment, and control segment. The *space segment* consists of 24 satellites, each in its own orbit located 11,000 nautical miles above Earth. The *user segment* consists of receivers, which you can hold in your hand or mount in your car. The *control segment* consists of ground stations (five of them, located around the world) that make sure that the satellites are working properly.

One trip around Earth in space equals one orbit. The GPS satellites each take 12 hours to orbit Earth. Each satellite is equipped with an accurate clock to let it broadcast signals coupled with a precise time message. The ground unit receives the satellite signal, which travels at the speed of light. Even at this speed, the signal takes a measurable amount of time to reach the receiver. The difference between the time the signal is sent and the time that it is received, multiplied by the speed of light, enables the receiver to calculate the distance to the satellite. To measure precise latitude, longitude, and altitude, the receiver measures the time it took for the signals from four separate satellites to get to the receiver. A GPS system can tell you your location anywhere on or above Earth to within about 300 feet. Even greater accuracy, usually within less than 3 feet, can be obtained with corrections calculated by a GPS receiver at a known fixed location.

Ground Control Stations

The GPS control or ground segment consists of unmanned monitor stations located around the world (Hawaii and Kwajalein in the Pacific Ocean; Diego Garcia in the Indian Ocean; Ascension Island in the Atlantic Ocean; and Colorado Springs, Colorado); a master ground station at Falcon Air Force Base in Colorado Springs, Colorado; and four large ground antenna stations that broadcast signals to the satellites. The stations also track and monitor the GPS satellites.

Receivers

GPS receivers can be hand carried or installed on aircraft, ships, tanks, submarines, cars, and trucks. These receivers detect, decode, and process GPS satellite signals. More than 100 different receiver models are already in use. The typical handheld receiver is about the size of a cellular telephone, and the newer models are even smaller. The handheld units distributed to U.S. armed forces personnel during the Persian Gulf war weighed only 28 ounces. Figure 6-4 shows the Garmin Street StreetPilot GPS System.

Uses for GPS

GPS has become important for nearly all military operations and weapons systems. In addition, it is used on satellites to obtain highly accurate orbit data and to control spacecraft orientation. Vehicle tracking is one of the fastest-growing GPS applications. GPS-equipped fleet vehicles, public transportation systems, delivery trucks, and courier services use receivers to monitor their locations at all times.

GPS is also helping to save lives. Many police, fire, and emergency medical service units are using GPS receivers to determine the police car, fire truck, or ambulance nearest to an emergency, enabling the quickest possible response in life-or-death situations. Automobile manufacturers are offering moving-map displays guided by GPS receivers as an option on new vehicles. The displays can be removed and taken into a home to plan a trip. Several Florida rental car companies are demonstrating GPS-equipped vehicles that give directions to drivers on display screens and through synthesized voice instructions.

Figure 6-4
Garmin StreetPilot GPS System.
(Courtesy of Garmin International, Inc.)

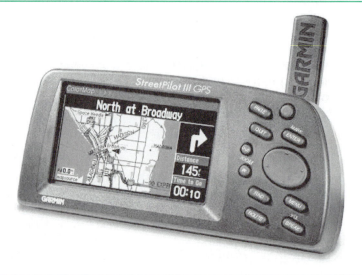

■ HANDHELD COMPUTERS

Another type of wireless communication device is the **handheld computer**, a portable computer that is small enough to be held in one's hand. Although extremely convenient to carry, handheld computers have not replaced notebook computers, because of their small keyboards and screens. The most popular handheld computers are those that are specifically designed to provide personal information manager functions, such as a calendar and address book. Some manufacturers are trying to solve the small keyboard problem by replacing the keyboard with an electronic pen. However, these pen-based devices rely on handwriting recognition technologies, which are still in their infancy.

The reason that handheld computers are mentioned in this chapter is that when they are supplied with manufacturer-installed or optional third-party communications software and with an added wireless modem, you can send, receive, read, and edit e-mail, as well as access a corporate or small-business network. If a standard mail server is used, a handheld computer can be set up to access e-mail while traveling. Some handheld computers are also capable of accessing the World Wide Web, but it requires configuration of accompanying software for the device and for the Internet service provider. Because the screens on handheld computers are small, standard browsing can be difficult.

Types of Handheld Computers

There are three types of handheld computers: Windows CE–based handheld PCs, palm-sized devices, and alternative devices. *Windows CE–based handheld PCs (HPCs)* run the Microsoft Windows CE operating system and are available in two versions: the first generation, simply called HPCs, and the newer HPC professional (Pro) models, often referred to by their development code name as *Jupiter devices*. Both types are intended primarily as portable devices that serve as PC companions, supplementing a primary desktop or notebook. Figure 6-5 shows the Compaq iPAQ BlackBerry H1100 Wireless Email Handheld Computer.

HPCs have a clamshell design, touch screens or touch pads, real keyboards rather than the onscreen virtual keyboards used by some other handhelds, and screen resolutions of 640×240 (half VGA), 640×480 (VGA), or 800×600 (SVGA). Most HPCs have color screens, although monochrome models still exist. All HPCs have voice recorders with an internal microphone and speaker, CompactFlash and PC card slots to add storage, and infrared transceivers. Many come with built-in modems, and most also use rechargeable batteries, with battery life ranging from 8 to 20 hours.

Software included on HPCs comprises limited versions of word processing, spreadsheet, and presentation software; personal information management applications to organize notes, schedules, tasks, and contacts; communication utilities; a clock; and a calculator. The HPC Pro models also have limited database capabilities and better ability to communicate with e-mail servers than the earlier models. Many of these are much larger as well,

Figure 6-5
Compaq iPAQ BlackBerry H1100
Wireless Email Handheld Computer.
*(Courtesy of Compaq Computer
Corporation.)*

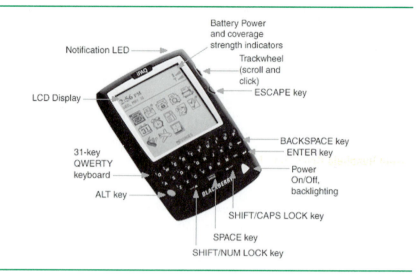

serving as notebook alternatives for executives who do not need access to full-fledged productivity applications

Palm-sized devices are designed to be held in one hand and are used to reference personal schedules, tasks, and contact lists as well as for minor editing. Lacking a keyboard, these small computers use a stylus and handwriting recognition as their primary means of data input. There are also tiny on-screen virtual keyboards if you want to tap out your entries. Palm-sized devices usually do not have standard internal modems, but all have infrared ports and can synchronize data with regular PCs using included synchronization software and cradles.

The two major categories of palm-sized PCs are the highly popular 3Com palm devices and Windows CE palm-sized PCs. Because of the size of the market and the devices' varied uses, both will probably continue as feasible choices with a growing range of hardware and software options and applications. For example, the 3Com devices have a devoted following, numerous third-party applications, and very simple operation, while the palm-sized PCs offer much more varied hardware options from different manufacturers and a growing array of third-party software.

Although all current 3Com models have monochrome screens, palm-sized PCs are available with either monochrome or color screens. Battery life ranges from approximately one week's typical use (palm-sized PCs) to one month (3Com devices). Both families of devices use internal ROM (read-only memory) and RAM (random access memory) for programs and data storage—palm-sized PCs also have CompactFlash memory-card slots.

Alternative devices that don't run Windows CE or the 3Com Palm OS include major brandname handheld computer models from Psion (particularly popular in Europe), Casio, Hewlett-Packard, and Sharp. Some of these manufacturers also make cellular devices. These devices all have small but functional screens, real keyboards, serial ports, and often, infrared ports for data transmission. They can all synchronize data with PCs.

Credit-card-sized handhelds, currently represented by the Franklin Rex and Rex Pro, are the smallest devices on the market today. If all you need are basic personal information management functions that you can take anywhere, the Rex cards can hold thousands of appointments, tasks, and contacts in little memory. The thickness of three credit cards, the Rex models run for six months on internal batteries. To synchronize data with primary computers, these devices can be inserted into a PC card slot in your notebook or even your primary handheld.

Using Handheld Computers for Communication

There are three ways to communicate using handheld devices: standard telephone-line modems, wireless modems, and networks. Most Windows CE HPCs and all HPC Pro models have internal modems. Most palm-sized personal digital assistants do not come with standard modems, but external models are available. Windows CE palm-sized PCs can also use CompactFlash modems. Although still in their infancy, wireless services let you send and receive e-mail, pages, and even access Web-based information with a handheld device when you are away from a telephone line. You'll have better luck with wireless coverage if you live and work in major metropolitan areas.

Accessing a corporate or small-business network with a handheld device is now possible with third-party accessories designed for specific product families or models. For example, Windows CE HPCs and HPC Pros can use PC card-based network interface cards (NICs) with special driver software. CompactFlash NICs are also available for devices with CompactFlash slots. To communicate using a handheld, you have to run applications built for the device, as desktop applications will not work. Most devices come with dial-up and terminal-emulation software, and many include software to send e-mail and browse the Web.

■ SUMMARY

In this chapter we discussed wireless communications as it pertains to pagers, cellular phones, global location/navigation systems, and handheld computers. Traditionally, communication technologies used wires (i.e., twisted pair, coaxial, fiber optic) as the media to connect a sender and receiver together to transmit a message. A wireless communication is, very simply, a communication without wires.

A pager is a wireless communication device that offers one- or two-way communication. The mobile user carries a small, pocket radio receiver, a pager or beeper. There are four different types of pagers: tone only, tone and voice, numeric pager display, and alphanumeric display.

A cellular phone is a type of wireless communication that is most familiar to mobile phone users. It is called "cellular" because the system uses many base stations to divide a service area into multiple cells. Cellular calls are transferred from base station to base station as a user travels from cell to cell.

Cellular phones send radio signals to low-power transmitters located within cells 5 to 12 miles in radius. It is useful to obtain an understanding of how your carrier charges for cellular use, as different companies utilize different methods. There are three types of cellular phones: handheld, transportable, and installed phones. The phones are available with a wide variety of features and options. The benefits of cellular phone use include: falling prices, eases living with others, and the possibility of keeping a single phone number. Drawbacks of cellular phones include interpreting charges, sharing a phone, and the problems encountered when using cellular phones to access the internet.

Global positioning systems (GPSs) are the only systems capable of showing your exact position on Earth anytime, in any weather, anywhere. GPS has three parts: the space segment, user segment, and control segment. A GPS system can tell you your location anywhere on or above Earth to within about 300 feet. Even greater accuracy, usually within less than 3 feet, can be obtained with corrections calculated by a GPS receiver at a known fixed location. GPS has become important for nearly all military operations and weapons systems. In addition, it is used on satellites to obtain highly accurate orbit data and to control spacecraft orientation. Vehicle tracking is one of the fastest-growing GPS applications.

A handheld computer is a portable computer that is small enough to be held in one's hand. Some handheld computers are equipped with a wireless modem, which permits the user to access e-mail and the World Wide Web, as well as accessing a corporate or small-business network. The three types of handheld computers are: Windows CE–based handheld PCs (HPCs), palm-sized devices, and alternative devices.

QUESTIONS

1. Traditionally, what media did communication technology use to connect a sender and receiver together to transmit a message?

2. What is meant by *wireless communication*?

3. Provide a brief overview of the evolution of wireless communication.

4. What is a pager?

5. Identify the beginning of the paging industry.

6. Discuss the evolution of paging technology.

7. Identify and discuss the four types of pagers discussed in the chapter.

8. What is a cellular phone?

9. Provide a brief overview of the evolution of the cellular phone.

10. What is the FCC?

11. Why can the FCC be blamed for the slow development of cellular phone technology?

12. Identify the methods by which cellular phone carriers charge users.

13. Name the three types of cell phones identified in the chapter.

14. Identify the benefits and drawbacks of using cell phones.

15. What is a global positioning system?

16. Briefly discuss the history of navigation.

17. Discuss the principles behind global positioning systems.

18. Identify the parts of global positioning systems.

19. Identify the uses of global positioning systems.

20. What is a handheld computer?

21. What types of handheld computers are available?

22. How can handheld computers be used for wireless communications?

PROJECTS AND PROBLEMS

1. Pick one of the following technologies: pagers, cellular phones, global position systems, handheld computers. Find a company in your area that sells any of these products or do research at the library or on the Internet and write a three-page report describing the capabilities, features, and shortcomings of a product that you have chosen.

2. Obtain a pager, cellular telephone, or handheld computer and demonstrate it to the class.

3. Interview someone who is currently using a pager in his or her job. Ask the following questions:
   (a) How is the pager being used by the person in his or her job?
   (b) What are the advantages of using the pager over alternative communication methods?
   (c) What are the disadvantages of using the pager over alternative communication methods?
   (d) What type of pager is being used?
   (e) What special features does the pager possess?
   (f) What features does the person wish that the pager possessed?

4. Conduct a survey of a group of at least 10 people who are using cellular phones. Ask them the following questions and report the results:
   (a) What were the reasons for purchasing a cellular phone?
   (b) Do the advantages of owning a cellular phone justify the cost?
   (c) What are the disadvantages of using a cellular phone?

   (d) Would you ever consider owning a cellular phone as your only phone? If you answered no, what improvements or enhancements in cellular technology would cause you to consider abandoning your wired telephones?

5. Conduct a survey of a group of at least 10 people who are using handheld computers. Ask them the following questions and report the results.
   (a) What type of handheld computer do you use?
   (b) What were the reasons for purchasing a handheld computer?
   (c) For what tasks do you use your handheld computer?
   (d) Do you use your handheld computer for communications? If yes, how?

6. Discuss the following in a small group:
   (a) What are various applications in which pagers and cellular telephones can be used in a business setting?
   (b) What dangers and/or problems are associated with using cellular telephones, such as using them while driving? Develop a safety guide.

7. Larry Schaffer does not understand how the global positioning system in his new car works. He asks you how the system can possibly determine where he is, to provide him instructions on what roads to use to get to his destination. He also wants to know if it will work if he takes a vacation in Canada or Mexico. Write a paragraph answering these questions.

Vocabulary

air/ground services	citizens' band (CB) radio	high-speed train service	tone-only pager
tone and voice pagers	global positioning system (GPS)	installed phone	transportable/car phone
alphabetic display pager	handheld computer	marine radio telephone	two-way radio
cellular phone	handheld phone	numeric pager display pager	wireless communication

References

Aerospace Corporation, "GPS Primer," http://www.aero.org/publications/GPSPRIMER.

Computer Shopper, "How to Buy Handhelds," http://www.zdnet.com/computershopper.

Goldberg, Jeff, "A Guide to Wireless Billing," http://www.point.com/article/823.

"Guide to Cell Phones," http://www.inventors.about.com/library/weekly/aa070899.htm.

Privacy Rights Clearinghouse, "Fact Sheet 2: Cordless/Cellular Phones," http://www.privacyrights.org/fs/fs2-wire.htm.

Rowe, Stanford H., II, *Telecommunications for Managers*, 4th ed., Prentice Hall, Upper Saddle River, NJ, 1999.

Tedesco, Eleanor Hollis, *Telecommunications for Business*, PWS-Kent, Boston, 1990.

Whelan, David, "Is Cutting the Telephone Cord Right for You?" http://www.point.com/article/833.

CHAPTER 7

Telecommuting and Electronic Data Interchange

I n this chapter we introduce you to telecommuting and electronic data interchange as additional communication technology applications.

WHAT YOU WILL LEARN

- Definition of telecommuting
- How to select telecommuters
- Benefits of telecommuting
- Drawbacks of telecommuting
- How electronic data interchange (EDI) is defined
- Advantages of EDI
- Types of EDI applications
- How EDI is implemented

■ INTRODUCTION TO TELECOMMUTING

Technology has brought many changes to the workplace. As we have seen in earlier chapters, some of these changes include the use of electronic mail, teleconferencing, voice processing, facsimile, wireless communications, and other technologies. Other changes that technology has made possible relate

97

to the work environment. For many workers, telecommuting is one of these changes.

Telecommuting has been defined as "the process of commuting to the office through a communications link rather than transferring one's physical presence" (Newton, 1998, p. 712). These communications links are often facilitated through the use of a laptop computer with a modem, facsimile machine, e-mail, and perhaps with teleconferencing. Another source defines telecommuting as "moving the work to the workers instead of moving the workers to work" (Nilles, 1994, p. xix). Most telecommuting programs have the workers working at home. However, others set up telework centers, in which workers work in a conventional office environment other than the person's normal company office. The advantage to using a telework center rather than a person's home is that equipment and transmission capabilities can be provided that would not be available in a home setting.

The U.S. Census Bureau reports that the number of workers who work out of their homes has nearly tripled: from 4 million in 1990 to 11 million in 1997. A Society of Human Resource Management survey found that 24 percent of human resource professionals indicated that their companies offer telecommuting. *USA Today* reports that approximately 40 percent of all employees participate in some form of telecommuting. Some jobs lend themselves better than others to teleconferencing. Table 7-1 lists telecommutable jobs.

There are several forces that have driven the proliferation of telecommuting. One of these forces is most certainly the advancement of technology. The advent of low-priced equipment, including laptop/notebook computers and desktop videoconferencing equipment, have been the primary technologies that have spawned the development of telecommuting. In addition, recent movements in the United States toward the development of a national information infrastructure have made the networking of off-site computer equipment to an organization's on-site local area network a reality. The telephone network is converting to a digital format, which means that it will become easier and more reliable for computers to talk to each other over the phone lines. Cellular telephone technology also adds mobility and versatility for the individual telecommunications user.

Table 7-1
Some Telecommutable Jobs

Job Title	Home-Based		Satellite or Local Center	
	Full-Time	Part-Time	Full-Time	Part-Time
Accountant	No	Yes	Yes	Yes
Actuary	Maybe	Yes	Yes	Yes
Advertising executive	Maybe	Yes	Yes	Yes
Applications programmer	Yes	Yes	Yes	Yes
Architect	Yes	Yes	Yes	Yes
Auditor	No	Yes	Yes	Yes
Author	Yes	Yes	Yes	Yes
Bookkeeper	No	Yes	Yes	Yes
CAD/CAM engineer	No	Yes	Yes	Yes

Table 7-1
Some Telecommutable Jobs
(*continued*)

Job Title	Home-Based		Satellite or Local Center	
	Full-Time	Part-Time	Full-Time	Part-Time
Central files clerk	No	No	Maybe	No
Civil engineer	Yes	Yes	Yes	Yes
Clerk-typist	Maybe	Yes	Yes	Yes
Clinical psychologist	No	Yes	Yes	Yes
Computer scientist	No	Yes	Yes	Yes
Counter clerk	No	No	Yes	No
Data-entry clerk	Yes	Yes	Yes	Yes
Data-search specialist	Yes	Yes	Yes	Yes
Department general manager	No	Yes	Maybe	Yes
Design engineer	No	Yes	Yes	Yes
Economist	Maybe	Yes	Yes	Yes
Financial analyst	Yes	Yes	Yes	Yes
General secretary	No	Yes	Yes	Yes
Graphic Artist	Yes	Yes	Yes	Yes
Industrial engineer	No	Yes	Yes	Yes
Journalist	Yes	Yes	Yes	Yes
Laboratory director	No	Yes	Maybe	Yes
Laboratory scientist	No	No	Maybe	Maybe
Lawyer	Maybe	Yes	Yes	Yes
Mail clerk	No	No	Yes	Yes
Mainframe operator	No	No	Maybe	No
Maintenance technician	No	Yes	Yes	Yes
Manager of managers	No	Yes	Yes	Yes
Manager of people	No	Yes	Yes	Yes
Manager, machine systems	Maybe	Yes	Yes	Yes
Market analyst	Yes	Yes	Yes	Yes
Marketing manager	No	Yes	Yes	Yes
Natural scientist	No	Yes	Yes	Yes
Office machine operator	No	No	Yes	Yes
Personnel manager	No	Yes	Yes	Yes
Purchasing manager	Maybe	Yes	Yes	Yes
Radio newscaster	Yes	Yes	Yes	Yes
Realtor	Yes	Yes	Yes	Yes
Receptionist	No	No	Yes	Yes
Risk analyst	Yes	Yes	Yes	Yes
School administrator	No	Yes	Yes	Yes
Software engineer	Yes	Yes	Yes	Yes
Statistician	Maybe	Yes	Yes	Yes
Stock analyst	Yes	Yes	Yes	Yes
Stockbroker	Yes	Yes	Yes	Yes
Supervisor	Maybe	Yes	Yes	Yes
Systems engineer	No	Yes	Yes	Yes
Systems programmer	No	Yes	Yes	Yes
Technical writer	Yes	Yes	Yes	Yes
Telemarketer	Yes	Yes	Yes	Yes
Telephone operator	Yes	Yes	Yes	Yes
Theoretical physicist	Yes	Yes	Yes	Yes
Traveling salesperson	No	Yes	Yes	Yes
University professor	No	Yes	Yes	Yes
Word processing secretary	Yes	Yes	Yes	Yes

Source: Copyright 1994 by JALA International Inc.

Another driving force for the continued development of telecommuting has been the desire to alleviate traffic problems, especially in metropolitan areas. Fewer employees traveling from their homes to their places of employment results in savings of cost and time. Obviously, fewer automobiles on the roads results in a reduction in air pollution. Although car pooling has helped to reduce air pollution, telecommuting can contribute to solving this environmental problem.

There was a time when workers could expect to experience lifetime employment from one employer. This is no longer a realistic expectation, as evidenced by the fact that most people change jobs at least five times during their lives. A job change in the past usually meant moving to another location. Some families found it difficult to adjust to new environments. Telecommuting has helped some workers to live where they want to live, regardless of where their jobs are located.

A change in management philosophy among many managers has also helped to provide impetus for the development of telecommuting programs. In the past, many managers were attendance oriented, believing that an employee under his or her supervision could be productive only under the manager's direct control. They believed that attendance at the job site was linked with productivity and that workers who were not monitored would not be productive. We now know that some employees are actually more productive telecommuting than they are in the traditional office setting. For telecommuting to work, managers today need to adopt this output orientation and believe that output, not attendance, is what is important.

There are three basic requirements for making a telecommuting project work: employee commitment, corporate support, and an intelligent use of the technology that permits the telecommuter to carry out his or her duties and to maintain a link to the corporate office (Roseberry, "About.com Guide"). The lack of any one of these may result in the potential failure of a telecommuting program. Many organizations have found that to obtain full employee commitment, it is essential to make participation in telecommuting voluntary. This helps to ensure that employees are fully motivated to making the program work. Telecommuting will not work well in businesses that do not support it or have reservations on how well it can work. Organizations must provide telecommuters with the computers, software, and communication links necessary to make telecommuting succeed.

■ SELECTING TELECOMMUTERS

Can all employees in all types of positions within an organization telecommute? The answer to this question is probably no. There are some types of jobs for which telecommuting works much better than for other jobs. For example, a technical writer would probably be well suited to telecommuting; but a bus driver would not. In these two examples it is fairly easy to determine whether or not telecommuting would work, but what about the thousands of jobs in which this determination is not as easy? How does a company determine which jobs are best suited for telecommuting? The answer to this question is that there must be a systematic method for making this determination. A system that can be used is explained below.

Analyze Job Tasks

The first step is to analyze the typical tasks that a person in a particular position would perform. The tasks should not be too detailed and should be the main tasks that are performed over a specific period of time, such as one week. Next, determine the percentage of time that is spent on each task. For example, a typical job might entail the tasks and time allotments shown in Table 7-2.

Determine Task Suitability for Telecommuting

The next step involves determining how well the employee can do some or all of his or her assigned tasks away from the office, assuming that the necessary equipment and files are available. Each task should be evaluated based on specific criteria that will establish its suitability or unsuitability for telecommuting:

- Face-to-face interaction required
- Concentration required
- Need for physical access to fixed resources
- Involvement of sensitive information requiring physical security

Any task that requires a high level of face-to-face contact, extended concentration, the need for physical access to special and/or fixed resources, or that involves sensitive information requiring physical security that is not available away from the office should not be completed while the employee is telecommuting.

Task Number	Task	Percentage
1	Analyze figures	15
2	Collate information	5
3	Compose letters and memos	5
4	Coordinate information	5
5	Copy information	5
6	Develop plans	20
7	Interact with the public	10
8	Prepare reports	15
9	Present information	5
10	Retrieve/provide information	15

Table 7-2

Job Task Time Allotments Example

*Source: EDI and Electronic Commerce Implementation in Wales, "The ABC of EDI,"
http://www.edi.wales.org/feature4.htm

■ BENEFITS OF TELECOMMUTING

Telecommuting has become an increasingly popular work option around the world, mainly because it offers substantial benefits to both employers and employees. Some telecommuters work from home one or two days a week, while others function outside the corporate environment for more extended periods. Whatever the situation, employers and employee should be aware of the main advantages of telecommuting before embarking on a pilot project to determine the desirability of using telecommuting throughout the organization. In addition, there are some benefits that telecommuting offers society. The following is a list of some of the key benefits of telecommuting.

Benefits for Companies

1. *Better able to recruit employees.* One of the benefits of telecommuting is that it allows companies to recruit employees from a wider geographic area. This is possible because workers can be linked to their offices using computer and telecommunications technology. It also makes the company more attractive to potential employees. Those qualified persons who might not have considered moving to a new location might apply for a position if they are permitted to telecomute for at least a portion of the normal workweek. In addition, employees who have children and would not normally consider working might be persuaded to consider employment that includes the possibility of telecommuting. Physically challenged persons who have specialized skills but because of their disabilities are not able to work in a traditional work arrangement may be employable if permitted to telecomute.

2. *Reduces costs.* Another benefit of telecommuting for companies is that the cost of maintaining office overhead can be reduced. Since telecommuters often work out of their homes for at least part of the workweek, the number of offices within the company that require setup is reduced. In addition, fewer support personnel, such as administrative assistants and secretaries, may be required, which results in additional cost savings.

3. *Increases employee productivity.* Although telecommuting may not work well for everyone, some people are able to produce more when telecommuting. Some studies have found that employee productivity is increased by 10 to 30 percent. This may be due to the fact that some people actually spend more time on tasks while doing them at home because of the reductions in both travel time and opportunities for socialization among co-workers. It also may be due to the fact that some telecommuters work in an environment that is more conducive to getting tasks completed, so that there is more time for other activities. Companies that have telecommuting programs also report that it helps to reduce employee absenteeism, thus increasing productivity.

4. *Reduces need for child care.* In addition to being able to recruit employees who desire to stay home to take care of young children, telecommuting

addresses the problem of child care for workers currently employed. Many parents who work find it very difficult to locate acceptable child care centers. To address this issue, some companies have established centers on company property. Telecommuting reduces this need for child care facilities.

5. *Improves employee retention rate.* Traditional work arrangements often result in employees who exhibit signs of increased stress and burnout. Telecommuting helps to improve morale and usually decreases turnover and the need to replace employees.

Benefits for Employees.   In addition to providing benefits to companies, telecommuting provides some distinct advantages to employees.

1. *Reduces travel time.* Telecommuting reduces the travel time necessary for employees to travel to work and back home. This helps to eliminate the stress associated with commuting to work, especially in high-traffic metropolitan areas and in situations where the worker encounters bad weather or road repair work.

2. *Improves quality of life.* Telecommuting helps to increase job satisfaction for those employees who maintain a positive attitude toward this work arrangement. As mentioned, it often increases work productivity, which results in a happier employee who is committed to his or her job. It allows for flexible work hours and permits a more balanced home life by providing extra time for family and leisure activities.

3. *Reduces costs.* Because telecommuters do not report to work on a daily basis, costs associated with maintaining a vehicle, auto insurance, and gas and oil costs are reduced. In addition, fewer clothes need to be purchased, and lunch costs are reduced.

Benefits to Society.   Listed below are some specific benefits that telecommuting provides to society.

1. *Reduction in traffic congestion and energy conservation.* Telecommuting helps to ease traffic congestion associated with rush-hour commutes. Thus the roadways are less congested for people who must commute to work, helping to alleviate some of the stress related to this activity. In addition, less traffic means less pollution caused by automobile emissions, which results in a cleaner environment. Because fewer persons work out of corporate facilities, energy resources are conserved at these locations.

2. *Community benefits.* One distinct benefit that telecommuting provides to communities is increased neighborhood safety as more people remain at home, making their homes less prone to break-in and burglary. In addition, telecommuting eases the strain on community child care programs.

■ DRAWBACKS OF TELECOMMUTING

Listed below are some specific drawbacks of telecommuting.

1. *Lack of socialization.* Humans are social beings and need to be able to interact with others. For many people, work provides the means for social interaction. Employees interact with co-workers, not only on matters pertaining to work, but also on topics relating to their home life and families. As long as this does not interfere with the completion of the tasks assigned to workers, employers usually do not prohibit this interaction. Being part of the social fabric of a workplace helps employees feel alive and in touch with the world. Some telecommuters don't realize the benefits of socialization until it is taken away from them.

2. *No escape from work.* Another drawback is that in one sense, telecommuters never leave work. The office is always a few steps away, and there is a temptation to sneak in after hours to finish a project or send e-mail. One of the great things about going to work in an office is that at the end of the day, you can go home and escape from the pressures of work. When you work at home, it's as if you can't get away.

3. *Opposition by some managers.* As mentioned earlier, for telecommuting to work, managers need to be process oriented as opposed to having an attendance orientation. Managers who feel that they need to have employees present to control them adequately will create problems for themselves and for their telecommuting employees.

4. *Opposition by unions.* Some unions oppose anything that might result in exploitation of employees. If telecommuting is compulsory rather than voluntary, as is recommended, unions will be more likely to oppose it.

■ ELECTRONIC DATA INTERCHANGE DEFINED

Electronic data interchange (EDI) is a standard format for exchanging business data. Carr and Snyder define it as "the process of direct computer-to-computer communication of information in a standard format between organizations or parties (companies) that, as a result of this communication, permits the receiver to perform a set of business functions (e.g., purchasing, invoicing)" (Carr and Snyder, 1997, p. 344). All sizes of businesses can utilize EDI, and software packages are available that are suitable for a variety of businesses.

The major issue relating to EDI is that different EDI standards are in use, making it difficult for one organization to exchange data with another. The standards in use are EDIFACT, ANSI X.12, TRADACOMS, and ODETTE.

The EDIFACT (EDI for administration, commerce, and transport) standard is the only EDI standard that is truly accepted worldwide. EDIFACT provides standard formats for business documents and incorporates features that meet international requirements. Consequently, the document structures are large, as they try to cater to all conceivable eventualities. It is therefore common to find that individual industry sectors use subsets of the EDIFACT standard.

Development of standards in the United States has been separate from that in Europe and has proceeded under control of the American National Standards Institute (ANSI). The X.12 committee has specified standards for transaction sets, a data element dictionary, and transmission control. These relate directly to messages, data elements, and service segments of the standards developed in Europe, but there are differences in the way they are used. The ANSI X.12 standard is used in the United States, Canada, and to a degree in Australia. Several industry-specific subsets are also in use.

The TRADACOMS standard was developed by the Article Numbering Association (ANA) in 1982 for the retail industry in the United Kingdom and is currently the most widely used standard in Great Britain within this market. TRADACOMS defines standards for more than 30 trading documents. ODETTE was developed by the Society of Motor Manufacturers and Traders (SMMT) in 1985 and provides more than 30 messages that reflect this industry's use of **just-in-time (JIT)** methods. Up until recently, ODETTE was based on the TRADACOMS segment directory. The latest releases are adopting EDIFACT message standards.

An EDI message contains a string of data elements, each of which represents a single fact, such as a price, product model number, and so on, separated by delimiters. The entire string is called a *data segment*. One or more data segments framed by a header and trailer form a *transaction set*, which is the EDI unit of transmission (equivalent to a message). A transaction set often consists of what would usually be contained in a typical business document or form. The parties who exchange EDI transmissions are referred to as *trading partners*. EDI messages can be encrypted and decrypted. EDI is one form of electronic commerce, which also includes e-mail and fax.

One type of EDI that has been gaining popularity recently is **Internet-EDI** (known as *I-EDI* or *EDI-INT*), which answers the needs of small and midsized companies that sell products or services to large companies. Traditional EDI functions were processed on private **value-added networks (VANs)** set up as electronic bridges between specific businesses using similar business forms. Common EDI applications include the transfer of purchase orders, invoices, shipping notices, and so on, primarily in manufacturing and engineering sectors. Internet-EDI functions on the World Wide Web, thereby opening up literal electronic commerce (banking, marketing, credit transactions, etc.). This is a much less expensive way of using EDI. In a survey of 50 Fortune 1000 companies by Cambridge, Massachusetts–based Forrester Research, 46 percent of respondents predict that they expect to use Internet-EDI by 2001 (Millman, 1998, p. 38).

BENEFITS OF EDI

The primary advantage of EDI is that it provides a significant opportunity to lower the cost of business between business partners (businesses, customers, vendors, etc.). This is due to the elimination of hard copies of invoices, purchase orders, and other business documents. EDI also strengthens the relationship between business partners. In fact, there have been instances in which businesses have chosen vendors primarily because of their willingness to conduct business via EDI. EDI offers a significant competitive advantage for those businesses that utilize this technology.

EDI systems can shorten the lead time between receipt and fulfillment of orders. When scheduling information is transmitted with ordering data, companies can plan production more accurately and thus reduce stock inventories. Reduction in inventory can result in major savings. The use of EDI to transmit invoice data and payments can improve a company's cash flow and may increase the amount of working capital, as accounts can be dealt with more efficiently.

In summary, it has now become apparent that the greatest value of EDI will emerge in strategic areas such as the provision of better levels of customer service and improved marketing competitiveness. Following is a list of the strategic, operational, and opportunity benefits of EDI from "The ABCs of EDI" (http://www.edi.wales.org/feature4.htm):

Strategic benefits include:

- Faster trading cycle
- Ability to adopt new business processes, such as just-in-time manufacturing techniques.
- Ability to win new business or retain existing customers, leading to improvements in business efficiency
- Ability to respond to highly competitive new market entrants

Operational benefits include:

- Reduced costs: paper and postage bills cut, reduction in money tied up in stock, reductions in manual processing costs (e.g. reductions in associated with verification, keying, and rekeying of documents and the cost of manual filing systems)
- Improved cash flow
- Security and error reduction
- Acknowledged receipt

Opportunity benefits include:

- Enhanced image
- Competitive edge
- Improved corporate trading relationships

■ EDI APPLICATIONS

Electronic data interchange applications extend to all business- and trade-related activities. The activities can be categorized in three main areas "The ABCs of EDI," http://www.edi.wales.org):

1. *Commerce:* trade and industry, manufacturing, finance and banking, tourism and travel

2. *Transportation:* road, rail, air, sea; forwarding and dispatching; warehousing
3. *Government:* customs and excise, national and international trade, statistics

As far as particular industries are concerned, EDI is being viewed increasingly as a business-enabling technology, facilitating any of the activities noted above. In the automotive industry, EDI has been used primarily because of *just-in-time* (JIT) activities. With JIT, a manufacturer orders and then receives parts from suppliers just before those parts are needed on the assembly line. EDI provides the transaction link that JIT requires.

Where a transaction involves import or export, customs declaration documents can now be submitted using EDI messages, which greatly reduces the processing time required and helps to expedite the entire process. For example, Singapore harbor implemented EDI techniques in the 1980s. Now renowned for its competitiveness, customs transactions, which previously took a day to complete, can now be done in minutes.

Banks and other financial institutions are supporting use of EDI in the area of **electronic funds transfer (EFT)**. EFT enables these organizations to operate much more efficiently by eliminating significant amounts of paperwork. This results in a beneficial "knock-on" effect to their customers, thereby reducing fees. Governments view EDI as an enabler to help manage such areas as procurement, taxation, logistics, and so on. Government departments deal with vast quantities of information. EDI can facilitate tracking, and therefore management, of this information. Governments are using EFT increasingly to process payments such as social insurance and unemployment benefits to people and organizations ("The ABCs of EDI").

IMPLEMENTING EDI

There are five main processes involved in the use of EDI: extracting data from a computer system, translating the data into a transmittable format, transmitting the message, translating/interpreting the message at the receiving end, and downloading the data in the receiving application. Once management has been committed to move forward with EDI, the next step is to establish a phased plan for EDI implementation. The following is a sample plan for implementing an EDI system ("The ABCs of EDI," http://www.edi.wales.org):

1. Nominate an EDI project chairperson.
2. Form an EDI project team.
3. Analyze and prioritize internal and external information flows.
4. Analyze manual/automated generation of information. Identify key trading partners in terms of order quantity, value, etc.
5. Identify and use EDI information sources: awareness centers, trade associations, EDI software vendors and network operators, EDI consultants, and EDI users.
6. Assess costs of implementation.
7. Plan pilot implementation based on all of the above.

8. Form agreements to pilot with selected trading partners.
9. Assess and agree on requirements for software, communications, and standards.
10. Run the pilot test and evaluate outcomes.
11. Progress with implementation to new business partners and new business functions.

EDI is implemented in the same way as any other major business strategy; that is, it is implemented piecemeal, each stage being proved and evaluated before moving on to the next. To prevent disruption of key processes, it is advised not to attempt to switch to full EDI operation overnight. It takes time for people, systems, and processes to adapt to the new methodology. Once a business is ready for full implementation of EDI, there are further considerations in relation to interchange agreements with trading partners, the specific responsibilities of each trading partner, and similar matters.

■ SUMMARY

Telecommuting has been defined as "the process of commuting to the office through a communications link rather than transferring one's physical presence" (Newton, 1998, p. 712). These communications links are often facilitated through the use of a laptop computer with a modem, facsimile machine, e-mail, and perhaps with teleconferencing.

Most telecommuting programs have the workers working at home. However, others set up telework centers, in which workers work in a conventional office environment other than the person's normal company office.

There are several forces that have driven the proliferation of telecommuting: the advancement of technology, the advent of low-priced equipment, including laptop/notebook computers and desktop videoconferencing equipment; recent movements in the United States toward the development of a national information infrastructure, the conversion of the telephone network to a digital format, and the widespread use and reliability of cellular telephone technology.

The three basic requirements for making a telecommuting project work are employee commitment, corporate support, and an intelligent use of the technology that permits the telecommuter to carry out his or her duties and to maintain a link to the corporate office. The most important factors that should be considered when determining whether or not an employee would be an effective telecommuter include an analysis of the employee's job tasks and a determination of the suitability of these job tasks to telecommuting.

Telecommuting offers benefits to employers, employees, and to society as a whole. The benefits to employers include reduced costs, increased productivity, reduction in the need for child care, appearing more attractive to potential employee candidates, and being able to meet the needs of physically challenged employees. The benefits to the employee include a reduction in travel time, improvement in the quality of life, and a reduction in costs. The benefits to the community and society include a reduction in traffic congestion and related pollution as well as energy conservation, and an ease on the strain of community child care programs. The drawbacks to telecommunicating include a lack of socialization, opposition by certain management philosophies, and opposition by certain labor unions.

Electronic data interchange (EDI) is a standard format for exchanging business data. It is defined as "the process of direct computer-to-computer communication of information in a standard format between organizations or parties (companies) that, as a result of this communication, permits the receiver to perform a set of business functions (e.g., purchasing, invoicing) (Carr and Snyder, 1997, p. 344).

Traditional EDI functions operated on private value-added networks (VANs) set up as electronic bridges between specific businesses using similar business forms. EDI is commonly used for the electronic transfer of forms such as purchase orders, invoices, and shipping notices, primarily in the manufacturing and engineering sectors. Internet-EDI functions on the World Wide Web, thereby opening up literal electronic commerce (banking, marketing, credit transactions, etc.). This is a much less expensive way of using EDI.

The primary advantage of EDI is that it provides a significant opportunity to lower the cost of business between business partners (businesses, customers, vendors, etc.). Other advantages of using EDI systems include a reduction in lead time between receipt and fulfillment of orders and a reduction in inventory levels. It has now become apparent that the greatest value of EDI will emerge in strategic areas such as the provision of better levels of customer service and improved marketing competitiveness.

EDI applications extend to all business- and trade-related activities. The activities can be categorized in three main areas: commerce, transportation, and government. There are five main processes involved in the use of EDI: extracting data from a computer system, translating the data into a transmittable format, transmitting the message, translating/interpreting the message at the receiving end, and downloading the data in the receiving application.

EDI is implemented in the same way as any other major business strategy; that is, it is implemented piecemeal, each stage being proved and evaluated before moving on to the next. To prevent disruption to key processes, it is advised not to attempt to switch to full EDI operation overnight. It takes time for people, systems, and processes to adapt to the new methodology.

QUESTIONS

1. What is telecommuting?

2. What changes have made telecommuting possible?

3. Identify three basic requirements that are necessary to make a telecommuting project successful.

4. What should be evaluated to determine if a particular employee is a good candidate for telecommuting?

5. Identify the benefits that telecommuting provides to employers.

6. Identify the benefits that telecommuting provides to employees.

7. Identify the benefits that telecommuting provides to society and the community.

8. Identify the drawbacks to telecommuting.

9. Define electronic data interchange (EDI).

10. Identify EDI standards.

11. What business documents would EDI be most commonly used to transfer?

12. What is Internet-EDI (IEDI)?

13. Identify the advantages of using EDI.

14. Identify the five main processes involved in the use of EDI.

15. In general, how should EDI be implemented?

16. Identify the steps involved in an EDI implementation plan.

PROJECTS AND PROBLEMS

1. Take a survey to determine what local companies in your city or region utilize telecommuting. Ask the following questions.
   (a) For which jobs do they use telecommuting?
   (b) Is telecommuting voluntary or compulsory?
   (c) How are telecommuting workers selected?
   (d) How frequently are telecommuting employees required to come to the company offices to work or attend meetings?
   (e) Do telecommuters work from their homes or from another location?
   (f) What telecommunications equipment do telecommuters utilize? Is this equipment provided to them by the company?
   (g) What do employees like most about telecommuting?
   (h) What do employees like least about telecommuting?

2. Study the telecommuting guidelines established by state governments in the United States. To do this, use a search engine to search on "telecommuting (name of state)"; for example, "telecommuting Minnesota."

3. You work in the Chicago national headquarters of a large multinational company. After years of fighting the smog and traffic, you and your fellow workers have decided to do something about it. They have elected you as a spokesperson to develop a recommendation for management to im-

plement a telecommuting program. Use PowerPoint or similar software to make a convincing presentation to management to adopt such as program. Your presentation must address such issues as benefits to the company, cost of hardware and software, selection process for those who will participate, and benefits to employees.

4. Visit a company of your choice to find out whether any business transactions, such as purchasing, sales, and shipping, are conducted using electronic data interchange (EDI).
   (a) If you find any companies that use EDI, describe how EDI works in each company.
   (b) If you don't find any companies that use EDI, describe the procedures that the company uses to purchase supplies. Could EDI be used by this organization? Is the organization considering its use?

5. Use a search engine to locate information on the Web about companies that provide EDI software.
   (a) What are the names of these software packages?
   (b) What are the capabilities of the software?
   (c) Is the software designed to meet the needs of a specific industry? If yes, what industry?
   (d) What hardware is required to run this software?
   (e) What is the cost of the software?

Vocabulary

electronic data interchange (EDI)

electronic funds transfer (EFT)

Internet-EDI

just in time (JIT)

telecommuting

telework center

value-added network (VAN)

References

Carr, Houston H., and Charles A. Snyder, *The Management of Telecommunications: Business Solutions to Business Problems*, Irwin/McGraw-Hill, Chicago, 1997.

EDI and Electronic Commerce Implementation in Wales, "The ABCs of EDI," http://www.edi.wales.org/feature4.htm.

Millman, Howard, "Easy EDI for Everyone," *InfoWorld*, Aug. 17, 1998.

Newton, Harry, *Newton's Telecom Dictionary*, Flatiron Publishing, New York, 1998.

Nilles, Jack M., *Making Telecommuting Happen: A Guide for Telemanagers and Telecommuters*, Van Nostrand Reinhold, New York, 1994.

Roseberry, Catherine, "About.com Guide to Telecommuting," http://www.telecommuting.about.com/business/business/telecommuting.

Stair, Ralph M., and George W. Reynolds, *Principles of Information Systems*, 4th ed., Course Technology, Cambridge, MA, 1999.

Sullivan, Colin, "Beyond Traditional EDI: Electronic Commerce Demystified," *Inform,* Nov. 1998.

Tedesco, Eleanor Hollis, *Telecommunications for Business*, PWS-Kent, Boston, 1990.

"The Different Standards," http://www.saaconsultants.com/EDI/edi_standards.html.

Ziff-Davis Corporation, "I Hate Telecommuting!" http://www.zdnet.com/zdtv/thesite/0197w2/work/work31jump4_010997.html.

"What Is EDI?" http://www.whatis.com/edi.htm.

PART THREE

The Internet and Intranets

In this part of the book we provide an introduction to the Internet and intranets, as well as a discussion of the major tools that are available through the Internet. These tools include discussion groups, newsgroups, World Wide Web browsers, telnet, gopher, Archie, and file transfer protocol (FTP). We also provide an introduction to hypertext markup language (HTML), used for the creation of World Wide Web pages.

8

Introduction to the Internet and Intranets

In this chapter we introduce you to the Internet and to intranets. You will learn how the Internet is defined, the history and uses of the Internet, as well as Internet addressing, connections, and protocols. In addition, you will learn how intranets are defined and used, and what the future holds for the Internet and for intranets.

WHAT YOU WILL LEARN

- Definition of the Internet
- History of the Internet
- Uses of the Internet
- Internet addressing
- Internet connections
- Internet protocols
- Definition of Intranets
- How Intranets are used
- Future of the Internet and intranets

■ THE INTERNET DEFINED

The Internet has been publicized a great deal recently. It seems as if everyone wants to obtain an Internet connection. However, there is some misunderstanding about what the Internet is, as well as its capabilities and uses. The **Internet** is a network of computer systems that are interconnected in approximately 130 countries. Figure 8-1 shows the types of Internet connections throughout the world. All the connected computer systems share a common protocol: **transmission control protocol/Internet protocol (TCP/IP)**. A **protocol** is the set of rules or conventions by which two machines talk to each other. TCP/IP allows computer systems of various types to communicate with each other.

■ HISTORY OF THE INTERNET

The Internet began in 1969 as the Advanced Research Projects Agency Network (ARPANET) by the U.S. Department of Defense. Later, the Department of Defense made ARPANET available to universities and other organizations. Initial research was conducted to determine if a network could be developed which would ensure that military communications could continue in the event of a nuclear war. In response to this charge, ARPANET became a packet-switched network where information gets broken into little packets which move independently of each other until they reach the destination.

The system continued to expand, and in 1983, split into two networks, ARPANET and MILNET. ARPANET was used for civilian (research) efforts

Figure 8-1
International Internet Connectivity.
(Courtesy of Larry Landweber and the Internet Society.)

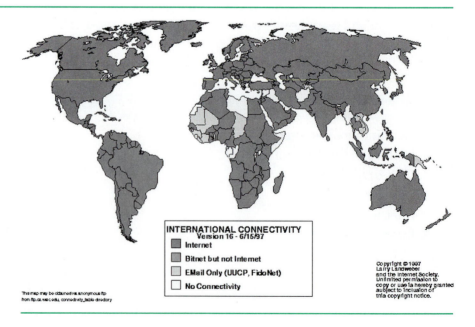

INTERNATIONAL CONNECTIVITY
Version 16 - 6/15/97
■ Internet
■ Bitnet but not Internet
□ EMail Only (UUCP, FidoNet)
□ No Connectivity

This map may be obtained via anonymous ftp
from ftp.cs.wisc.edu, connectivity_table directory

Copyright © 1997
Larry Landweber
and the Internet Society.
Unlimited permission to
copy or use is hereby granted
subject to inclusion of
this copyright notice.

and MILNET was reserved for military use. Also in the early 1980s, several other new networks were formed to serve other groups and organizations. One of these was the Because It's Time Network (BITNET) for academic communities. Another network was the Computer Science Network (NSNET), which connected researchers together for the sharing of information. In 1986, the National Science Foundation connected researchers across the country with five supercomputer centers, which became known as NSFNET. This network formed a backbone of transmission lines—fiber optic wires, satellite links, and microwaves—to carry large amounts of traffic very quickly over long distances. The NSFNET backbone became the basic infrastructure for the Internet.

USES OF THE INTERNET

The Internet today has four main uses: electronic mail, remote logon, file transfer, and multimedia. Electronic mail (e-mail), which is the most widely used application, permits people who have an Internet connection and have been assigned user identification (e.g., jsmith@psu.edu) to send electronic messages to others connected to the Internet. Remote logon (or telnet) allows people to log on to any computer connected to the Internet from another computer which has an Internet connection. These users are able, for example, to check for e-mail messages and perform other tasks. **File transfer** is the ability to transfer a file from a computer connected to the Internet to another computer that has an Internet connection. One utility that permits this to occur is **file transfer protocol (FTP)**. Other Internet utilities, which assist in file transfer, are archie and veronica, which provide the means for searching the Internet for information pertaining to a particular topic.

Multimedia is the fourth and newest use of the Internet. **Multimedia** is the use of more than one medium such as text, graphics, sound, and video. Before this application became available, it was only possible to view and communicate information in simple text. Because the Internet had been used in the past mainly by the government and academia for research, nongraphical interfaces were adequate. Today, the need for multimedia is extensive and the **World Wide Web** (commonly called the Web) is the part of the Internet that provides us with multimedia applications. One of the ways in which businesses have recently been using the Web is for electronic commerce. **Electronic commerce** is the buying and selling of goods and services, and the transfer of funds, through digital communications. Additional information on the World Wide Web is provided in Chapter 10.

INTERNET ADDRESSING

Every network and computer that is connected to the Internet is assigned an address. Addresses are made up of a sequence of four numbers separated by periods (e.g., 129.219.30.21). Each of the numbers is in the range 0 through 255. Starting from the left, the numbers in the address identify a network, and the number(s) on the right identify a specific host or computer system. In the sample address on the previous page, the network portion of the address is 129.219.30 and the host portion is 21. On networks with more hosts, the last two or three numbers are used. An address in number form is called an **IP address**. Information sent from one site on the Internet to another is divided into packets, and each packet has the IP address of the sender and the IP address of the destination.

The problem with numerical IP addresses is that it is difficult for people to remember and type them correctly, especially since every Internet site is assigned a different number. For this reason, many Internet sites are also assigned domain names. The domain name for 129.219.30.21 is www.eas .asu.edu, which is the site for the College of Engineering and Applied Sciences at Arizona State University. The number of words in a domain name varies but is always at least two, with two to four words commonly used. The words, which are separated by periods, are more specific on the left and more general as you move to the right, which is just the opposite of the arrangement of a numerical address.

The Internet is made up of a collection of networks which are divided into groups called domains. The **domain name** either identifies the geographical location or a type of organization. For instance, in our previous example, www.eas.asu.edu is an educational institution, since the word on the right side of the domain name is *edu*, which is used by most schools, colleges, and universities. All the major domain types are identified in Table 8-1.

■ INTERNET CONNECTIONS

Access to the Internet is available in the following ways: an electronic mail connection, a direct connection, an ISDN connection, a shell connection, a SLIP/PPP connection, a cable connection, or through a commercial online service. The easiest way to obtain Internet access is by working for a company with an Internet connection or by becoming a student. Most colleges and universities, including community colleges, now provide Internet access to all enrolled students. In addition, some public libraries have Internet terminals for anyone to use. Also, many communities offer connections to a service called Free-Net, which you can use from a library or school or by dialing in to it.

Table 8-1
Major Domain Types

Domain	Type of Organization
com	Commercial organization
edu	Educational institution
gov	Government (U.S.)
mil	Military (U.S.)
net	Network
org	Nonprofit organization

Electronic Mail Connection

An **electronic mail connection**, usually through a company or other organization, limits users to send mail electronically within or outside the organization via the Internet. Remote login and file transfer are generally not available, and this type of connection would not be a good choice for using multimedia on the Internet.

Direct Connection

A **direct** (or **dedicated) connection**, which is the preferred way of accessing the Internet at this time, is through a company, educational institution, or other organization. Some organizations provide dial-up access via a modem. This connection is usually accomplished through the purchase of a T1 transmission line. The speed of transmission for a T1 line is 1.544 megabytes, as compared with a speed of up to 56 kilobytes for a voice transmission line.

ISDN Connection

An alternative method that also provides relatively fast connection speed is the **integrated services digital network (ISDN) connection**. ISDN is designed to carry large amounts of information at a fast rate of speed. It is especially well suited for the transmission of high-quality audio and video materials and for desktop videoconferencing for those without a direct connection. The regional telephone companies in the United States are gradually making ISDN available in more localities. Currently, there is better than 75 percent coverage, and this percentage will be increasing in the near future. Most long-distance ISDN connections within the United States are between 56 and 128 kilobytes.

Shell or SLIP/PPP Connection

Private providers provide either a **shell connection** or a **SLIP/PPP connection** to the Internet. A *shell connection* is a dial-up service in which the subscriber accesses the account with terminal emulation software. The Internet software runs on the provider's host computer and the emulation software displays the link between the local host and the Internet computers. With a *SLIP/PPP connection*, your computer becomes physically connected to the Internet. The connection is made through a private provider via dial-up, but special software provides the capability of transmitting TCP/IP packets between the Internet-connected computer and your computer. This is seen as the second-best connection, after a direct or ISDN connection. Subscribers to these Internet providers usually pay an installation fee and a per-month fee that will either provide them with an unlimited number of hours of access, or will limit them to a specific number of hours before additional charges are incurred.

Cable Connection

An alternative way to connect to the Internet is through your television cable provider. Cable companies are spending billions of dollars to upgrade TV networks to handle the two-way traffic needed to deliver the Internet. A special television cable modem is required for this type of connection. Cable modems, which connect to computers via an Ethernet network card, support Internet download and upload speeds of up to 30 megabits per second. A file that takes 10 minutes to download with a 28.8 kilobit-per-second modem will arrive in less than 30 seconds with a cable modem. Figure 8-2 shows how a cable Internet connection works.

Figure 8-2

How Cable Connections Work.
(Reprinted from the November 1999 issue of Maximum PC. *Copyright Imagine Media, Inc. All rights reserved.)*

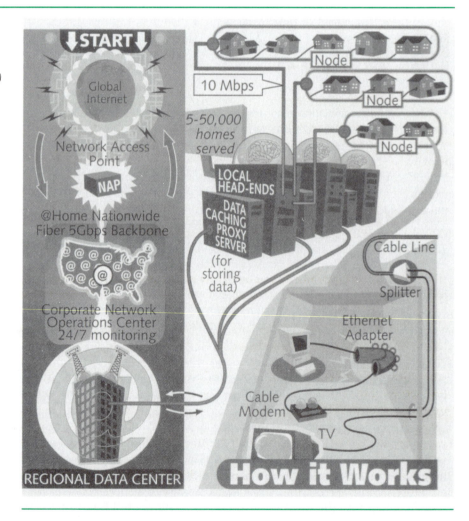

Commercial Online Service Connection

The final alternative to gaining Internet access is through commercial online services such as America Online, CompuServe, or Prodigy. Each of these providers offers a number of Internet services. All of them allow for electronic messages to be transferred to people connected to the Internet. Many online carriers have recently added ways to provide subscribers access to Internet servers which provide information in multimedia format. Subscribers are usually charged a monthly fee for a specific number of hours of basic services. Special services often result in additional fees above the basic fee. There are also several free commercial online services, such as NetZero. A disadvantage of these free services is that users have to contend with advertising banners that appear on their screens when these services are used.

■ INTERNET PROTOCOLS

Several different protocols are used on the Internet: http, ftp, gopher, and telnet.

http

The **http (hypertext transport protocol)** service is used by World Wide Web clients and servers to exchange documents. The following actions occur when http is used: A client opens a connection to a server, the client requests a particular document, the server answers the request, and the connection is closed.

ftp

The FTP (file transfer protocol) is used to exchange files on the Internet. The FTP usually means that the file can be retrieved by anonymous FTP so that a password is not required.

Gopher

Gopher servers can be accessed through addresses that indicate the path to these servers. Each gopher connection results in a different list of menu items. Additional information on gopher is provided in Chapter 12.

Telnet

Telnet allows you to log on to a remote computer connected to the Internet to access information or to run programs. Additional information on telnet is provided in Chapter 12.

■ INTRANETS DEFINED

An **intranet** represents a local area network within an organization which may or may not be connected to the Internet, but which has some similar functions. In this situation, World Wide Web servers may be on a company's internal networks so that employees have access to the organization's Web documents. A World Wide Web browser such as Microsoft Internet Explorer or Netscape Navigator is used to access the documents. In fact, it might be difficult to know whether the origin of the documents is within the organization or from the Internet.

■ INTRANET USES

A number of information resources and transactions are potential candidates for an intranet.

Documents

Every corporation has reams of business information that it must distribute to internal employees or external customers and suppliers. The following list provides examples of the types of documents that companies traditionally distribute: policy and procedure manuals, quality manuals, work instructions, employee benefits programs, orientation materials, software user guides, hardware manuals, quick reference guides, online help style guides and other standards, training manuals and tutorials, company newsletters and announcements, scheduling information, maps and schematic drawings, computer reports of customer data, sales and marketing literature, specifications, price lists, product catalogs, and press releases. Intranets provide a way to put all of these documents online for instant access by authorized users.

Electronic Resources

Companies also have a number of electronic resources stored on computer that are traditionally distributed by transportable media or by copying across network nodes. These may include test data, customer data, spreadsheet templates, documentation templates, software applications and utilities, and programmer toolkit components. In the past, many of these resources may have been hidden away in rarely accessed cavities of the network. Using appropriate Web applications, these resources can be cataloged online for user review and distributed automatically through a single mouse-click across a network to any authorized user who requests them.

Interactive Communication

Finally, there are various types of two-way communication within a corporation that can be facilitated by Web technologies. These include surveys and feedback; program notification and enrollment; progress inquiries and reporting; memo distribution, comment, and reply; spontaneous data entry and data collection; interactive database queries; and product promotion and ordering. A Web browser gives us a way to communicate with employees, customers, or suppliers, present information, capture feedback, and process the feedback automatically through databases or scripting mechanisms. It also supports spontaneous user searches of information archives or databases.

■ FUTURE OF THE INTERNET AND INTRANETS

Many organizations are working on standards related to both hardware and software that will define the next-generation Internet. Two dominant initiatives are spearheading the research and development of Internet infrastructure, the underlying backbone crucial to the transmission and flow of all Net traffic. The *Next Generation Internet* (NGI) Initiative is funded entirely by the U.S. federal government and is working primarily on projects for government agencies. *Internet2* (I2), on the other hand, is an effort undertaken by a coalition of universities and companies that have contributed both funding and research resources. Twelve members, primarily universities, will be the initial beneficiaries of its research and development. It is likely that the work of both NGI and I2 will find their way into the public Net. Both initiatives suggest significant improvements over the Internet we use today. The key features of NGI and I2 proposals are in the areas of optical networks, reliability, and better use of bandwidth:

1. *Ultrafast optical networks.* Much faster switches and routers will be able to replicate information throughout the Net, reducing congestion and bottlenecks. These switches and routers will be smarter, enabling them to negotiate priorities and bandwidth capacity for specific data streams, acting much like air traffic controllers at busy airports.
2. *Greater reliability and security.* One of the key goals for the Internet of the future is to guarantee specific levels of high-quality service, based on individual needs. E-mail and e-commerce systems will be significantly more robust, offering much greater security than do today's systems.
3. *Better use of bandwidth.* New *multicast* technology will send data to multiple recipients at the same time, and the system will be able to reserve bandwidth for real-time applications. This will eliminate the present choppy or low-resolution audio and video.

Beyond providing sizzling speed and rock-solid reliability, the next-generation Internet will spawn a whole new array of applications. At a basic level, TV and radio broadcasters will probably abandon their analog equipment and migrate entirely to the Internet, enhancing their programming with a variety of interactive features. Current videoconferencing and computer conferencing capabilities will be transformed into *tele-immersion*, in which you will enter fully three-dimensional virtual worlds and appear to interact physically with other Net users in real time. People will be able to attend classes at colleges and universities anywhere in the world. Surgeons will be able to operate on patients via remote controls. Virtual tourism, of both Earth and extraterrestrial locations, will become commonplace.

What is the timeline for this development? The future Internet is already in use by its developers. You'll probably start to see parts of these predictions make their way into "our" Internet in the immediate future.

■ SUMMARY

The Internet is a network of computer systems that are interconnected in approximately 130 countries. All the connected computer systems share a common protocol: transmission control protocol/Internet protocol (TCP/IP). TCP/IP allows computer systems of various types to communicate with each other.

The Internet began in 1969 as the Advanced Research Projects Agency Network (ARPANET) by the U.S. Department of Defense. Later, the Department of Defense made ARPANET available to universities and other organizations. The system continued to expand, and in 1983 split into two networks, ARPANET and MILNET. ARPANET was used for civilian (research) efforts and MILNET was reserved for military use. Also in the early 1980s, several other new networks were formed to serve other groups and organizations. In 1986, the National Science Foundation connected researchers across the country with five supercomputer centers, which became known as NSFNET. This network formed a backbone of transmission lines—fiber optic wires, satellite links, and microwaves—to carry large amounts of traffic very quickly over long distances. The NSFNET backbone became the basic infrastructure for the Internet.

The Internet today has four main uses: electronic mail, remote logon, file transfer, and multimedia. Electronic mail (e-mail), which is the most used application, permits people who have an Internet connection and have been assigned user identification (e.g., jsmith@psu.edu) to send electronic messages to others connected to the Internet. Remote logon (or telnet) allows people to log on to any computer connected to the Internet from another computer which has an Internet connection. File transfer is the ability to transfer a file from a computer connected to the Internet to another computer that has an Internet connection. Finally, the need for multimedia today is extensive, and this demand is being addressed through the World Wide Web.

Every network and computer that is connected to the Internet is assigned an address. Addresses are made up of a sequence of four numbers separated by periods (e.g., 129.219.30.21). An address in number form is called an IP address. Information sent from one site on the Internet to another is divided into packets, and each packet has the IP address of the sender and the IP address of the destination. The problem with numerical IP addresses is that it is difficult for people to remember and type them correctly, especially since every Internet site is assigned a different number. For this reason, many Internet sites are also assigned domain names. The domain name for 129.219.30.21 is www.eas.asu.edu, which is the site for the College of Engineering and Applied Sciences at Arizona State University. The number of words in a domain name varies but is always at least two, with two to four words commonly used. The words, which are separated by periods, are more specific on the left and more general as you move to the right, which is just the opposite of the arrangement of a numerical address.

The Internet is made up of a collection of networks which are divided into groups called domains. The domain name either identifies the geographical location or a type of organization.

Access to the Internet is available in the following ways: an electronic mail connection, a direct connection, an ISDN connection, a shell connection, a SLIP/PPP connection, a cable connection, or through a commercial online service.

Several different protocols are used on the Internet: http, ftp, gopher, and telnet. The service http (hypertext transport protocol) is used by World Wide Web clients and servers to exchange documents. The ftp (file transfer protocol) is used to exchange files on the Internet. Gopher servers can be accessed through addresses that indicate the path to these servers. Telnet allows you to log on to a remote computer connected to the Internet to access information or to run programs.

An intranet represents a local area network within an organization which may or may not be connected to the Internet, but which has some similar functions. A number of information resources and transactions are potential candidates for an intranet. Every corporation has reams of business information that it must distribute to internal employees or external customers and suppliers. Companies also have a number of electronic resources stored on computer that are traditionally distributed by transportable media or by copying across network nodes. Finally, there are various kinds of two-way communication within a corporation that can be facilitated by Web technologies.

Two dominant initiatives are spearheading the research and development of Internet infrastructure, the underlying backbone crucial to the transmission and flow of all Net traffic. The *Next Generation Internet* (NGI) Initiative is funded entirely by the U.S. federal government and is working primarily on projects for government agencies. *Internet2* (I2), on the other hand, is an effort undertaken by a coalition of universities and companies that have contributed both funding and research resources.

Further developments in the future of the Internet and Intranets might include ultrafast optical networks. Much faster switches and routers will be able to replicate information throughout the Net, reducing congestion and bottlenecks. One of the key goals for the Internet of the future is to guarantee specific levels of high-quality service, based on individual needs. E-mail and e-commerce systems will be significantly more robust, offering much greater security than do today's systems.

New multicast technology will send data to multiple recipients at the same time, and the system will be able to reserve bandwidth for real-time applications. The will eliminate the present choppy or low-resolution audio and video.

QUESTIONS

1. What is the Internet?

2. What is TCP/IP? What is a protocol?

3. Give a brief history of the Internet.

4. List and discuss the four principal uses of the Internet.

5. Discuss briefly Internet addressing.

6. What is the difference between an IP address and a domain name?

7. What are domains? List examples of major domain types.

8. List and discuss the ways that Internet access is made available to users.

9. List and discuss the various protocols that are used on the Internet.

10. What is an intranet?

11. Identify and provide examples of uses of an intranet.

12. Discuss the future trends of the Internet and intranets.

PROJECTS AND PROBLEMS

1. Take a survey of local companies and other organizations in your city or region that use the Internet or intranet(s). Ask the following questions:
   (a) What type of Internet connection do they have? Are they satisfied with the speed of this connection?
   (b) For what purposes do they use the Internet or intranet(s)?

2. Prepare a brief proposal for developing a business based on electronic commerce (e-commerce). Describe what products and/or services you will offer. Describe how users will inter-act with the Web site. How will you get people to visit your site? Develop a simple spreadsheet to analyze income and expenses.

3. Install one of the free Internet service providers (i.e., Netzero: http://www.netzero.com). How do these services work? How can they provide Internet access without charging for it? Do you think that there will be a trend toward the development of more free service providers?

Vocabulary

cable connection

cable modem

commercial online service connection

direct (or dedicated) connection

domain name

electronic commerce

electronic mail connection

file transfer

file transfer protocol (FTP)

gopher protocol

hypertext transport protocol (http)

integrated services digital network (ISDN) connection

Internet

intranet

IP address

multimedia

protocol

shell or SLIP/PPP connections

transmission control protocol/Internet protocol (TCP/IP)

World Wide Web

References

Ackerman, Ernest. *Learning to Use the World Wide Web,* Franklin, Beedle & Associates, Wilsonville, OR, 1997.

"Computer-Currents High Tech Dictionary," http://www.currents.net/resources/dictionary.

Del Rizzo, Brian, "Broadband: Our Complete Guide to Riding the Bucking Bronco of High-Speed Internet Access," *Maximum PC*, Nov. 1999.

Gehris, Dennis, *Microsoft Internet Explorer 5.0.* South-Western Educational Publishing, Cincinnati, OH, 2000.

Gehris, Dennis, *Using Multimedia Tools and Applications on the Internet*, Wadsworth, Belmont, CA, 1998.

IntraMark Resources, http://www.intramark.com/resources/sem_1.html.

Stair, Ralph M., and George W. Reynolds, *Principles of Information Systems*, 4th ed., Course Technology, Cambridge, MA, 1999.

"The Next Generation Internet," http://www.websearch.about.com/internet/websearch/library/weekly/aa050799.htm.

9

Electronic Mail Discussion Groups and Newsgroups

I n this chapter we discuss the use of electronic mail discussion groups and newsgroups. You will learn how to find, subscribe to, and unsubscribe from and communicate with discussion groups and how to use newsgroups.

WHAT YOU WILL LEARN

- Definition of electronic mail discussion groups
- How to find electronic mail discussion groups
- How to subscribe to an electronic mail discussion group
- How to communicate with and contribute to an electronic mail discussion group
- Proper etiquette or behavior in a discussion group
- How to unsubscribe from an electronic mail discussion group
- Definition of newsgroups
- How to use a newsgroup reader

■ DEFINITION AND NATURE OF ELECTRONIC MAIL DISCUSSION GROUPS

In Chapter 3 you learned that electronic mail has become one of the most often used communication technology applications. It is defined as electronic messaging that permits people who have an Internet or intranet connection and have been assigned a user identification (e.g., jsmith@psu.edu) to send electronic messages to others connected to the Internet or to an intranet.

There are several methods that allow people who have similar interests and wish to ask questions, share information, or discuss issues related to a common topic or theme to form groups through the use of electronic mail. One method is by the use of **discussion groups**, sometimes called *discussion lists*.

Membership in a discussion group permits you to read the e-mail messages that other members have sent to the group. Some groups are set up only to make announcements about upcoming events, products, or the like. Although these groups do not encourage you to send return messages, most other groups permit you to respond to the messages of others. Because the title of the group often does not fully describe the topic of discussion, you probably should read the messages for a time until you decide to respond.

Another option when using discussion groups is to try to initiate a discussion of your own on a topic of your choice which relates to the theme of the group. This can be done by asking a question. For example, in a group about computer printers or computing peripherals, you might ask a question such as: "Can anyone recommend an inkjet printer that offers good print quality?" Another way to start a discussion would be by stating your opinion and asking the members of the group to react to it. For example, state the following: "I believe that the Epson Color 800 printer has good print quality. Does anyone agree or disagree?"

Several words of caution are in order when using discussion groups. Most discussion groups are **unmoderated**. This means that no one has been assigned to screen the messages that are posted in a group. For this reason, some people do not stick to the topic that is being discussed. This can be frustrating, especially when you are trying to obtain information about something and several members are speaking about an entirely different subject. In addition, be prepared for messages that scold, berate, insult, or contain profanity. This type of message is called a *flame*. Some people lose their self-control and return a *flaming message* in return. It is best to ignore any message that you read that is offensive and send only polite messages to the group.

Many discussion groups are called **Listserv lists**. This is commercial mailing list manager software that is marketed by L-Soft International. At the time of writing of this book, there were 151,087 Listserv lists (29,573 private lists and 121,514 public lists).

Most management of a list, such as adding **(subscribing)** and removing members who choose to leave **(unsubscribing)**, is done automatically by software running on the server that serves as the host system for the list. Some lists allow you to retrieve archives or collections of past discussions or obtain a summary of the discussions that have taken place over a period of time as opposed to getting the messages when they are posted by subscribers. Users may select how often they prefer to receive the messages posted to the list. The following three options are often provided to subscribers for receiving messages (L-Soft Web site: http://www.lsoft.com):

1. *Single messages.* List subscriber will receive the e-mail messages individually and immediately after they are posted to the list.
2. *Digest mode.* List subscriber will receive one posting that includes all the individual messages delivered during that digest cycle, which can be set to daily or weekly cycles.
3. *Index mode.* Similar to the digest mode, the list subscriber will receive one posting that contains an index of the subject topics for all messages distributed during that digest cycle. Subsequently, the list subscriber may retrieve any message(s) of interest.

■ FINDING ELECTRONIC MAIL DISCUSSION GROUPS

To subscribe to an electronic mail discussion group, you must be able to find the list or group address so that you can communicate with the list via e-mail. There are reference books that list the various discussion groups that are available, along with instructions on how to subscribe to them. One of these books is *Cyberhound's Guide to International Discussion Groups* (see the reference list). The problem with such books is that they soon become out-of-date, as entries are changed, deleted, and added. A better way of finding discussion lists is to use a Web browser to link to a search page. One such page is L-Soft's Catalist, which is found at http://www.lsoft.com/lists/listref.html. This is a catalog of Listserv lists which allows you to enter a search term to search or browse the database of the lists that use Listserv. For example, if we were searching for lists relating to "Telecommunications," we might key this term in the search box (see Figure 9-1). After clicking on the Start the Search! button, the results appear as shown in Figure 9-2. Clicking on any of these links provides information relating to each list.

Obviously, there are other search sites on the Web to find discussion lists. Another one of these is called Liszt, which is found at http://www.liszt .com/. This page allows you to key in a topic in a search box or click on topical areas such as books, computers, education, and nature to find a list (see Figure 9-3). Since we are seeking information about lists relating to telecommunications, we would need to click on "Computers" and then "Telecommunications."

Still another search page is the Publicly Available Mail List (http://www .neosoft.com/internet/paml/), which contains names, addresses, and information about lists available through the Internet and is maintained by Stephanie de Silva. Another search page is found at http://www.tile.net/ lists, which provides all of the information that you need to join a list, along with hyperlinks that make it easy to subscribe.

Figure 9-1
L-Soft's Catalist Search Page. *(Courtesy of L-Soft International, Inc.)*

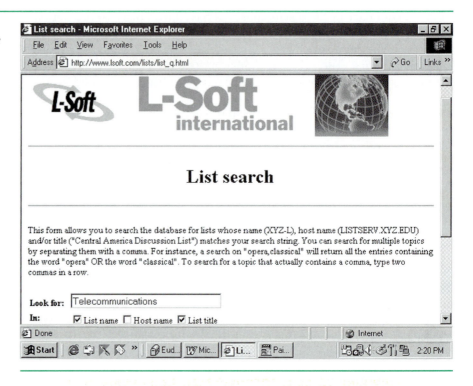

Figure 9-2
L-Soft Catalist Search Results. *(Courtesy of L-Soft International, Inc.)*

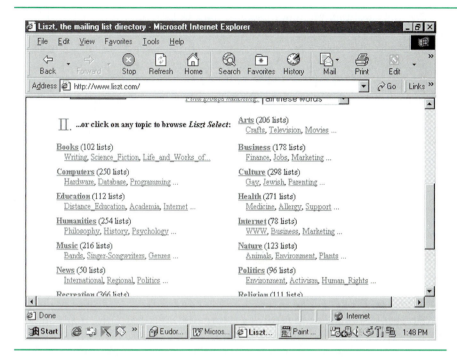

Figure 9-3
Liszt Discussion List Topical Areas.
(*Microsoft Internet Explorer™ screen shot reprinted by permission from Microsoft Corporation*)

■ SUBSCRIBING TO AN ELECTRONIC MAIL DISCUSSION GROUP

After you perform a search to find a discussion group that you want to join, two types of e-mail addresses will be provided: an administrative address and a list address. The administrative address is the one that you use to subscribe to a list. It is also used to unsubscribe from the list when you no longer want to receive e-mail messages from the list. The administrative list is the one that is provided after you do a search using one of the Web search pages. For example, if we clicked on "EDSS-295@LIST.UVM.EDU, Telecommunications and the Information Highway *(135 subscribers)*," we would obtain the results shown in Figure 9-4.

EDSS-295@LIST.UVM.EDU

Telecommunications and the Information Highway

List name: EDSS-295
Host name: LIST.UVM.EDU
Subscribers: 135
  • Features: Spam filter
  • Archives
  • Web archive interface
  • Digests (with MIME support)
  • Indexes
  • Database functions

To subscribe, send mail to LISTSERV@LIST.UVM.EDU with the command (paste it!):

Figure 9-4
Information about the "Telecommunications and the Information Highway" Electronic Mail Discussion Group

In this example, we would send e-mail to LISTSERV@LIST.UVM.EDU, placing nothing in the subject line and SUBSCRIBE EDSS-295 in the body of the message. The original e-mail message from the list server should also provide the list address, which is the address to which you send original messages. Note that this is usually a different address than the administrative address to which you sent the subscribe command. Sometimes the message will instruct you to send another message or click on a Web link to confirm that you want to subscribe to the list. See Figure 9-5 for an example of the confirmation e-mail message that was received after sending the subscribe command to the LISTSERV@LIST.UVM.EDU address to join the "Telecommunications and the Information Highway" discussion group. You will note that the instructions indicate that EDSS-295@LIST.UVM.EDU is the address to which messages are to be sent.

■ COMMUNICATING WITH AND CONTRIBUTING TO AN ELECTRONIC MAIL DISCUSSION GROUP

After you send a subscribe message to the administrative address of the discussion group, you should receive a return message indicating that you have been accepted as a subscriber. Depending on the activity level of the list, you may start to receive e-mail messages from the group almost immediately or it may take anywhere from several hours to several days to receive them. Sometimes you may want to reply to a message you've received from a member of the list. You can send e-mail that either goes to everyone in the group or only to the person who originated the message. The e-mail program you use will allow you to reply to a message. If you reply to a message from the group, it will be sent to all the members of the group. You'll need to decide whether to reply to the list or to the person.

■ PROPER ETIQUETTE OR BEHAVIOR IN A DISCUSSION GROUP

Ernest Ackerman offers the following rules of etiquette or behavior when working with a discussion group (Ackerman, 1997, pp. 124–125):

1. Send messages going to the entire list to the list address. Send commands or requests to be interpreted by the software that manages the list to the administrative address. Send special requests or questions that cannot be resolved to the address of the list owner, administrator, or moderator.
2. Spend some time getting to know the list. When you join a list, take a little while to see the types of items discussed and the tone of the discussion. You may also find that your questions are being answered.
3. Write easy-to-read messages. The material you write to the list should be grammatically correct, concise, and thoughtful. It's a lot easier to read something that is well written, and many members of the list may not have the time to deal with writing that is incorrect, longwinded, and

Date: Mon, 27 Dec 1999 15:12:40 -0500
From: "L-Soft list server at UVM (1.8d)" <LISTSERV@LIST.UVM.EDU>
Subject: You are now subscribed to the EDSS-295 list
To: "Dennis O. Gehris" <dgehris@EPIX.NET>
Reply-To: EDSS-295-request@LIST.UVM.EDU
X-LSV-ListID: EDSS-295
Message-Id: <19991227201241.TKKO8453.almond@smtpgate.uvm.edu>

Mon, 27 Dec 1999 15:12:40

Your subscription to the EDSS-295 list (Telecommunications and the
Information Highway) has been accepted.

Please save this message for future reference, especially if this is the
first time you are subscribing to an electronic mailing list. If you ever
need to leave the list, you will find the necessary instructions below.
Perhaps more importantly, saving a copy of this message (and of all
future subscription notices from other mailing lists) in a special mail
folder will give you instant access to the list of mailing lists that you
are subscribed to. This may prove very useful the next time you go on
vacation and need to leave the lists temporarily so as not to fill up
your mailbox while you are away! You should also save the "welcome
messages" from the list owners that you will occasionally receive after
subscribing to a new list.

To send a message to all the people currently subscribed to the list,
just send mail to EDSS-295@LIST.UVM.EDU. This is called "sending mail to
the list," because you send mail to a single address and LISTSERV makes
copies for all the people who have subscribed. This address
(EDSS-295@LIST.UVM.EDU) is also called the "list address." You must never
try to send any command to that address, as it would be distributed to
all the people who have subscribed. All commands must be sent to the
"LISTSERV address," LISTSERV@LIST.UVM.EDU. It is very important to
understand the difference between the two, but fortunately it is not
complicated. The LISTSERV address is like a FAX number that connects you
to a machine, whereas the list address is like a normal voice line
connecting you to a person. If you make a mistake and dial the FAX number
when you wanted to talk to someone on the phone, you will quickly realize
that you used the wrong number and call again. No harm will have been
done. If on the other hand you accidentally make your FAX call someone's
voice line, the person receiving the call will be inconvenienced,
especially if your FAX then re-dials every 5 minutes. The fact that most
people will eventually connect the FAX machine to the voice line to allow
the FAX to go through and make the calls stop does not mean that you
should continue to send FAXes to the voice number. People would just get
mad at you. It works pretty much the same way with mailing lists, with

Figure 9-5
Example of a Discussion Group
Confirmation Message

(continued)

Figure 9-5 (Continued)

the difference that you are calling hundreds or thousands of people at the same time, and consequently you can expect a lot of people to get upset if you consistently send commands to the list address.

You may leave the list at any time by sending a "SIGNOFF EDSS-295" command to LISTSERV@LIST.UVM.EDU. You can also tell LISTSERV how you want it to confirm the receipt of messages you send to the list. If you do not trust the system, send a "SET EDSS-295 REPRO" command and LISTSERV will send you a copy of your own messages, so that you can see that the message was distributed and did not get damaged on the way. After a while you may find that this is getting annoying, especially if your mail program does not tell you that the message is from you when it informs you that new mail has arrived from EDSS-295. If you send a "SET EDSS-295 ACK NOREPRO" command, LISTSERV will mail you a short acknowledgement instead, which will look different in your mailbox directory. With most mail programs you will know immediately that this is an acknowledgement you can read later. Finally, you can turn off acknowledgements completely with "SET EDSS-295 NOACK NOREPRO".

Following instructions from the list owner, your subscription options have been set to "REPRO" rather than the usual LISTSERV defaults. For more information about subscription options, send a "QUERY EDSS-295" command to LISTSERV@LIST.UVM.EDU.

Contributions sent to this list are automatically archived. You can get a list of the available archive files by sending an "INDEX EDSS-295" command to LISTSERV@LIST.UVM.EDU. You can then order these files with a "GET EDSS-295 LOGxxxx" command, or using LISTSERV's database search facilities. Send an "INFO DATABASE" command for more information on the latter.

This list is available in digest form. If you wish to receive the digested version of the postings, just issue a SET EDSS-295 DIGEST command.

Please note that it is presently possible for anybody to determine that you are signed up to the list through the use of the "REVIEW" command, which returns the e-mail address and name of all the subscribers. If you do not want your name to be visible, just issue a "SET EDSS-295 CONCEAL" command.

More information on LISTSERV commands can be found in the LISTSERV reference card, which you can retrieve by sending an "INFO REFCARD" command to LISTSERV@LIST.UVM.EDU.

without any real point. If the posting must go on for several screens, it is a good idea to summarize it and invite others to ask you for more information.

4. If you're writing a response to something from the list, include only the pertinent portions of the original message. Let's say that someone starts

a discussion in the group and writes something about 40 lines long. You want to respond, but only to one portion of it. Include only the portion that's relevant to your response in your follow-up message. Members of the group may not have the time or space to deal with long e-mail messages.

5. When you ask a question of the members of the list, be sure to post a summary of the responses you receive. That way everyone on the list can benefit from the responses to your question. Naturally, this applies only if you get several responses and the answers to the question would be of general interest.

6. Posting or sending a message to the group is a public act. Everything you write to the list may be distributed to all members of the list. If the list is moderated, your messages may be read first by the moderator(s) and then passed on to the list. If you're working with a list that isn't moderated (most aren't), your messages go directly to all the members of the list. Don't embarrass yourself. A friend, relative, or supervisor may also be a member of the list.

7. The members of a list are people like yourself and need to be treated with respect and courtesy. Respond to messages as if you were talking face to face. A member may be from a different culture, may not be familiar with your language, and may have views and values different from yours. Don't respond too quickly to something that upsets you, and don't criticize others too hastily or without good reason. It's better to think before you write than to be sorry afterward.

8. Avoid sarcasm and be careful with humor. You are communicating entirely by your words. You don't have the benefit of facial expression, body language, or tone of voice to let somebody know you're "only kidding" when you make a sarcastic remark. Members of the list will appreciate well-written, humorous pieces or responses, but be sure your writing will be interpreted that way.

9. Think about whether a response to a message should go to the list or to an individual. Messages to the list should be of general interest, or a request on your part for advice or for help in solving a problem. You'll know the e-mail address of the person who made the original request, and you can send a response to that person if it is appropriate.

UNSUBSCRIBING FROM AN ELECTRONIC MAIL DISCUSSION GROUP

To unsubscribe from an electronic mail discussion group, you need to send a command to the administrative address of the list. The specific command, which is placed in the body of the message, is often UNSUBSCRIBE (Name of List), sometimes followed by your name. In Figure 9-5 the message instructs us to use the command SIGNOFF EDSS-295. After sending this message, you should receive another message which indicates that you have been removed as a subscriber from the list.

■ DEFINITION AND NATURE OF NEWSGROUPS

A **newsgroup** is somewhat similar to an electronic mail discussion group because it also uses electronic mail as a way of communicating with people who are interested in a specific topic. For example, a person wishing to contact a newsgroup will use their e-mail account to send a message to the newsgroup. However, it differs from a discussion group in the way that the messages are delivered. A discussion group delivers messages via a person's e-mail inbox, along with any other e-mail that is received. Alternatively, in a newsgroup, the messages are read with the use of a newsgroup reader.

A newsgroup is also somewhat similar to a public bulletin board, which is covered with messages that you might see at your local supermarket. However, there are a few basic differences. One difference is that you will be able to read the responses to your messages that other people leave for you and others to read.

There are thousands of newsgroups that are organized around special topics that interest people. Newsgroups are housed on news servers, which are computer systems that collect, archive or store, and distribute newsgroup messages. Millions of people send and receive information using newsgroups. As one person posts a message to a news server, others can respond to the message if they choose. Most newsgroups are unmoderated, which means that no one edits your message or the responses to it. You post directly to the newsgroup without any censorship or editorial control over what you say.

One of the oldest and most popular types of newsgroups is called **Usenet**. Each newsgroup has a name that gives the topic or topics for the articles in the group. The groups are arranged or named according to a hierarchy that contains between two and six levels. When you look at the name of a newsgroup, you'll see several words or names separated by periods. The first part of the newsgroup name is the name of the top level of the hierarchy. Moving to the right, the names become more specific. Here are some examples: comp.infosystems.www.browsers.ms-windows; rec.music.artists.mariah-carey; and soc.genealogy.german. There are over 14,000 newsgroups and several major, top-level categories. Some of the top-level categories are listed in Table 9-1.

■ USING A NEWSGROUP READER

As mentioned earlier, a **newsgroup reader** is needed to read and post (send) newsgroup messages. Newsgroup readers are often packaged as a companion program to a Web browser. **Outlook Express** is an e-mail and newsgroup reader that is packaged with Microsoft Internet Explorer. **Posting is** the process of placing a message that you have composed on a newsgroup for others to read. The people who read your posting may decide to post another message in response to your original posting. When you post a message, you should make sure that you have a feeling for the subject that's being discussed. If you post a message that has nothing to do with the newsgroup's purpose, you not

Table 9-1
Usenet Hierarchies

Name	Newsgroups Dealing With:
alt	Alternative views of the world
bionet	Topics in biology
biz	Discussions related to business
comp	Discussions related to computers
K12	Issues dealing with teachers and students in kindergarten through grade 12
misc	Miscellaneous topics
news	Use and discussion of the Usenet
rec	Artistic activities, hobbies, or recreational activities
sci	Scientific topics
soc	Social issues and various cultures
talk	Talking or discussing

only needlessly congest the network, you also break the continuity of ongoing discussions.

Parts of the Outlook Express News Window

Before we start using Outlook Express, let's examine the Outlook Express "News" window (see Figure 9-6).

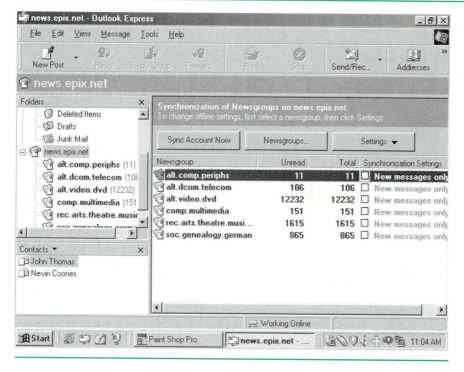

Figure 9-6
The Outlook Express "News" Window.
(*Microsoft Outlook Express™ screen shot reprinted by permission from Microsoft Corporation*)

Menu Bar. The Menu bar gives you access to all the menu options. Simply click on a menu name to display a list of related menu commands, and then click the command you want to use.

Title Bar. The Title bar displays the name of the program, Outlook Express, preceded by the Outlook Express icon.

Subscribed Newsgroup List. The Message list displays the newsgroups to which you subscribe.

Tips. Tips are helpful hints for using Outlook Express more efficiently.

Starting Outlook Express as a Newsreader

You have two options for starting Outlook Express as a newsreader. One way is to choose "News" from the Go menu in Internet Explorer. If you don't have Internet Explorer loaded and you only want to use Outlook Express, you can load it by selecting it from "Programs" on the Start menu of Windows.

When you start Outlook Express from the Start menu, the left side of the window will show several options ("Read Mail," "Read News," "Compose a Message," etc.). You need to click on "Read News" to work with Outlook Express as a newsreader (see Figure 9-7). The Outlook Express window can be minimized or maximized by clicking on the appropriate button in the upper right corner of the window.

Downloading Newsgroups

The first time that you connect to your newsgroup server, all newsgroups that are available need to be downloaded to your computer so that you can decide the newsgroups to which you want to subscribe. This may take several minutes, as there may be thousands of newsgroups. You may see a message displayed which indicates that you have not yet subscribed to any newsgroups and then a question asking you if you want to download the newsgroups. You should click on "Yes." If you don't see this message, you need to click on the "Newsgroups" button on the toolbar of Outlook Express. While the newsgroups are downloading, you will see the message shown in Figure 9-8.

Subscribing to Newsgroups

The next thing that you need to do after downloading the available newsgroups is to subscribe to the newsgroups that interest you. This will allow you to participate by reading posted messages and posting messages of your own. **Subscribing** is the process of marking the newsgroups that will be displayed each time you start as a newsreader. Since there are thousands of newsgroups, how do you know what groups are available? One way is to access one of the newsgroups that list all the available newsgroups. The names of these newsgroups are news.lists, news.groups, news.announce.newusers, news.announce.newsgroups, and news.answers.

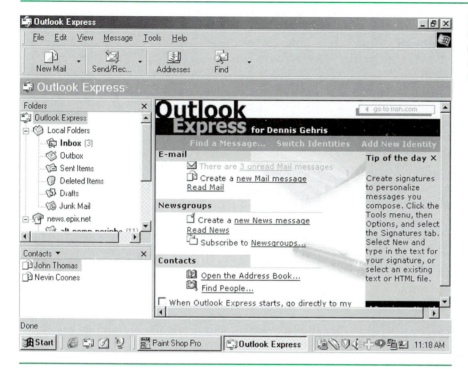

Figure 9-7
Outlook Express Loaded from Windows.
(*Microsoft Outlook Express™ screen shot reprinted by permission from Microsoft Corporation*)

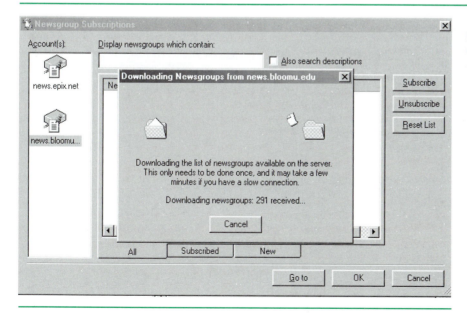

Figure 9-8
Downloading Newsgroups Message.
(*Microsoft Outlook Express™ screen shot reprinted by permission from Microsoft Corporation*)

Another way to know which newsgroups are available for subscribing is simply to enter a topic in Outlook Express's search box and see if any newsgroups are displayed. For example, suppose that we are interested in genealogy. We click on the "Newsgroups" button on the Outlook Express tool bar. When the "Newsgroups" window is displayed, key in "genealogy" in the "Newsgroups Which Contain" box at the top of the window. All available newsgroups that deal with telecommunications will be displayed (see Figure 9-9).

To subscribe to any of the newsgroups displayed, click on one to select it and click on the "Subscribe" button on the "Newsgroups" window. For example, if we decide to subscribe to the group soc.genealogy.german, click on it, and then click on the "Subscribe" button; an icon appears next to the newsgroup name (see Figure 9-10).

In this manner you can subscribe to as many additional newsgroups as you desire. After you have completed indicating the newsgroups to which you want to subscribe, you click on the "OK" button. You will be returned to the Outlook Express main window.

Unsubscribing from Newsgroups

You may decide to unsubscribe from a newsgroup if you find that the newsgroup does not interest you after you have looked at the messages that have been posted. To do this, point the mouse cursor on the newsgroup's name in the "Subscribed Newsgroup" list and click the right button. Click "Unsubscribe from this Newsgroup" on the shortcut menu that appears (see Figure 9-11). If necessary, click "Yes" to confirm the action.

Figure 9-9
Displaying Available Genealogy Newsgroups. (*Microsoft Outlook Express™ screen shot reprinted by permission from Microsoft Corporation*)

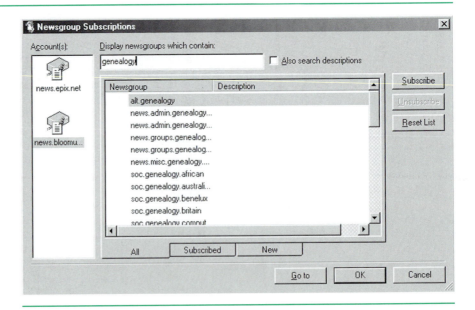

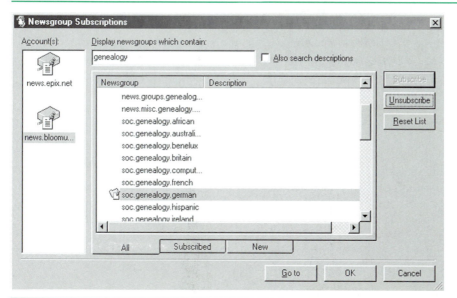

Figure 9-10
Subscribing to a Newsgroup.
(*Microsoft Outlook Express™ screen shot reprinted by permission from Microsoft Corporation*)

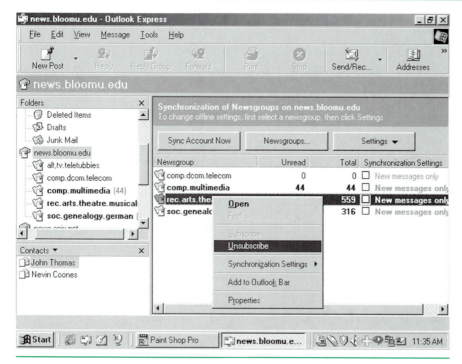

Figure 9-11
Unsubscribing from a Newsgroup.
(*Microsoft Outlook Express™ screen shot reprinted by permission from Microsoft Corporation*)

Reading Newsgroup Postings

To read newsgroup postings, first double-click on the newsgroup name in the "Newsgroup" list portion of the window. Next, click on a message in the "Message" list that appears. A portion of the message should be displayed in the "Preview" pane (see Figure 9-12).

Posting Messages

Much of the fun of working with newsgroups is that you can participate in an ongoing discussion, respond privately to a message's author, or start a new discussion by posting your own message on a topic of your choice. If you post a new message to a newsgroup and others respond to it, the original message header will be preceded by a "+." Clicking on the "+" will reveal the responding messages, which will be preceded by "Re:". The original message and the responses to it are commonly referred to as a *thread*. Posted messages can be printed by clicking on "Print" from the File menu.

Posting a New Message. To post a new message, select a newsgroup to which you want to post a message. Click the "Compose Message" button on the Outlook Express tool bar. Key a subject for your message. Make sure that you

Figure 9-12
Reading Newsgroup Postings.
(*Microsoft Outlook Express™ screen shot reprinted by permission from Microsoft Corporation*)

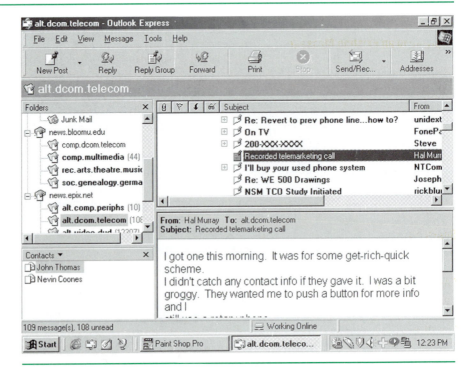

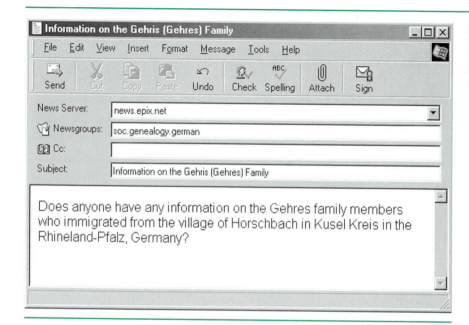

Figure 9-13
Posting a New Newsgroup Message.
(*Microsoft Outlook Express™ screen shot reprinted by permission from Microsoft Corporation*)

choose a subject that accurately reflects the content of your message, so that people can decide whether they want to read it (see Figure 9-13). Next, click the "Post Message" button on the tool bar. If necessary, click "Yes" to confirm that your message was posted.

Replying to an Existing Message. To reply to an existing message, click on the message header to which you want to reply. Next, you have several options. You can click on the "Reply to Group" button on the tool bar to post your response to the newsgroup. As an alternative, you can click on the "Reply to Author" button on the tool bar to send a private e-mail message to the message's author. Finally, you can click on the Compose menu and then click on "Reply to Newsgroup and Author" to reply to both the entire newsgroup and the message's author at the same time.

You then type the message and delete parts of the original message that might be unrelated to your reply (see Figure 9-14). Finally, you click the "Post Message" button on the tool bar to send the message.

Shortcuts. A shortcut is a single-cut link to the Outlook Express start page, the Internet Explorer start page, or the Microsoft Corporation home page.

Folder List. The folder list contains all the folders in Outlook Express. You can customize the folders to meet your needs.

Tool Bar. The tool bar contains buttons for commands you use in Outlook Express. The buttons change depending on which folder of Outlook Express you are using.

Figure 9-14
Replying to an Existing Newsgroup.
Message. (*Microsoft Outlook Express™
screen shot reprinted by permission from
Microsoft Corporation*)

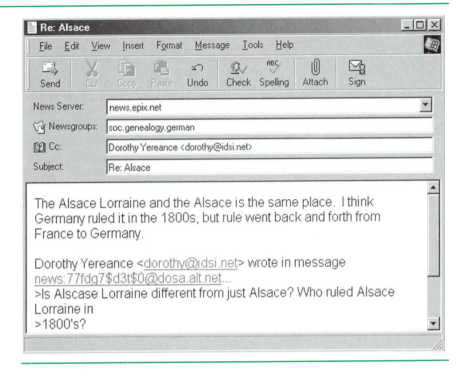

SUMMARY

There are several methods that allow people who have similar interests and wish to ask questions, share information, or discuss issues related to a common topic or theme to form groups through the use of electronic mail. One method is by the use of discussion groups, sometimes called discussion lists.

Membership in a discussion group permits you to read the e-mail messages that other members have sent to the group. Most discussion groups are unmoderated. This means that no one has been assigned to screen the messages that are posted in a group. Many discussion groups are called Listserv lists. This is commercial mailing list manager software that is marketed by L-Soft International. Most management of a list, such as adding new members (subscribing) and removing members who choose to leave (unsubscribing), is done automatically by software running on the server that serves as the host system for the list.

To subscribe to an electronic mail discussion group, you must be able to find the list or group address so that you can communicate with the list via e-mail. There are reference books that list the various discussion groups that are available, along with instructions on how to subscribe to them. A better way of finding discussion lists is to use a Web browser to link to a search page. After you perform a search to find a discussion group that you want to join, two types of e-mail addresses will be provided: an administrative address and a list address. The administrative address is the one that you use to subscribe to a list and to unsubscribe from a list when you no longer want to receive e-mail messages from the list. After you send a subscribe message to the administrative address of the discussion group, you should receive a return message indicating that you have been accepted as a subscriber. The original e-mail message from the list server should also provide the list address, which is the address to which you send original messages. Everyone should always adhere to proper etiquette or behavior when participating in a discussion group. To unsubscribe from an electronic mail discussion group, you need to send a command to the administrative address of the list.

A newsgroup is somewhat similar to an electronic mail discussion group because it also uses electronic mail as a way of communicating with people who are interested in a specific topic. However, it differs from a discussion group in the way that the messages are delivered. A newsgroup is also somewhat similar to a public bulletin board, which is covered with messages that you might see at your local supermarket. However, there are a few basic differences. One difference is that you will be able to read the responses to your messages that other people leave for you and others to read. There are thousands of newsgroups that are organized around special topics that interest people. Newsgroups are housed on news servers, which are computer systems that collect, archive or store, and distribute newsgroup messages. Millions of people send and receive information using newsgroups. As one person posts a message to a news server, others can respond to the message if they choose.

Most newsgroups are unmoderated, which means that no one edits your message or the responses to it. You post directly to the newsgroup without any censorship or editorial control over what you say. One of the oldest and most popular types of newsgroups is called Usenet. A newsgroup reader is needed to read and post (send) newsgroup messages. Newsgroup readers are often packaged as a companion program to a Web browser. Outlook Express is an e-mail and newsgroup reader that is packaged with Microsoft Internet Explorer.

Posting is the process of placing a message that you have composed on a newsgroup for others to read. The people who read your posting may decide to post another message in response to your original posting. When you post a message you should make sure that you have a feeling for the subject that's being discussed.

The first time that you connect to your newsgroup server, all newsgroups that are available need to be downloaded to your computer so that you can decide the newsgroups to which you want to subscribe. The next thing that you need to do after downloading the available newsgroups is to subscribe to the newsgroups that interest you and in which you'd like to participate by reading posted messages and posting messages of your own.

Subscribing is the process of marking the newsgroups that will be displayed each time you start a newsreader. Much of the fun of working with newsgroups is that you can participate in an ongoing discussion, respond privately to a message's author, or start a new discussion by posting your own message on a topic of your choice. You may decide to unsubscribe from a newsgroup if you find that the newsgroup does not interest you after you have looked at the messages that have been posted.

QUESTIONS

1. Define *electronic mail*.

2. Define *discussion groups*.

3. How might a discussion group be helpful to an individual or group?

4. Identify two ways to find discussion groups.

5. Identify the procedure for subscribing to a discussion group.

6. What differentiates an administrative address from a list address?

7. How do you send a message to a discussion group?

8. How do you reply to a message sent to a discussion group?

9. Identify some examples of proper etiquette when participating in a discussion group.

10. How do you unsubscribe from a discussion group?

11. What is a newsgroup?

12. How is a newsgroup like a discussion group, and how is it different?

13. What is Usenet?

14. What is a newsgroup reader? Provide an example of one type.

15. Is it necessary to download newsgroups before subscribing to one?

16. What are the procedures for subscribing to a newsgroup?

17. What are the procedures for unsubscribing to a newsgroup?

18. What does *posting* a message to a newsgroup mean? How is it done?

19. How do you reply to an existing message in a newsgroup?

PROJECTS AND PROBLEMS

1. Determine if there are any electronic mail discussion groups to which you may be interested in subscribing by accessing http://www.lsoft.com/lists/listref.html on the Web. If you are interested in any of these groups, subscribe to one of them. After subscribing to the group, what were your experiences?

2. Determine the following about the system you use to read Usenet news at your school.
   (a) What is the Internet domain name of the news server?
   (b) Which newsreader is available on your network?
   (c) Have any special groups been set up at your school? What are they? For which groups are they designed?

3. Use your newsreader to subscribe to the news.newusers .questions newsgroup. Answer the following questions about the group.
   (a) How many articles are listed?
   (b) Read one of the articles. What is its title? Who is the author?
   (c) Find a response to an original article. How did you know that it was a response rather than an original posting?

4. If you have used both electronic mail discussion groups and newsgroups, which do you prefer? Why?

5. Blatant business use of noncommercial Usenet newsgroups is generally frowned on by the Internet community. There are, however, methods that can be used by businesses to market their products which do not upset users of the newsgroups and can even enhance the culture of the Internet. These methods are as follows.

   - *Short advertisement in newsgroup.* A short advertisement for company products, separate from any relevant thread in the newsgroup, is posted. This is not likely to upset too many people, provided that it is relevant to the newsgroup. It is, however, not likely to be read by many people. A better method is to answer a problem as part of a subject thread, which needs to be specific to one of your company's products, and then mention your company product. This will provide a combination of "expert" advice on a type of product as well as specific information on your company product.
   - *Acting as an expert.* This involves giving regular expert advice in a newsgroup on a variety of topics relevant to your business area, and including at the bottom of your posting your company name and address. Users of the newsgroup will associate you and your company with the newsgroup activity. This method of "brand awareness" avoids all direct advertising and over time will

generate inquiries, but it does require regular, time-consuming postings.

(a) Comment on the effectiveness of each method. Under what circumstances would each best be used?

(b) If you were working for a company considering the use of newsgroups to promote your company's products, which method would you use? Why?

Vocabulary

discussion group	newsgroup reader	subscribing	Usenet
Listserv list	Outlook Express	unmoderated	
newsgroup	posting	unsubscribing	

References

Ackerman, Ernest, *Learning to Use the World Wide Web*, Franklin, Beedle & Associates, Wilsonville, OR, 1997.

"Commercial Use of the Internet Case," http://www.et.brad.ac.uk/BEGIN/casestudy/index.htm.

CyberHound's Guide to International Discussion Groups, Farmington Hills, MI, 1996.

Gehris, Dennis, *Microsoft Internet Explorer 5.0*, South-Western Educational Publishing, Cincinnati, OH, 2000.

L-Soft Web site, http://www.lsoft.com.

Pfaffenberger, Bryan, with David Wall, *Computer & Internet Dictionary*, 6th ed., Que Corporation, Indianapolis, IN, 1995.

10

World Wide Web

I n this chapter we describe the World Wide Web and discuss how information is accessed. We look at the features and types of World Wide Web browsers, how they are used, and discuss how information is found.

■ WORLD WIDE WEB DEFINED

The **World Wide Web (WWW or Web) is** what makes multimedia applications possible on the Internet. Officially, the Web is described as a wide-area hypermedia information retrieval initiative aiming to give universal access to a large universe of documents. Some people believe incorrectly that the Web and the Internet are the same thing. This is probably because many people use the Web and no other parts of the Internet. In reality, the Web is only a part of the Internet. There are servers connected to the Internet that make it possible to use other Internet services, such as gopher and file transfer protocol. These other services are discussed in Chapter 12.

The Web started in 1989 at CERN, the European Laboratory for Particle Physics in Geneva, Switzerland and was funded by 18 European member states. The CERN researchers developed a system that would allow physicists and other scientists to share information with others and to provide for information in textual form. There was no intention of adding video or sound, and the capability of transmitting images was not considered. The basis for the development of the WWW was the **hypertext transfer protocol (HTTP).** Hypertext transfer protocol remains the standard protocol used to access Web documents. Once the CERN researchers established this specification, client and server software was written and the Web was on its way to becoming a reality.

The first piece of Web software was introduced on a NeXT computer. It had the capability to view and transmit hypertext documents to other people on the Internet and came with the capability to edit hypertext documents on the screen. Demonstrations were given to CERN committees and seminars, as well as to the Hypertext Conference in 1991. Today, one estimate is that the Web has been expanding at a rate of 1 percent per day. At this rate the Web is doubling in size in a period of less than 10 weeks.

The advantage of working with the Web becomes apparent to anyone who has used any of the other Internet services: file transfer protocol (FTP), gopher, and so on. With the Web, less time is spent in learning the procedures for obtaining information on the Internet and more time is available to actually obtain information. As an example, gopher, which works with a system of menu items, can be very inefficient and time consuming. The advantage of the Web over gopher is obvious. The menu items simply may not represent the type of information desired. Users often end up aimlessly wandering through menus. These problems can be avoided when using the Web, provided that the information is presented in a helpful way. Web pages may also use lists, but text is generally used to describe the information.

Hypermedia is made up of hypertext and other multimedia elements that allow you to move from item to item and back again without having to follow a predefined path. The term *hypertext* was coined in the 1960s by Ted Nelson as a means of moving through text in a nonlinear manner. Nelson, currently Project Professor at the Keio Shonan Fujisawa Campus in Japan, invented the concept for a term project while a graduate student at Harvard. The paths are called *links* and are connected to other resources on the Internet. The links can be part of a sentence or paragraph or may be connected to an image or digitized sound. When the link is in the form of hypertext, the text is often underlined with a graphical browser. Because it is underlined, the user knows that clicking on the word or words with the mouse cursor results in a connection to a predefined place on the Internet. When a link is connected to an image, text will usually instruct the user to click on the image for a connection. There is also a way of reconnecting with previous links, so that if you wish, you can return to places where you've been.

Web pages are developed with the use of the **hypertext markup language (HTML)**. HTML provides a system for marking up text documents and a way to integrate multimedia and the use of hyperlinks. Although not a difficult language to use, it uses special tags through a specific structure.

It is assumed that in the past the largest segment using the Web consisted of students at four-year college campuses within the United States. Due partly to the Web's availability through online services (America Online, CompuServe, Prodigy, etc.), it is obvious that many more people will have the opportunity to experience the power of the Web in the future. Through these services, users will be able to experience the value of retrieving information in a variety of multimedia formats.

ACCESSING INFORMATION ON THE WEB

Each of the links as defined in hypermedia documents on the World Wide Web represents a **uniform resource locator (URL)**. Users need to know the URL if a link to a location on the Internet doesn't happen to be displayed on the Web page on which they are currently working. URLs are often mentioned in articles and advertisements and represent a starting point for linking to other URLs through hypermedia. Web users will often use a URL as a starting point, often referred to as *home pages*.

The basic form of a URL is *service://domain name/full path name*. An example is the URL for Bloomsburg University's Department of Business Education and Office Information System Web page: http://www.bloomu.edu/departments/beois/beois.htm. In this example, "http" is the service, www.bloomu.edu, is the domain name, and "/departments/beois/beois.htm is the path. Sometimes a path is not specified and only the service and the domain name are indicated. This type of URL is usually for the main page for the site. For example, http://www.bloomu.edu is Bloomsburg University's main Web page.

Types of URLs

There are several different types of URLs: http, ftp, gopher, and telnet, which correspond to the Internet protocols discussed in Chapter 8. It should be noted that not all of these types may be available on all browsers.

http.   The service http (hypertext transport protocol) is used by Web clients and servers to exchange documents. An example of a URL of this type would be http://www.yahoo.com, which is for the Yahoo list of Web resources.

ftp.   The service ftp (file transfer protocol) is used to exchange files on the Internet. The ftp URLs usually mean that the file can be retrieved by an anonymous FTP, so that a password is not required. An example of an FTP URL is ftp://ftp.microsoft.com.

gopher.   Gopher servers can be accessed through URLs which indicate the path to these servers. Each gopher connection results in a different list of menu items, which on a browser is represented by a series of labeled folders. The user clicks on the folders to use the various services or to access submenus, which are also represented by a folder list. An example would be gopher://marvel.loc.gov, which would connect you to the gopher server at the Library of Congress.

Telnet.   Telnet allows you to log on to a remote computer connected to the Internet to access information or to run programs. It should be noted that not all browsers permit you to use telnet, and some browsers require that you configure a helper application program on your hard disk for telnet. An example of a telnet URL is telnet://locis.loc.gov, which is another way to connect to the Library of Congress.

■ FEATURES OF WORLD WIDE WEB BROWSERS

Once you have an Internet connection, a **Web browser** (also known as a *Web client*) is the software program that is needed to make access to Web servers on the Internet possible. All Web browsers have similar basic features that they need to perform:

■ Provide an easy and simple procedure for installing the browser. Fortunately, the latest versions of most Web browsers possess this feature.
■ Send requests for data to Web servers in the correct Internet and World Wide Web formats. This is a very necessary feature and is incorporated into all Web browsers.
■ Receive and display information that is sent back from Web servers or display error messages to the user. This also is a necessary feature that all Web browsers possess.

There are several additional browser features that are desirable. It should be noted that not all browsers possess all of these features. A browser that has most of the features might work well for an inexperienced user.

■ Display information in the design format originally intended by the authors of documents. Displaying Web pages in the formats designed by the authors is not always possible, especially when using a nongraphical browser. This may also be a problem for some graphical browsers.
■ Save documents that arrive via requests made by the user. This gives you the ability to view the text and layout information for home pages later, without having to connect to them again.
■ Store **bookmarks** or *hotlist* entries of locations that the user might want to revisit. This is a real time saver because it provides an opportunity for the user to link very quickly to pages that were accessed during previous sessions.

- Maintain a history of links. This is often done by use of a **cache**, which is saved on the hard disk of the user. This provides a means of revisiting previous links without having to download them again during the same session.

- Turn in-line images on and off. **In-line images** are graphic images that are transmitted over the Web. This is a valuable feature for those users who are using a dial-up connection to the Internet, since it greatly improves the speed at which information is received.

- Print pages. There are times when you might want to have a hard copy of a Web page, especially if it contains information that is being used for research.

- Copy information from a home page to the Windows Clipboard. This feature provides the ability to clip information from the browser program to another Windows program (such as a word processing program).

- Display the first screen of text while the graphical elements are downloading. This provides the user with the ability to start reading the text while the rest of the information is being received.

- Indicate the percentage of a page that remains to be retrieved. This information is often displayed at the bottom of the screen and provides a means for the user to make a decision as to whether he or she wants to wait before trying to access the remainder of the information.

TYPES OF WEB BROWSERS

Now that you know what a browser is and what features are necessary and desirable, let's look at the various types of browsers that are available. We'll limit our discussion to today's most commonly used browsers.

Lynx and Other Nongraphical Browsers

There are two main categories of World Wide Web browsers: nongraphical and graphical. **Nongraphical browsers**, such as Lynx for IBM/IBM PC compatibles from the University of Kansas, only display text and are not suitable for multimedia use since other multimedia elements—audio, graphics, and full-motion video—cannot be displayed or played. It should be noted that although text is the only element that can be displayed, it may be possible to download graphics, audio, and video files that can be used in other multimedia players and programs.

Graphical Browsers

Graphical browsers, most commonly used, have full multimedia capabilities and can display or play text, audio, graphics, and full-motion video. Graphical browsers can be divided into two subcategories: those that are free of charge and those that must be purchased from a vendor. Purchasing a browser gives the user a legal right to use it. The main advantage of purchasing a browser is that the vendor will usually provide the product along with technical support. This may be important to a novice user who would not have anyone to turn to if problems occur or questions arise. Many software vendors provide access to an Internet provider as an option to the purchaser.

The two most popular graphical browsers in use today are **Microsoft Internet Explorer** by Microsoft Corporation and **Netscape Communicator** by the Netscape Communications Corporation.

Microsoft Internet Explorer. There was much controversy when Windows was first issued, as Microsoft Corporation provided a means of connecting automatically to the Microsoft Network, which is an Internet service provider (ISP). Several commercial online services took legal action to try to block Microsoft from offering the Microsoft Network automatically to anyone who installs Windows. More recently, the U.S. Justice Department has filed suit against Microsoft because of its alleged monopolistic practices, which include providing Internet Explorer as the only browser available to purchasers who install Windows software.

There are seven parts to the Microsoft Internet Explorer browser (see Figure 10-1). Although the Netscape browser is somewhat different from Internet Explorer, many of the features are similar. The *Menu bar* (A) contains all of the commands you need to access and move around Web pages, customize the browser, and get help. The *Title bar* (B) displays the program name preceded by the name or address of the Web page you are viewing. The *Standard tool bar* (C) provides buttons to access and move around Web pages and to work with Internet Explorer. The *Links tool bar* (D) contains buttons to link to several Microsoft Web sites. The *Address bar* (E) displays the address of the current document or Web page and lets you type a new filename or Web

Figure 10-1
Parts of the Internet Explorer Browser.
(*Microsoft Internet Explorer™ screen shot reprinted by permission from Microsoft Corporation*)

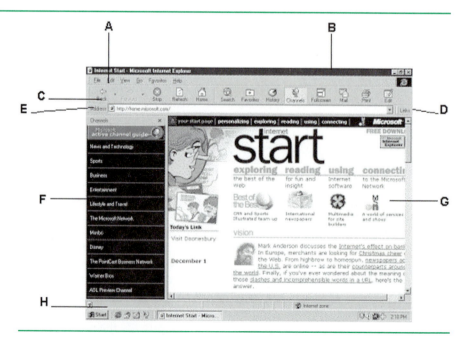

page address or search for other files or Web sites. The *Explorer bar* (F) displays links to Web pages from your research results, favorites list, history list, and channels. The *Browser pane* (G) displays the current document or Web page. The *Status bar* (H) indicates the progress of loading a Web page and provides other messages about commands.

Netscape Communicator. The latest versions of Netscape (see Figure 10-2) contain features that make it the browser of choice for many users. Some of the superior features that Netscape possesses are listed below. As mentioned earlier, Internet Explorer contains some of the same features.

■ Netscape provides *visual clues* during the downloading process. The program indicates when it has connected to a site and displays the percentage of bytes that have been downloaded, the percentage of bytes remaining to be downloaded, along with the number of bytes. It also indicates when the browser has completed the download.

■ Netscape phases in graphics that are a part of a Web page being downloaded. A low-resolution version of the image first appears and updates of the image are made until the entire image is seen.

■ Netscape recognizes special extensions to the HTML Web language, which enhances the appearance of the pages after they are downloaded. For example, one extension allows backgrounds of different colors and textures to be viewed.

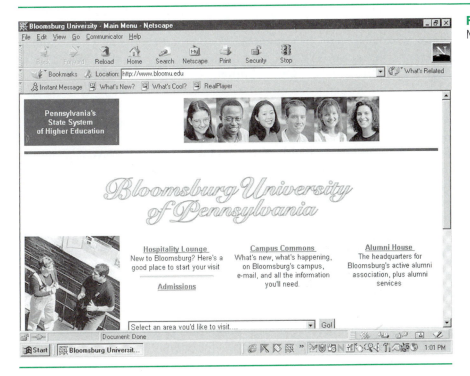

Figure 10-2
Netscape Communicator Browser

- Netscape possesses the ability to send and receive electronic mail messages, as well as a means of viewing Usenet newsgroups.
- Netscape supports live objects and other interactive multimedia content, such as Java applets, frames, and inline plug-ins.
- Netscape possesses automatic features for assigning digital IDs that allow you to conduct online financial transactions, and send and receive e-mail and newsgroup messages securely with state-of-the-art message encryption and digital signatures.
- Netscape also includes features such as client-side image mapping and support for multiple, simultaneous streaming of video, audio, and other data formats, as well as support for the Progressive JPEG file format.
- Netscape's *frame feature* is a sophisticated page-presentation capability that enables the display of multiple, independently scrollable frames on a single screen, each with its own distinct URL. It should be noted that frames can also be viewed with the Internet Explorer browser.

USING A WEB BROWSER

To use a Web browser to move to another location on the Web, you need to enter the URL into the browser. There are several ways to do this with any browser. One way is to click the mouse cursor on the Address bar and key the URL there. To have the browser go to the site, press the "Enter" key or click on the "Go" button with Internet Explorer. The Address bar will always display the URL of the Web page to which you are currently connected, even if you got to the page without keying the address in the Address bar. Another way to enter a URL is to click on "Open" on the File menu in Internet Explorer (or "Open Page" in Netscape). When you do this, the "Open" dialog box appears. You can key the URL into this box. To have the browser go to the site, click the "OK" or "Open" button.

Links are connections to other Web sites on the Internet. By clicking on a link, you instruct the browser to follow the link and display the document associated with it. Links take various forms. The most common form is the hypertext link. You can recognize a hypertext link easily because the text is usually blue and it is underlined. In addition, you can see part or all the linked URL on the Status bar by moving a mouse cursor over the hypertext link. The mouse cursor will turn into a pointing hand and the linked URL will be displayed on the Status bar at the bottom of the window. With many browsers, including Internet Explorer, the link will change color (usually purple) to indicate that you have followed this link within the past 20 days or whatever you have indicated on the "General" tab on Internet Options.

Another type of link is a link that is connected to a graphic image. You can determine if the image is linked by moving the mouse cursor over the graphic. If it changes to a pointing hand and a URL appears on the Status bar, you know that the graphic image is linked. Sometimes an image map is used to link a Web page. An image map is a graphic image in which clicking on various places on the image will link you to different Web pages.

■ FINDING INFORMATION WITH A WEB BROWSER

You can locate information on the Web through the process of searching. It is possible to search Web sites, directories, guides, and newsgroups for information. Three mechanisms on the Web that are available for researching a specific topic are **search engines** (or **spiders**), **resource** (or **subject**) **trees**, and **meta search engines.** Many search engines contain resource tree search mechanisms, and most resource or subject trees also have built-in search engines. It's up to you which of these you use, as each will produce similar but slightly different results.

Search Engines (or Spiders)

A number of online search engines (or spiders) are available for searching for sites relating to a particular topic on the World Wide Web. They allow you to search by title or headers of documents, by words or phrases in the documents themselves, or by searching other indexes or directories. By pressing the "Search" button on the standard toolbar in Internet Explorer or Netscape you will be able to access some of the popular search engines. Figure 10-3 shows the Snap.com search engine.

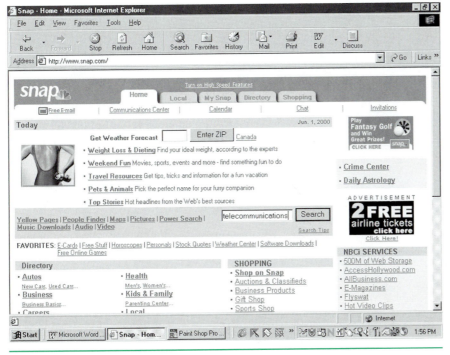

Figure 10-3
Snap.com Search Engine.
(*Microsoft Internet Explorer™ screen shot reprinted by permission from Microsoft Corporation*)

Resource (or Subject) Trees

An alternative way of finding resources on the Web is to use what can be called a resource or subject tree. These sites list Web sites by topics and subtopics and may also have a search utility that helps you to search for topics within the categories.

The most popular and best resource (or subject) tree is *Yahoo* (http://www.yahoo.com). Yahoo stands for "Yet Another Hierarchically Odoriferous Oracle." The main topics in Yahoo at the time of writing this book were *Arts and Humanities* (Literature, Photography, . . .); *Business and Economy* (B2B, Finance, Shopping, Jobs, . . .); *Computers and Internet* (Internet, WWW, Software, Games, . . .); *Education* (College and University, K-12, . . .); *Entertainment* (Cool Links, Movies, Humor, Music, . . .); *Government* (Elections, Military, Law, Taxes, . . .); *Health* (Medicine, Diseases, Fitness, . . .); *News and Media* (Full Coverage, Newspapers, TV, . . .); *Recreation and Sports* (Sports, Travel, Autos, Outdoors, . . .); *Reference* (Libraries, Dictionaries, Quotations, . . .); *Regional* (Countries, Regions, U.S. States, . . .); *Science* (Animals, Astronomy, Engineering, . . .); *Social Science* (Archaeology, Economics, Languages, . . .); and *Society and Culture* (People, Environment, Religion, . . .) (see Figure 10-4).

To use a resource tree, you click on a heading or subheading, which will produce a list of additional subtopics. Clicking on a link to a subtopic will either produce another subtopic list or a list of sites. Clicking on the links to the

Figure 10-4
The Yahoo Resource Tree

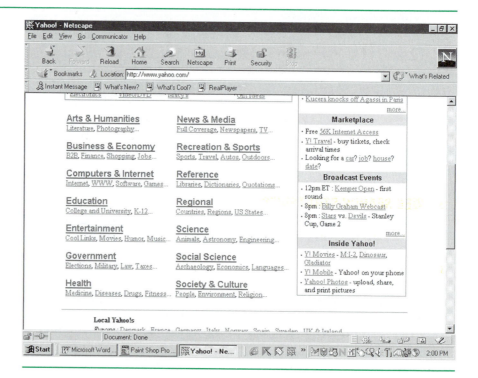

sites will retrieve the Web page for that site. For example, if you wanted to use Yahoo to find information on organizations that sponsor telecommuting programs, you would first click on *Computers & Internet*, then *Telecommunications*, then *Telecommuting*, then *Organizations*.

Developed by two students at Stanford University, it is updated every five days. A search utility is a part of Yahoo. To use Yahoo, either enter a word or words into the search bar and click on the "Search" button or click on one of the hyperlinked main topics. Yahoo's search engine provides the capability of searching the Yahoo site, Usenet, and e-mail addresses. You can configure the search to find new listings added during various lengths of time and to display various number of listings per page.

Here are some additional popular search engines and subject trees.

- *Excite* (http://www.excite.com). The Excite database contains more than 1 million Web documents that can be searched. It also contains the past two weeks of Usenet newsgroup messages and classified advertisements.
- *InfoSeek Net Search* (http://www.infoseek.com). InfoSeek Net Search is a fast, accurate, and comprehensive way to search the Web. This engine allows you to enter a question or as many words or phrases as you need to describe what you want to find.
- *Lycos* (http://www.lycos.com). The Lycos engine searches for Web documents by document title, headings, links, and keywords.

Meta Search Engines

Meta search engines simultaneously search multiple search engines for the search term entered. As an example, MetaCrawler (http://www.metacrawler .com) is a multithreaded search site that can take your search terms and simultaneously feed them to nine sites: Open Text, Lycos, WebCrawler, InfoSeek, Excite, Inktomi, Alta Vista, Yahoo, and Galaxy. It organizes the results into a uniform format and displays them. With the MetaCrawler, you also have the option of sorting the hits, so that the list that is displayed can be sorted in a number of different ways, such as locality, region, and organization. MetaCrawler can even eliminate invalid URLs.

■ WEB SEARCH STRATEGIES

The following strategies for searching the Web are suggested.

- *Understand the search engine's limitations.* Does it only include information for Web documents or does it search other areas of the Internet? Understanding what's in the database will help you devise more effective search terms.
- *Access the search engine.* Don't try to search during peak usage hours (12 to 3 P.M. Eastern Time). This is the time of heaviest Internet use and consequently, will be slow.

- *Type one or more search words in the text box.* Start with fairly specific terms. Type the most important words first. For example, if you're searching for business careers in accounting, use "accounting careers" instead of "business careers."
- *Click the "Start search" or "Submit" button.* Most search engines contain a "Start Search" or "Submit" button. Clicking this button initiates the search.
- *View the list of documents retrieved.* Most search engines rank the search results numerically, with the first document having the highest score. If you find a document that looks like it's relevant, click the cited hyperlink.
- *Refine and repeat the search if necessary.* Common problems include too many or too few documents. For example, if you want to learn about voice processing as it pertains to voice recognition and you get too many responses when searching on "voice processing," narrow your search to "voice recognition."
- *Check your spelling.* Make sure that you don't have incorrect spellings that will negate your search results.
- *Don't use commonly occurring articles or Web terms.* Articles or terms to avoid are "and," "the," and "http."
- *Don't type plurals.* Always type the singular form of all search words of the hyperlinked main topics.

■ SUMMARY

The World Wide Web (WWW or Web) is what makes multimedia applications possible on the Internet. Officially, the Web is described as a wide-area hypermedia information retrieval initiative aiming to give universal access to a large universe of documents. The basis for the development of the Web was the hypertext transfer protocol (http). Hypertext transport protocol is used by Web clients and servers to exchange documents. The advantage of working with the Web becomes apparent to anyone who has used any of the other Internet services: file transfer protocol (FTP), gopher, and others. With the Web, less time is spent in learning the procedures for obtaining information on the Internet and more time is available to actually obtain information.

Hypermedia is made up of hypertext and other multimedia elements that allow you to move from item to item and back again without having to follow a predefined path. The paths are called links and are connected to other resources on the Internet. The links can be part of a sentence or paragraph or may be connected to an image or digitized sound. When the link is in the form of hypertext, the text is often underlined with a graphical browser. Because it is underlined, the user knows that clicking on the word or words with the mouse cursor results in a connection to a predefined place on the Internet. When a link is connected to an image, text will usually instruct the user to click on the image for a connection. There is also a way of reconnecting with previous links, so that if you wish, you can return to places where you've been. Web pages are developed with the use of the hypertext markup language (HTML). HTML provides a system for marking up text documents and a way to integrate multimedia and the use of hyperlinks.

Each of the links as defined in hypermedia documents on the World Wide Web represents a uniform resource locator (URL). The basic form of a URL is service://domain name/full path name. There are several different types of URLs: http, ftp, gopher, and telnet. It should be noted that not all of these types may be available on all browsers.

Once you have an Internet connection, a Web browser (also known as a Web client) is the software program needed to make access to Web servers on the Internet possible. All Web browsers have similar basic features that they need to perform. In addition, there are several browser features that are desirable. It should be noted that not all browsers possess all of these features. A browser that has most of the features might work well for an inexperienced user.

There are two main categories of World Wide Web browsers: nongraphical and graphical. Nongraphical browsers, such as Lynx for IBM/IBM PC compatibles from the University of Kansas, only display text and are not suitable for multimedia use since the other multimedia elements—audio, graphics, and full-motion video—cannot be displayed or played. Graphical browsers have full multimedia capabilities and can display or play text, audio, graphics, and full-motion video. Graphical browsers can be divided into two subcategories: those that are free of charge and those that must be purchased from a vendor. The two most popular graphical browsers in use today are the Microsoft Internet Explorer and the Netscape Communicator.

To use a Web browser to move to another location on the Web, you need to enter the URL into the browser. We discussed several ways to do this with any browser. You can find things on the Web through the process of searching. It is possible to search Web sites, directories, guides, and newsgroups for information. Three mechanisms on the Web that are available for researching a specific topic are search engines (or spiders), resource (or subject) trees, and meta search engines. Many search engines contain resource tree search mechanisms, and most resource (or subject) trees also have search built-in engines. It's up to you which of these you use, as each will produce similar but slightly different results.

Finally, a number of strategies for searching the Web were suggested. These included understanding the search engine's limitations, typing one or more search words in the text box, refining and repeating the search, checking your spelling, not using commonly occurring articles or Web terms, and avoiding the use of plurals.

QUESTIONS

1. What is the World Wide Web (Web)? Explain its growing popularity.

2. What is http?

3. What is hypermedia?

4. What is hypertext markup language?

5. What is a URL? What types of URLs are available?

6. What is a Web browser?

7. Identify the basic features common to all Web browsers.

8. Identify several additional features that some Web browsers might possess.

9. Identify the two major categories or types of Web browsers. What is the primary difference? Which is more commonly used?

10. Identify the two most commonly used graphical browsers.

11. Identify the three main mechanisms on the Web that are available for researching a specific topic. How do they differ?

12. Identify some strategies for searching the Web effectively.

PROJECTS AND PROBLEMS

1. If you have access to both the Internet Explorer and Netscape browsers, use both browsers and do a brief report listing the similarities and differences when using each browser to do the following: do a search using the "Search" button, add an item to the list of bookmarked (or favorite) sites, and change the size of the cache. What other similarities or differences did you find?

2. Use the Internet Explorer or Netscape browsers with an Internet connection to link to the following sites. Provide a description of the nature and purpose of each site. What do these sites have in common? *Note:* If any of these sites are not active, use a search engine to search on the description (e.g., "telecommuting jobs") or on the general term "online jobs" to find the correct URLs.
   (a) Telecommuting jobs (http://www.tjobs.com)
   (b) Monster Job Service (http://www.monster.com)
   (c) World Wide World Employment Office (http://www.employmentoffice.net)

3. Use the following search engines to find information about the various types of *10 Base T Hubs* used in networks. Which one produced the best results?
   (a) Excite (http://www.excite.com)
   (b) Lycos (http://www.lycos.com)
   (c) MetaCrawler (http://www.metacrawler.com)

4. Use a resource tree such as Yahoo (http://www.yahoo.com) to find information about the following topics. Explain specifically what you needed to click on to get a list of usable sites.
   (a) Family reunions that have been scheduled
   (b) Marine archeology organizations
   (c) Location of foreign embassies and consulates in the United States

5. Use search engines and/or subject trees to conduct research to determine if there are any graphical browsers available other than Internet Explorer and Netscape. What are their names? How are they similar? How are they different?

6. Investigate the pros and cons of purchasing merchandise online and the potential security problems, especially related to using a credit card.

7. Conduct a Web search on electronic commerce (e-commerce). What is it? What are the various forms of e-commerce? How does a company or other organization use it?

8. Joyce Peters, a friend who is returning to college after raising a family, asks your advice about the best way to conduct information for a report that she is doing on the current telecommunications legislation. She is familiar with traditional methods of finding information by doing library searches for books and periodicals but does not understand how to conduct a search using a Web browser. Prepare a written explanation of the advantages of using the Web as a research tool in this situation. List the steps that Joyce should follow to conduct the search using a Web browser.

Vocabulary

bookmark

cache

graphical browser

hypermedia

hypertext markup
language (HTML)

hypertext transfer
protocol (HTTP)

in-line image

Microsoft Internet
Explorer

Netscape Communicator

nongraphical browser

resource or subject tree

search engine (or
spider)

uniform resource locator
(URL)

Web browser

World Wide Web (WWW
or Web)

References

Gehris, Dennis, *Microsoft Internet Explorer 5.0*, South-Western
Educational Publishing, Cincinnati, OH, 2000.

Gehris, Dennis O., *Using Multimedia Tools and Applications on
the Internet*, Wadsworth Publishing, Belmont, CA, 1998.

Pfaaffenberger, Bryan, *Discover the Internet*, IDG Books Worldwide, Foster City, CA, 1997.

11

Creating Web Pages

I n this chapter we examine how Web browsers use hypertext mark-up language (HTML) to process information. The basic HTML tags are presented, as well as instructions for using a popular HTML editor to create Web pages.

WHAT YOU WILL LEARN

- Definition of hypertext markup language (HTML)
- Benefits of HTML
- Drawbacks of HTML
- How to use HTML tags
- How to use an HTML editor to create a Web page

HTML DEFINED

The **hypertext markup language (HTML)** is the basis for the pages that appear on the World Wide Web. HTML's purpose is to transmit the structure of documents between users of the Web. Web browsers such as Internet Explorer and Netscape read the HTML files that have been created in standard American Standard Code for Information Interchange (ASCII) format and stored on servers connected to the Internet. The HTML was standardized to prevent confusion among users. Browsers are also able to read specially developed **HTML**

extensions, which give pages a special appearance. HTML requires the programmer to think in terms of rules that will result in a specific document content. This differs from word processors, which require you to concentrate on formatting and how the document will appear when it is printed.

■ BENEFITS OF HTML

Although HTML possesses some limitations, it does have advantages, four of which are:

1. It is easy to learn because it is not necessary to memorize HTML codes.
2. It is compatible with any Web browser.
3. Its files are small and take up little storage space.
4. It is possible to create and define a numbered list that can be displayed with bullets or with Roman or Arabic numbers.

The first obvious advantage is that it is easy to learn compared to other programming languages, since you don't need to memorize HTML codes. This is because a number of editors are available that can be used to create the HTML files containing the codes. In this chapter we discuss the various types of editors that are available and explain how to use one of the editors. The second advantage is that HTML is compatible with any Web browser and can be displayed on any computer that supports HTML. In effect, anyone with an IBM PC–compatible computer or Macintosh computer, an Internet connection, and a Web browser is able to read a Web page created with HTML. The third advantage is that HTML files are small and take up very little storage space compared with other types of program files. Program files created for other applications often need to be compressed so that they can fit on a floppy disk. This is not necessary with an HTML file.

The fourth advantage is that an HTML author is able to use the language to create and define a list which can be displayed with bullets or Roman or Arabic numerals. This feature, which illustrates the structured nature of HTML, provides the user with a great deal of flexibility in viewing a document. But nothing is perfect, and HTML is not an exception.

■ DRAWBACKS OF HTML

Although HTML possesses the advantages noted above, it also has some limitations:

1. It lacks WYSIWYG (what you see is what you get) capabilities.
2. It is limited to predetermined codes.

The first disadvantage of HTML is that while composing a document, you can't see exactly how the document will appear when it is viewed with a Web browser. In other words, HTML lacks WYSIWYG capabilities. The only way to see the document as it will actually appear is to open the file with a Web browser. This is often time consuming and frustrating to someone who is trying to develop a Web document. Some HTML editors display the created pages nearly the way they will be displayed in a browser or have a built-in test feature in which the editor will connect to a Web browser that you have configured in advance.

The other principal disadvantage of HTML is that you are limited to the predetermined codes that are currently available. Therefore, you are unable to create special effects for which code has not been written. This may limit the creativity of layout and design experts who desire to exhibit their creativity. It should be noted that the newer HTML versions contain more codes than did previous versions. In addition, subsequent versions of HTML will probably contain many more codes, which will result in Web pages with varied layouts.

■ USING HTML

HTML uses **tags**, instructions to the browser about how to display text and other elements. Tags are constructed by enclosing the identifier in "less than" (<) and "greater than" (>) symbols, which separates them from the remainder of the text. The basic format is <identifier>. The tags are not case-sensitive, so the tags can be in lowercase, uppercase, or a mixture. Thus, all of the following tags would be acceptable: <html>, <HTML>, and <HtMl>. Some HTML editors use uppercase tags and some use lowercase. In this book we use uppercase tags to make them easier to differentiate from text. There are two basic types of tags: **single-element** and **symmetric**. *Single-element tags* consist of one tag only. An example of a single-element code is <p>. *Symmetric tags* are used in pairs. One of these can be seen as an "on" code and the other as an "off" code. A tag without a slash (e.g., <HTML>) is the "on" code, and a tag with a slash (e.g., </HTML>) is the "off" code. Information required, including text and other tags, is placed between the "on" and "off" codes.

HTML is also composed of six specific types of tags. Each command is of equal importance and has a particular purpose. The HTML file that is created is a text file with either an .htm extension if an MSDOS computer is being used or .html with a UNIX-based computer. When using a Macintosh computer, the HTML file is saved without an extension, since these computers do not use file extensions.

HTML is composed of six different types of tags: structural, paragraph-formatting, character-formatting, list-specification, hyperlink, and multimedia. Each type of tag has a specific purpose and use. Depending on the type of document you are preparing with HTML, you may or may not need to know all of the possible variations of tags in each type. Figure 11-1 is a sample of an HTML document file. We will refer to it as we discuss the various types of HTML tags.

Figure 11-1
Sample HTML File

```
<HTML><HEAD><TITLE>Sample HTML Document File</TITLE></HEAD>
<BODY><H1><I>"Communication Technologies"</I></H1>
<BR><B><CENTER>by Dennis O. Gehris, Ed.D., and Linda Szul, Ed.D.</B><A HREF=
    "http://www.bloomu.edu/departments/beois/welcome2.au">
<BR>Click here for an audio welcome.</A></CENTER>
<HR>
<H2>The text contains the following sections:</H2>
<BR>
<OL>
<LI>Communication Technology: Introduction, History, and Future
<LI>Communication Technologies Applications
<LI>The Internet/Intranets
<LI>Networking Fundamentals
</OL>
<HR>
<P><IMG SRC="http://www.bloomu.edu/departments/beois/lsmiley.gif">For more
    information, contact
<ADDRESS>Prentice Hall Publishing Company
One Lake Street, Upper Saddle River, NJ 07458</ADDRESS> or
visit the company's site at <A HREF="http://www.prenhall.com">
Prentice Hall's Web Site</A>.
</BODY></HTML>
```

Structural Tags

Structural HTML tags identify a file as an HTML document and provide information about the data in the HTML file. The following are structural tags: <HTML> </HTML>, <HEAD></HEAD>,<TITLE></TITLE>, and <BODY> </BODY>. The sample HTML document shows correct order for these tags:

<HTML><HEAD><TITLE>Sample HTML Document File</TITLE></HEAD></HTML>

<HTML></HTML>	This tag informs the browser what kind of document it is so that it can be displayed properly. The "on" code is placed at the beginning of the document and the "off" code at the end of the document.
<HEAD></HEAD>	This tag allows the server software to discover information about the document.
<TITLE></TITLE>	The information that appears between these "on" and "off" codes will appear on the title bar of the window and is used for index information by Web search engines.
<BODY></BODY>	The information that appears between these "on" and "off" codes represents the main part of your document.

Paragraph-Formatting Tags

Paragraph-formatting tags specify the paragraphs and heading levels. The paragraph-formatting tags are <P></P>, <BR>, <HR>, <H1></H1>, <H2></H2>, <H3></H3>, <H4></H4>, <H5></H5>, <H6></H6> and <PRE></PRE>.

<P></P>	The paragraph tag is used to designate the beginning of a paragraph. Earlier HTML versions did not require an "off" code, but later versions do require this code. Without this tag, browsers will not be able to tell when a paragraph begins and ends, because unlike a word processor, pressing the Enter key in an HTML editor has no effect on the line endings.
 	The line break tag allows you to break a line without adding a space between the lines. It does not require an "off" code.
<HR>	The horizontal rule tag instructs the browser to create a horizontal line across the width of the display window.
<H1...6></H1...6>	Each of the six header tags represents different type styles and sizes. The type style of the heading will vary depending on the browser that is being used. Figure 11-2 shows the appearance of text in each of the six header styles using Netscape. The sample HTML document file uses an H2 code as follows:

<H2>The text contains the following sections:</H2>

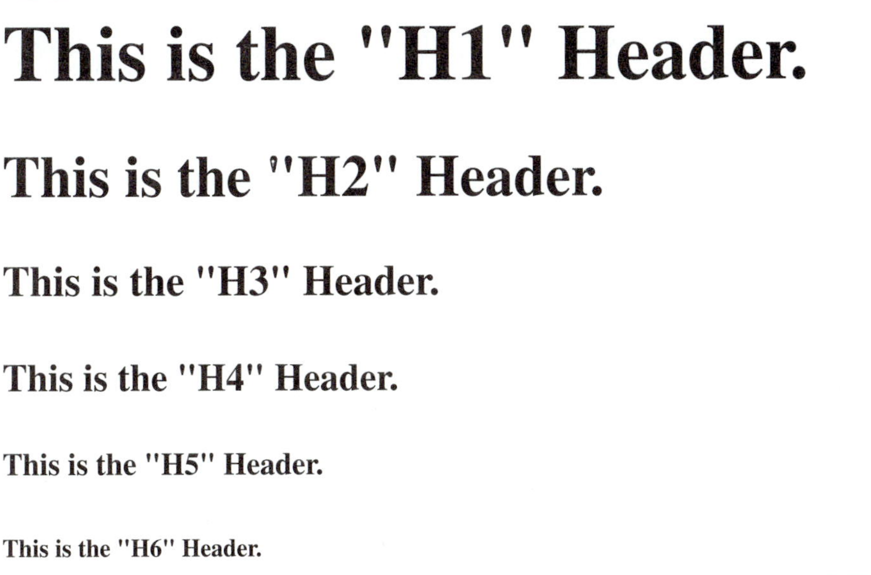

This is the "H1" Header.

Figure 11-2
Six HTML Header Styles

This is the "H2" Header.

This is the "H3" Header.

This is the "H4" Header.

This is the "H5" Header.

This is the "H6" Header.

<PRE></PRE>   The preformatted paragraph tag is used to create a block of text in a particular format. If you have a table with columns of text or numbers, you can preserve it by using this tag. It is also useful for displaying charts, graphs, and diagrams. The text will appear in the Courier font with most browsers.

```
<BODY>
<H1>Sales Report</H1>
<H3>Here is the sales report for September, October, and November.</H3>
<PRE>
                    Sales Report

            Sept.         Oct.          Nov.
            _____         ____          ____
Jones       394.23        223.83        256.55
Smith       212.45        323.21        423.33
Yuber       563.33        343.22        443.56

</PRE></BODY></HTML>
```

Figure 11-3 shows how the file appears in the Netscape browser.

Figure 11-3

Preformatted Text Displayed in Netscape. *(From Microsoft Internet Explorer 5.0 Textwork Book, 1st edition, © 2000. Reprinted with permission of Course Technology, a division of Thomson Learning. Fax 800-730-2215)*

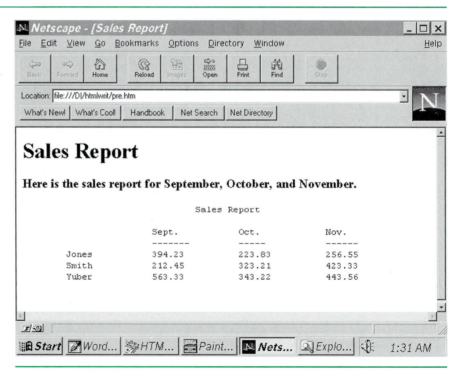

Character-Formatting Tags

Character-formatting tags allow for the application of various styles (such as bold, underline, or italics) to the characters in documents. The most popular character-formatting tags are <B></B>, <U></U>, <I></I>, <CENTER></CENTER>,<TT></TT>, <EM></EM>, <STRONG></STRONG>, <CITE></CITE>, and <ADDRESS></ADDRESS>. There are also special character commands. For example, because HTML uses the < and > characters to start and end a tag, "&lt" is used for a "less than" character (<) and "&gt" for a "greater than" (>) character. Some of the other special character commands are "&amp" for an ampersand (&), and "&quot" for double quotes (A) There are also several obscure character-formatting tags, including <SAMP></SAMP>, <CODE></CODE>, <KBD></KBD>, <VAR></VAR>, and <DFN></DFN>. However, the discussion here focuses on the most popular tags. Figure 11-4 shows text that uses each of the more popular tags.

<B></B>	The bold tag permits you to boldface text.
<U></U>	The underline tag underlines text.
<I></I>	The italics tag produces italicized text.
<CENTER></CENTER>	The center code centers horizontally text placed between the "on" and "off" codes. It can also be used to center a hyperlinked element. The sample HTML document file uses this tag as follows:

<CENTER>by Dennis O. Gehris, Ed.D. and Linda Szul, Ed.D.</B><A HREF="http://www.bloomu.edu/departments/beois/welcome2.au">
Click here for an audio welcome.</A></CENTER>

This text illustrates the "B" tag.

This text illustrates the "I" tag.

<u>This text illustrates the "U" tag.</u>

This text illustrates combining tags: **bold,** *italics,* <u>underline.</u>

This text illustrates the "TT" tag.

This text illustrates the "EM" tag.

This text illustrates the "STRONG" tag.

This text illustrates the "CITE" tag.

This text illustrates the "ADDRESS" tag.

Figure 11-4
Text Using the Most Popular HTML Character-Formatting Tags. *(From Microsoft Internet Explorer 5.0 Textwork Book, 1st edition, © 2000. Reprinted with permission of Course Technology, a division of Thomson Learning. Fax 800-730-2215)*

<ADDRESS> </ADDRESS>   The address tag is used for an electronic mail address and/or to identify the author of a document, or the Webmaster. The output will appear in italicized text. The sample HTML document file uses this tag as follows:

```
<ADDRESS>Prentice Hall Publishing Company
One Lake Street, Upper Saddle River, NJ 07458</ADDRESS>
```

List-Specification Tags

List-specification tags allow you to format several different types of lists: ordered (numbered), unordered (bulleted), directory (for short lists), menu (with each item one line long) and glossary (definition). Glossary lists are those in which each item has a term and a definition. Creating a list involves starting the section with the correct "on" command as shown below. In every type of list, except for a glossary list, the <LI> tag is used before each item in the list. After all items are keyed in the list, the "off" command is used as shown below. The sample HTML document file uses the following list-specification tags:

```
<OL>
<LI>Communication Technology: Introduction, History, and Future
<LI>Communication Technologies Applications
<LI>The Internet/Intranets
<LI>Networking Fundamentals
</OL>
```

<UL></UL>   This is the tag for an unordered list. This is a list with bulleted items that can be arranged in any order. Other tags, such as those for bold and hypertext, can be included within the list. The following is an example of the HTML tags for an unordered list:

```
<HTML><HEAD><TITLE>Example of an Unordered List</TITLE></HEAD>
<BODY>
<P><H1>Example of an Unordered List in HTML</H1>
<P><H3>The Types of HTML Lists</H3>
<UL>
<LI>Unordered Lists
<LI>Ordered Lists
<LI>Directory Lists
<LI>Menu Lists
<LI>Glossary Lists
</UL></BODY></HTML>
```

Figure 11-5 shows how this file would be displayed in a browser.

Example of an Unordered List in HTML

The Types of HTML Lists

- Unordered Lists
- Ordered Lists
- Directory Lists
- Menu Lists
- Glossary Lists

Figure 11-5
Unordered List Displayed in Browser.
(From Microsoft Internet Explorer 5.0 Textwork
Book, 1st edition, © *2000. Reprinted with
permission of Course Technology, a division of
Thomson Learning. Fax 800-730-2215)*

<OL></OL>   This is the tag for an ordered list, in which the items are preceded with numbers. The items do not need to be in any particular order and will be numbered consecutively. You do not need to number the items, the numbers will be displayed automatically when using a browser. The following is an example of the HTML tags for an ordered list:

```
<HTML><HEAD><TITLE>Example of an Ordered List</TITLE></HEAD>
<BODY>
<P><H1>Example of an Ordered List in HTML</H1>
<P><H3>My Shopping List</H3>
<OL>
<LI>Bread
<LI>Milk
<LI>Eggs
<LI>Cheese
<LI>Margarine
</OL>
</BODY></HTML>
```

Figure 11-6 shows how this file would be displayed in a browser.

<DIR></DIR>   Directory lists and menu lists are variations of unordered lists and are intended for lists with short items that can be displayed in a compact style.

<MENU></MENU>   Menu lists usually contain no bullets, numbers, or other labels. However, some browsers display menu and directory lists with bullets.

<DL></DL>   Glossary (definition) lists are intended for lists of terms and their corresponding definitions. Each list item contains a term and the definition of the term. The term is preceded with a <DT> tag and the definition is preceded with a <DD> tag. Following is an example of a glossary list.

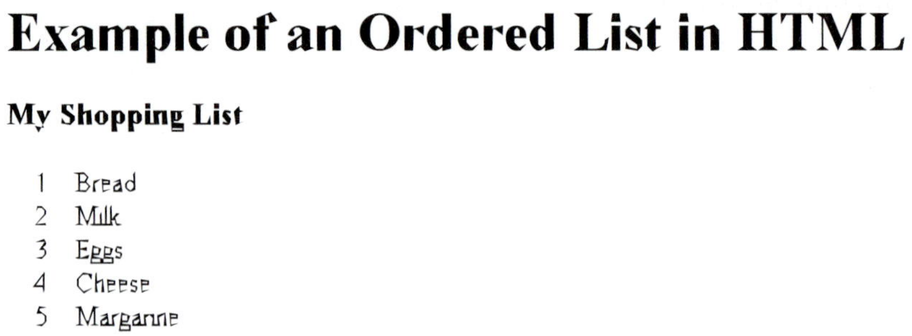

Figure 11-6
Ordered List Displayed in a Browser.
(From Microsoft Internet Explorer 5.0 Textwork Book, 1st edition, © 2000. Reprinted with permission of Course Technology, a division of Thomson Learning. Fax 800-730-2215)

Example of an Ordered List in HTML

My Shopping List

1 Bread
2 Milk
3 Eggs
4 Cheese
5 Margarine

<HTML><HEAD><TITLE>Example of a Glossary (Definition) List</TITLE></HEAD>
<BODY>
<P><H3>Example of a Glossary (Definition) List in HTML</H3>
<P><H4>Internet/Multimedia Definitions</H4>
<DL>
<DT><B>Internet</B>
<DD>A network of computer systems that are interconnected in about 130 countries.
<DT><B>Multimedia</B>
<DD>The integration of at least two media: text, audio, graphics, and full-motion video.
<DT><B>World Wide Web</B>
<DD>A wide-area hypermedia information retrieval initiative aiming to give universal access to a large universe of documents.
</DL>
</BODY></HTML>

Figure 11-7 shows how this file would be displayed in a browser.

Hyperlink Tags

Hyperlink tags allow for the specifications related to moving from one hyperlink to another on the Web. Hyperlink tags make it possible to link from a place in the present document to another place. You can hyperlink to complete documents or to graphic images, audio clips, and video clips. In order

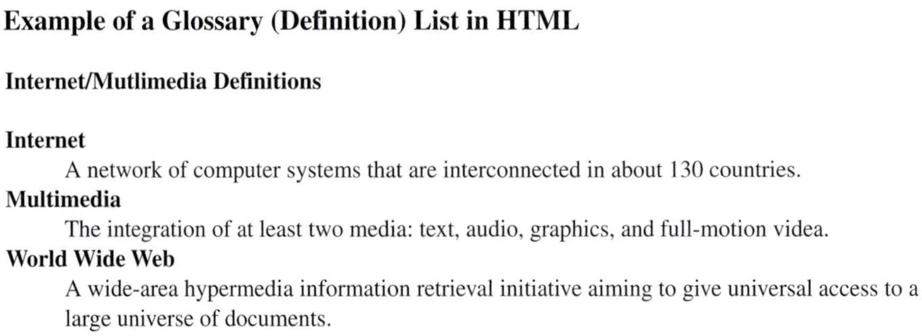

Figure 11-7
Glossary List Displayed in Browser.
(From Microsoft Internet Explorer 5.0 Textwork Book, 1st edition, © 2000. Reprinted with permission of Course Technology, a division of Thomson Learning. Fax 800-730-2215)

Example of a Glossary (Definition) List in HTML

Internet/Mutlimedia Definitions

Internet
   A network of computer systems that are interconnected in about 130 countries.
Multimedia
   The integration of at least two media: text, audio, graphics, and full-motion video.
World Wide Web
   A wide-area hypermedia information retrieval initiative aiming to give universal access to a large universe of documents.

to hyperlink the spot in your document, you must know the URL of the place or file to which you want to link and the text that you want to use to create the link. The sample HTML document uses the following hyperlink:

```
visit the company's site at <A HREF="http://www.prenhall.com">
Prentice Hall's Web Site</A>.
</BODY></HTML>
```

When using the correct hyperlink tags, the hyperlinked text appears in a different color and with most browsers, is usually underlined. There are three types of hyperlinks:

1. *Local hyperlink:* one that jumps to a place inside your file
2. *Remote hyperlink 1:* one that links to another file on another computer
3. *Remote hyperlink 2:* one that jumps to a named location in another file

Each type of hyperlink uses the <A></A> anchor tag, but in a slightly different manner.

Local Hyperlink   The format of the hyperlink tag that will jump to a specific place in the same document is as follows:

```
<A HREF="#TargetName">Linked Word(s)</A>
```

"#TargetName" would be replaced with the actual name of the target that is marked with the next tag. "Linked Words" would be replaced with the actual hyperlinked text.

```
<A NAME=#TargetName></A>Target Location
```

The hyperlink tag for the location to which to jump is as follows: "#TargetName" would be replaced with the actual name of the target that is marked with the next tag. "Linked Words" would be replaced with the actual hyperlinked text.

Following is an example of a file that uses these two hyperlink tags.

```
<HTML><HEAD><TITLE>Example of Local Hyperlink</TITLE></HEAD>
<BODY>
<P><H3>Example of a Local Hyperlink in HTML</H3>
<A HREF="#address">Click here to jump to the address.</A>
<H3>ABC University offers a wide variety of course offerings in all of the popular
    disciplines.</H3>
<A NAME="address"></A>
<ADDRESS>ABC University<BR>
320 University Boulevard<BR>
State University, NJ 08648</ADDRESS>
</BODY></HTML>
```

Remote Hyperlink 1   The format for the hyperlink code that is used to jump to another document is as follows:

<A REF="Document=s URL">Linked Word(s)></A>

"Document's URL" would be replaced with an actual URL. "Linked Word(s)" would be replaced with actual hyperlinked text. Following is an example of a file that uses this hyperlink tag.

```
<HTML><HEAD><TITLE>Example of Remote Hyperlink #1</TITLE></HEAD>
<BODY>
<P><H3>Example of a Remote Hyperlink #1 in HTML</H3>
<A HREF="http://www.microsoft.com">Click here to access Microsoft's Web Page.</A>
<H3>ABC University offers a wide variety of course offerings in all of the popular
    disciplines.</H3>
<ADDRESS>ABC University<BR>
320 University Boulevard<BR>
State University, NJ 08648</ADDRESS>
</BODY></HTML>
```

Remote Hyperlink 2   The format for the hyperlink code that is used to jump to a remote computer's URL and the name of the target-document file is as follows:

<A HREF="http://www.domain.name/path/filename.html#Target Name">Linked Word(s)</A>

The "http://www.domain.name/path/filename.html#TargetName" would be replaced with an actual URL, path, filename, and target name. "Linked Word(s)" would be replaced with actual hyperlinked text. Following is an example of a file that uses this hyperlink tag.

```
<HTML><HEAD><TITLE>Example of Remote Hyperlink #2</TITLE></HEAD>
<BODY>
<P><H3>Example of a Remote Hyperlink #2 in HTML</H3>
<A HREF="http://www.abc.edu/faculty/abc.html#faculty">Click to view a listing of our
    faculty</A>
<H3>ABC University offers a wide variety of course offerings in all of the popular
    disciplines.</H3>
<ADDRESS>ABC University<BR>
320 University Boulevard<BR>
State University, NJ 08648</ADDRESS>
</BODY></HTML>
```

Multimedia Tags

Multimedia (or asset-integration) tags provide access to multimedia applications relating to graphical images, video, and audio.

Graphic Image Tags. There are two graphic image file formats that can be used on a Web page. One is **graphical interchange format (GIF)**, which was originally developed for the CompuServe Online Service, to facilitate the transfer of graphics among the various computer brands connected to the service. The other graphic image format is the **Joint Photographic Experts Group (JPG or JPEG) format**, which takes advantage of human perceptional characteristics and does not deal with less essential information.

The syntax for the main HTML tags needed to access graphic images is as follows:

```
<IMG SRC="http://www.domain.name/path/sample.gif">
```

This is the tag format used to place a graphic image located on a remote computer on your Web page. If the graphic image file is located on the local server, the "http://www.domain.name" part of the address can be eliminated. When graphic images are combined with text, you can add an ALIGN= code to the tag so that the graphic is aligned at the top, bottom, or middle relative to the existing text. For example, if you wanted to indicate a middle alignment, the tag would be as follows:

```
<IMG ALIGN=MIDDLE SRC="http://www.domain.name/path/sample.gif">

<IMG SRC="http://www.domain.name/path/sample.gif"[Textual Description]>
```

This tag format would be used to provide a textual description of the image, which is displayed in text-only browsers.

The following tag format would be used to designate a graphic image as a hyperlink:

```
<A HREF="http://www.domain.name/path/file"><IMG SRC="http://www.domain.name/path/sample.gif"></A>
```

By clicking on the graphic, the user jumps to the appropriate hyperlink target. The sample HTML document file uses the following graphic image tag:

```
<IMG SRC="http://www.bloomu.edu/departments/beois/lsmiley.gif">
```

Audio and Video Tags. Five main audio file formats are used on the Internet. **Macintosh audio information file format (AIFF)** is used on Macintosh computers, and the **audio-file format on UNIX machines (SND, AU)** is used on computers running the UNIX operating system. PCs use either the **Microsoft Windows audio (WAV)** or **musical instrument digital interface (MID or MIDI) formats**. In addition, four video file formats are used on the Internet. The **quicktime cross-platform video file format (MOV)** was devised for use with the Macintosh computer long before anything similar was developed for Windows computers. The **audio video interleave (AVI)** format is the standard for Microsoft Windows, and the **Moving Picture Experts Group digital-video standard format (MPG** or **MPEG)** has become the defacto standard for digital video transmitted on the Web.

The syntax for the main HTML tags needed to access audio and video files will be sufficient. The sample HTML document file contains the following sound tag:

```
<A HREF="http://www.bloomu.edu/departments/beois/welcome1.au">.
```

Following is the tag format for downloading the file video.avi from the local Web server:

```
<A HREF="file://video.avi">Click here for video</A>
```

The "Click here for video" or other appropriate text would be hyperlinked text, so that when the user clicks on the text, the video file would be accessed and an external application would be launched.

The tag format for downloading the file video.avi from the remote Web server is as follows:

```
<A HREF="http://www.server/path/video.avi">Click here for video</A>
```

The tag format for downloading the file audio.wav from the local Web server is as follows:

```
<A HREF="file://audio.wav">Click here for audio</A>
```

The "Click here for audio" or other appropriate text would be hyperlinked, so that when the user clicks on the text, the audio file would be accessed and an external application would be launched.

The tag format for downloading the file audio.au from a remote Web server is as follows:

```
<A HREF="http://www.server/path/audio.au">Click here for audio.</A>
```

Next we examine the various types of software utility programs that can be used to prepare HTML documents.

■ HTML SOFTWARE UTILITY PROGRAMS

Internet Explorer and Netscape allow you to view the HTML tags in a document that has been loaded by choosing "source" or "Document source" from the View menu. However, it is not possible to edit the codes from within the browser. It is possible to use a basic word processing program or a text editor to create text files containing the HTML tags. However, this is a time consuming and very tedious procedure. A much better approach is to use some type of software utility program that is specially designed to produce HTML files. Although these programs are a great help to people producing HTML files, knowledge of HTML is usually required. Numerous *HTML utility programs* are available for both IBM/IBM-compatible and Macintosh computers. Some programs are available free or require a small shareware fee. Other programs can be purchased from software companies.

Utilities can be placed in two categories: converters and editors. *HTML Converters* can be used if you have an existing document such as a brochure or newsletter that is already saved on a file. Converters are usually built into an existing add-on word processing or desktop publishing application. Programs such as Microsoft Word and PageMaker possess an HTML conversion feature. *HTML editors* are used when you are creating a Web document from scratch and the document does not already exist in any type of file. The discussion here is limited to FrontPage Express, which is a free HTML editor available from Microsoft.

Using the FrontPage Express Editor

Microsoft's FrontPage Express (formerly FrontPad) is an HTML editor. Although no longer available from Microsoft, it will serve as an example of how most HTML editors are used. With FrontPage Express you don't have to worry about keying HTML codes, as the program adds the codes for you automatically as it creates the HTML file. Because FrontPage Express is a Microsoft product, the program's interface is very similar to that of other Microsoft software, such as Microsoft Word. If you already know Microsoft Word, you'll find FrontPage Express very easy to use. Even if you don't know Microsoft Word, you will still find the program very user friendly!

Parts of the FrontPage Express Window

It is wise to learn the parts FrontPage Express before using it. Figure 11-8 shows the parts of the FrontPage Express window. Below is an explanation of each of the parts shown.

Menu Bar.   The Menu bar gives you access to all the menu options. Simply click on a menu name to display a list of related menu commands, and then click the command you want to use.

Title Bar.   The Title bar displays the name of the program, FrontPage Express, and the name of the Web page. "Untitled" is a temporary name that FrontPage Express uses until you assign a new one.

Standard, Format, and Forms Tool Bars.   These tool bars contain buttons that give you quick access to a variety of commands and features. Moving the mouse pointer over a button will display the name of the tool bar button. It is possible to hide each of these tool bars by deselecting the tool bars on the View menu of FrontPage Express.

Figure 11-8

Parts of the FrontPage Express Window. *(From Microsoft Internet Explorer 5.0 Textwork Book, 1st edition, © 2000. Reprinted with permission of Course Technology, a division of Thomson Learning. Fax 800-730-2215)*

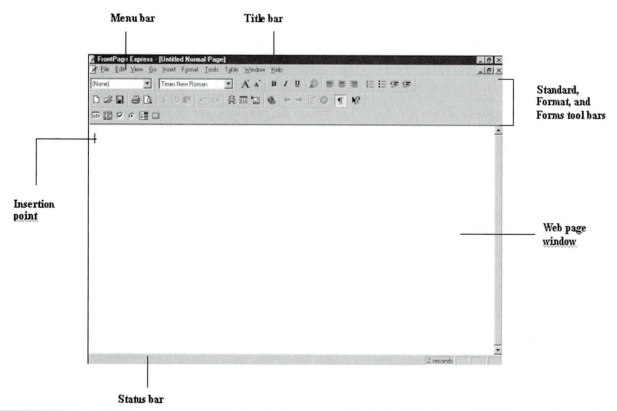

The *Standard tool bar*, which is the tool bar in the middle, contains buttons that handle the common file operations (New, Open, Save), printing, cutting, copying, pasting, and undo/redo. You can also insert tables, images, and hyperlinks with Standard tool bar buttons. The *Format tool bar* (the tool bar at the top) allows you to use drop-down lists of fonts and HTML styles and contains buttons that control font size, color, effects, and alignment. The *Forms tool bar* (the lower tool bar) contains buttons for inserting text boxes, radio buttons, check boxes, multiline text windows, drop-down lists, and action buttons.

Web Page Window.   This is where you enter text and graphics. The Web Page window can be maximized or minimized independent of the program window. **Status bar.** The Status bar provides you with information about current settings and commands. The time indicated on the status bar is the estimated time it would take to download the current Web page with a 28.8-kilobyte per second (kbps) modem.

Insertion Point.   The blinking insertion point (cursor) shows you where the next character that you key will appear.

Starting FrontPage Express

FrontPage Express can be started from the Windows Start menu. After clicking on the Start menu, choose "Programs" and then "Internet Explorer Folder." Finally, select "FrontPage Express."

FrontPage Express can be started from within Internet Explorer if you're using an upgraded version of the browser to revise an existing Web page. First load the Web page into Internet Explorer. Next, click on the "Edit" button on the tool bar. FrontPage Express will load automatically.

Using FrontPage Express

There are several ways to use FrontPage Express. One way is to use the built-in wizards, interactive help utilities that guide the user through each step of a multistep operation, offering helpful information and explaining options along the way. FrontPage Express contains several wizards. The Personal Web Page Wizard is designed to create a Web page to fit your personal needs. The Form Page Wizard helps you collect data by asking you to select the information that you want to collect. To use either of these wizards, choose "New" from the File menu, click on the name of the wizard, and click on "OK" (see Figure 11-9).

The second way to create a Web page using FrontPage Express is by deciding what you want the Web page to contain and then adding these features by selecting the items from the tool bar buttons or from the selections on the menus. This process is initiated by choosing "Normal Page" in the

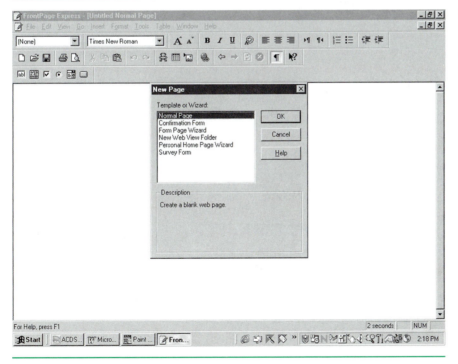

Figure 11-9

FrontPage New Page Dialog Box. *(From Microsoft Internet Explorer 5.0 Textwork Book, 1st edition, © 2000. Reprinted with permission of Course Technology, a division of Thomson Learning. Fax 800-730-2215)*

Figure 11-10
Page Created with FrontPage Express
*(From Microsoft Internet Explorer 5.0 Textwork
Book, 1st edition, © 2000. Reprinted with
permission of Course Technology, a division of
Thomson Learning. Fax 800-730-2215)*

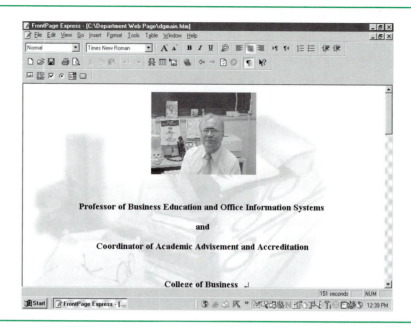

New Page dialog box. Figure 11-10 shows a page created in this manner with FrontPage Express.

■ SUMMARY

The hypertext markup language (HTML) is the basis for the pages that appear on the World Wide Web. HTML's purpose is to transmit the structure of documents between users of the Web. The advantages of HTML include the following.

1. It is easy to learn. It is not necessary to memorize HTML codes.
2. It is compatible with any Web browser.
3. Its files are small and take up little storage space.
4. It is possible to create and define a numbered list that can be displayed with bullets or Roman or Arabic numbers.

Although HTML possesses the advantages mentioned above, it also has some limitations.

1. It lacks WYSIWYG capabilities.
2. It is limited to predetermined codes.

HTML uses tags, instructions to the browser about how to display text and other elements. Tags are constructed by enclosing the identifier in "less than" (<) and "greater than" (>) symbols, which separates them from the remainder of the text. There are two basic types of tags: single-element and symmetric. Single-element tags consist of one tag only. Symmetric tags are used in pairs. HTML is composed of six specific types of tags: structural, paragraph-formatting, character-formatting, list-specification, hyperlink, and multimedia. Each type of tag has a specific purpose and use. Structural HTML tags identify a file as an HTML document and provide information about the data in the HTML file. Paragraph-formatting tags specify the paragraphs and heading levels. Character-formatting tags allow for the application of various styles (such as bold, underline, or italics) to the characters in documents. List-specification tags allow you to format several different types of lists: ordered (numbered), unordered (bulleted), directory (for short lists), menu (with each item one line long) and glossary (definition). Glossary lists are those in which each item has a term and a definition. Hyperlink tags allow for the specifications related to moving from one hyperlink to another on the Web.

HTML utility programs are available for both IBM/IBM-compatible and Macintosh computers. Some programs are available free or require a small shareware fee. Other programs can be purchased from software companies. Utilities can be placed in two categories: converters and editors. Converters can be used if you have an existing document such as a brochure or newsletter that is already saved on a file. Converters are usually built into an existing add-on word processing or desktop publishing application. Programs such as Microsoft Word and PageMaker possess an HTML conversion feature. HTML editors are used when you are creating a Web document from scratch and the document does not already exist in any type of file. In this chapter we examined the use of FrontPage Express, a free HTML editor available from Microsoft.

Microsoft's FrontPage Express (formerly FrontPad) is an HTML editor that comes packaged with the Internet Explorer browser. With FrontPage Express you don't have to worry about keying HTML codes, as the program adds the codes for you automatically as it creates the HTML file. Because FrontPage Express is a Microsoft product, the program's interface is very similar to that of other Microsoft software, such as Microsoft Word.

There are several ways to use FrontPage Express. One way is to use the built-in wizards, interactive help utilities that guide the user through each step of a multistep operation, offering helpful information and explaining options along the way. FrontPage Express contains several wizards. The Personal Web Page Wizard is designed to create a Web page to fit your personal needs. The Form Page Wizard helps you collect data by asking you to select the information that you want to collect. The second way to create a Web page using FrontPage Express is by deciding what you want the Web page to contain and then adding these features by selecting the items from the tool bar buttons or from the selections on the menus.

QUESTIONS

1. What is HTML, and what is it used for?

2. Discuss the advantages of HTML.

3. Discuss the disadvantages of HTML.

4. What is meant by the term *tag* as it is used in HTML?

5. Differentiate between single-element and symmetric tags.

6. What are structural tags?

7. What are paragraph-formatting tags?

8. What are character-formatting tags?

9. What are list-specification tags?

10. What are hyperlink tags?

11. What are the three main types of hyperlink tags?

12. What are multimedia tags?

13. What are HTML software utility programs?

14. What are wizards, and how they can be used in FrontPage Express?

PROJECTS AND PROBLEMS

1. Use a Web browser to open the following documents relating to HTML at the URLs indicated. Study each document. Use a Web search engine to find other sites that explain HTML.

    "Beginner's Guide to HTML," http://www.davesite.com/webstation/html

    "HTML Primer," http://www.htmlprimer.com

2. Identify each of the following HTML tags, providing the type of tab (structural, paragraph-formatting, character-formatting, list specification, hyperlink, or multimedia), the name of the tag, and the tag's function.
    (a) <BODY></BODY>
    (b) <ADDRESS></ADDRESS>
    (c) <B></B>
    (d) <OL>
    (e) <A HREF="http://www.bloomu.edu">Bloomsburg University's Web Site.</A>
    (f) <CENTER></CENTER><LI>
    (g) <LI>
    (h) <U></U>
    (i) <H3></H3>
    (j) <IMG SRC="sample.gif">
    (k) <HTML></HTML>
    (l) <UL>
    (m) A HREF="file://scream.wav:>Click here to hear a scream!</A>
    (n) <HR>

3. Use an HTML editor to create a personal Web page that contains the following elements.
    (a) Your name centered in a large font size.
    (b) A graphic of yourself or other GIF or JPEG file. (*Hint:* If you are using a graphic file from a scanned picture or other local file, it should be in the same hard drive subdirectory or on the same diskette as the HTML file when saved.)
    (c) A background consisting of a color or GIF file.
    (d) A list of your favorite Web links, names of the sites, and hyperlinks to them.
    (e) An e-mail link to your e-mail address. [*Hint:* Create a hyperlink for "mailto:(your e-mail address)."]

4. Use an HTML editor to create a Web document that describes who you are, your hobbies and interests, and why you are enrolled in this class. Make sure to include graphics and hyperlinks and change the background color. Create an e-mail link to your e-mail address on the page [mailto:(your e-mail address)].

5. Use an HTML editor to create a form that asks for the following input: contact, personal, and date and time that the person completed the form. Change the background color of the form.

6. Use an HTML editor to create a page that promotes a campus or organizational event. Include appropriate graphics and hyperlinks.

7. If available, use another HTML editor to create a Web page. How does this editor differ from the one you normally use? How is it similar?

Vocabulary

audio video interleave (AVI)

audio-file format on UNIX machines (SND, AU)

character-formatting tag

graphical interchange format (GIF)

HTML converter

HTML editor

HTML extensions

HTML tag

HTML utility program

hyperlink tag

hypertext markup language (HTML)

Joint Photographic Experts Group format (JPG or JPEG)

link-specification tag

Macintosh audio information file format (AIFF)

Microsoft Windows audio format (WAV)

Moving Picture Experts Group digital-video standard format (MPG or MPEG)

multimedia (or asset-integration) tag

musical instrument digital interface format (MID or MIDI)

paragraph-formatting tag

quicktime cross-platform video file format (MOV)

single-element tag

structural tag

symmetric tag

wizard

References

Gehris, Dennis, *Microsoft Internet Explorer 5.0*, South-Western Educational Publishing, Cincinnati, OH, 2000.

Gehris, Dennis O., *Using Multimedia Tools and Applications on the Internet*, Wadsworth Publishing, Belmont, CA, 1998.

12

Additional Internet Utilities

I n this chapter we deal with the following Internet utilities: telnet, gopher, archie/FTP search engine, and file transfer protocol (FTP). A definition is provided for each tool as well as an explanation of how each is used.

WHAT YOU WILL LEARN

- Definition of telnet
- How to use telnet
- Definition of gopher
- How to use gopher
- Definition of Archie/FTP search engine
- How to use an FTP search engine
- Definition of file transfer protocol
- How to use file transfer protocol

TELNET DEFINED

When you are working on a computer that is connected to the Internet, you are a part of a system of networks composed of millions of computers. Network administrators design networks to allow users on one computer on the network to access another, connected computer. The Internet allows this to happen through a program called **telnet**. After you use telnet to connect to another computer or subnetwork on the Internet, you are connected directly to the remote site and are able to access files, data, software, and so on. Telnet provides a system of security through login names and passwords, so that people who have access can be controlled. There are frequent stories in the news of people who somehow are able to gain illegal access to company and government networks by entering legitimate, but unauthorized login names and passwords using telnet. There are some sites that don't require a login name and a password and allow anyone to gain access to their computers through telnet.

Telnet operates in a client/server environment in which one host, the computer you are using that is running client telnet, negotiates opening a session on another computer, the remote host running server telnet. During the behind-the-scenes negotiation process, the two computers agree on the parameters governing the session. One of the first things they determine is the terminal type to be used, which is a line-by-line network virtual terminal. **Virtual terminal** refers to a set of terminal characteristics and sequences that both sides of a network connection agree to use to transmit data from terminals across the network, regardless of the terminal used.

Hytelnet uses telnet to reach Internet-accessible sites, including library systems, freenets, bulletin board systems, and other information sites. There are also World Wide Web gateways that are available that contain links to hytelnet sites. One of these is http://www.einet.net/hytelnet/START.TXT .html

■ USING TELNET

Telnet is a program that is built into the UNIX operating system of most computers connected to the Internet. If you are directly connected to UNIX, you enter the word *telnet* and then the name of the remote computer and press the Enter key. If you are successful in connecting to the remote computer, you will be prompted for your login name and password. If you are using Microsoft Windows, it contains a built-in telnet program that can be used easily if you are connected to the Internet. To use it, select "Run" from the Start menu. In the "Open" box, key "telnet://(name of computer)" and click on "OK." A telnet window will appear on which will be login and password prompts (see Figure 12-1). Another way to access Windows telnet is by using a telnet URL through a Web browser using the same syntax.

You can also use a telnet software program that provides a window for you to view the UNIX prompt. There are numerous freeware and shareware programs of this type. One shareware program, CRT, is available for Microsoft Windows. This program allows you to save a list of sites in a session list. When you want to log in to a remote computer, you choose the site from the list. The login name and password prompts then appear.

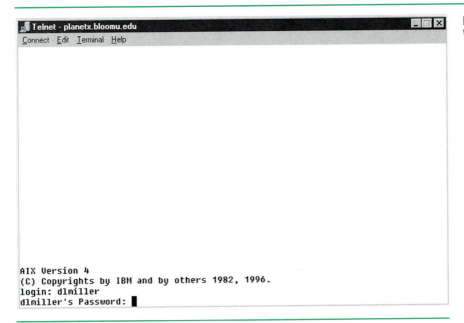

Figure 12-1
Windows Telnet Window

GOPHER DEFINED

Gopher is a UNIX-based, menu-driven program that helps you find files, programs, definitions, and other resources on topics that you specify. It was developed at the University of Minnesota and named after the school's mascot. In fact, the gopher server at Minnesota is referred to as the "mother gopher." Gopher is an older Internet tool, which was developed prior to the World Wide Web and considered by some to be obsolete. However, it is still used by those who prefer a quick, text-based information system. A term associated with gopher is **gopherspace,** which refers to the vast number of servers and areas of interest accessible through the Internet. There are two search mechanisms that work within gopherspace. One, called **veronica,** enables you to search gopherspace by directory titles and resources that match the key words that you supply. **Jughead** is a search service that enables you to search all of gopherspace for key words appearing in directory titles, but not menu items.

USING GOPHER

The easiest way to use gopher is to use it with a Web browser. You simply enter "gopher://(name of gopher server)" as the URL. For example, gopher://gopher.tc.umn.edu will link you to the "mother gopher" at the University of Minnesota, as shown in Figure 12-2. To navigate around in a

Figure 12-2
University of Minnesota Gopher

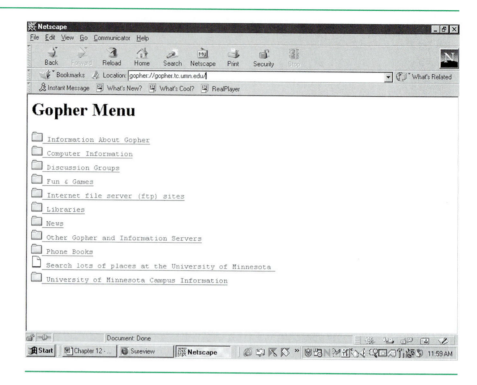

gopher, simply click on the link on a gopher menu line, which will produce another list of items. You continue to click on links until you find a file containing the information that you are seeking. If you are using the Netscape browser, a text file will have a page icon preceding the linked title. Clicking on the title will display the contents of the file on the screen.

The menu item "Other Gopher and Information Servers" or something similar to this will produce a list of additional places where gopher servers can be found arranged by world region (Africa, Asia, North America, etc.). Clicking on any of these will provide a list of countries in each region. If you're searching for a gopher server in the United States, click on "North America," and then "USA," which will display a list of states. Clicking on one of the states will produce a list of servers in the state.

On the University of Minnesota's gopher listing, the veronica search program is also located on "Other Gopher and Information Servers." Note that every gopher is set up differently and the menu items will contain a variety of descriptors, so veronica may be found at a different place. On this gopher, the item "Search All the Gopher Servers in the World" is where veronica is found. Similar to a Web search engine, a search box should appear in which you key a search term representing the information that you are seeking. For example, if you are looking for information on data transmission, you might key the term *modem* in the box and press the "Enter" key (see Figure 12-3).

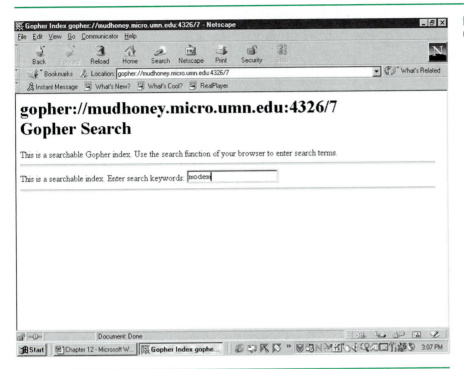

Figure 12-3
Conducting a Veronica Search

ARCHIE AND FTP SEARCH ENGINES DEFINED

Those who desire to make information available to anyone have created files located on servers connected to the Internet. The only problem is that without some way of knowing the server's name and the path or location on the server, these "public" files are useless. In the past, **Archie** was an Internet tool for finding specific files that are available in publicly accessible archives and that can then be retrieved using file transfer protocol (FTP), which is explained in the next section. It has been replaced by other FTP search engines that perform the same functions as Archie once did. Although these are useful utilities, one major drawback is that to retrieve the file, you must know the precise spelling of some or all of the file names.

USING FTP SEARCH ENGINES

The easiest way to use FTP search engines is to key in a URL for an FTP search engine in the "Address" box of a Web browser. Below are some sites for FTP search engines at the time of writing this book. You can use a regular search engine to search on "FTP search." Please note that some FTP search engines are designed to search for specific types of files.

Lycos Advanced FTP Search: http://www.download.lycos.com/static/advanced_search.asp

FTPFind: http://www.ftpfind.com

FTPSearch: http://archie.is.co.za/ftpsearch

FTPSearch: http://www.ftpsearch.de

We'll use the first one on our list—the one at Lycos—as an example to show you how to use an FTP search engine. The utility is very similar to the Archie request forms that were on the Internet when the Archie utility was still being used extensively. The first step is to key in the URL for the FTP search engine in the "Address" box of your browser. In this case it is http://www.download.lycos.com/static/advanced_search.asp. Then press the Enter key. The request form should appear as shown in Figure 12-4.

A search term is keyed in the search-for box, which can either be a file name or a directory title. We'll use ftp.faq ("faq" stands for "frequently asked questions") as the file name we'll be searching, as displayed in Figure 12-5. It is a way of learning about various topics relating to computers and other topics.

It is also necessary to specify the search case. This will tell the search form whether you want to search for the file name or directory exactly as we have

Figure 12-4
Lycos Advanced FTP Search Form.
(©2000 Lycos, Inc. Lycos® is a registered trademark of Carnegie Mellon University. All rights reserved.)

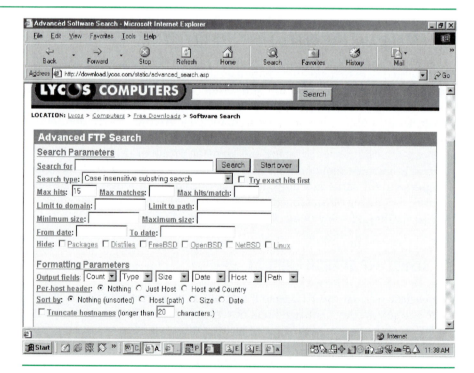

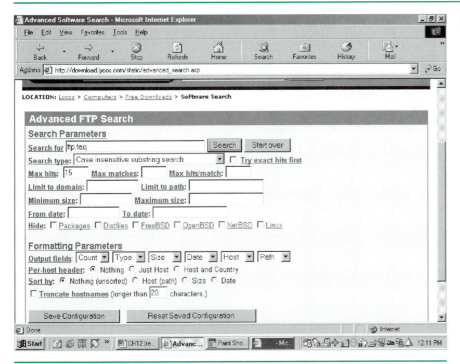

keyed it, and whether it is case sensitive (capital or lowercase letters). In our example we'll click to choose "Case-insensitive substring search" for case. We also need to indicate the output format. This is what the search engine will return when it gives us the results. Selecting "15" as the "Max Hits" will give us the number of hits the server should report. For efficiency across slow networks, it is recommended to keep this number low (100 or less). "Max matches" will indicate the maximum number of matches (unique file names) the server should report. Selecting "Max Hits/match" will give us the ability to limit the number of hits the server should report for each match (unique file name).

It is also possible to limit the search to certain places on the Internet and to specific file sizes and dates. For example, keying edu in the "Limit to domain" block would exclude hits from everywhere *but* *.edu. It is also possible to indicate formatting parameters to let you decide the gateway's output layout. You can have up to six fields, and each field has a selector to let you choose what that field will display. Accepting the defaults for the matches/hits and the formatting parameters and depressing the search button at the top of the form, our search produces the result shown in Figure 12-6. You will notice that the results show the count, type of file, size, date, host, and path. To display the results or save the file, you simply click on the file name on the right side of the path. To display more results, click on the hyperlink for "MORE Results" at the bottom of the form.

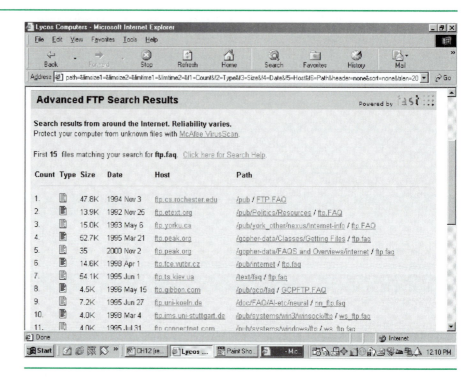

FILE TRANSFER PROTOCOL DEFINED

A **protocol** is the set of rules or conventions by which two machines talk to each other. **File transfer protocol (FTP)** is an Internet standard for the exchange of files between local and remote computers. FTP supports several commands that allow bidirectional transfer of binary and ASCII files between computers. The FTP client is installed with the TCP/IP connectivity utilities. TCP/IP is the protocol that all computers connected to the Internet possess.

USING FILE TRANSFER PROTOCOL

There are several types of FTP servers on the Internet: an **anonymous FTP server** and a **nonanonymous FTP server**. The difference is that with an *anonymous FTP server*, you don't need a special login or password to download files. If you are using the UNIX operating system, anyone who wants to download files simply logs on as "anonymous" and uses his or her e-mail address as the password. With a Web browser, however, you don't need to worry about entering the login or password. As you learned in Chapter 8, you key the FTP URL into the "Address" box of Internet Explorer.

If you are using a *nonanonymous FTP server*, you are required to log on with a validated user name and password. If you don't have a valid login or password, you can't access the files on this type of server. Businesses and educational institutions often establish nonanonymous FTP servers for use by employees that can be used to store files that can be accessed anywhere through an Internet connection.

An FTP utility program can be used to transfer the file from the remote computer to the user's computer. Several types of FTP utility programs can be used. A very commonly used Windows FTP utility program is called WS_FTP (see Figure 12-7).

Before you can search for files, you should understand the different types of files that you will encounter on the Internet. Several major types of files are available. One major type of file is a **text file**. Another name for this type of file is **ASCII** (pronounced "askee"). Text files can be read into most text editors, such as Windows Notepad, and into most word processing programs, such as Microsoft Word and WordPerfect. Text files sometimes, but not always, have the file extension "txt".

The other major type of file that you will encounter on the Internet is a **binary file**. There are several types of binary files. One type is an **application file**, sometimes called an *exec file*, which is an executable file that will run some type of program or routine. These files may have "exe" as the file extension.

Three types of software can be downloaded from the Internet: public domain software, freeware, and shareware. You also need to know that there is

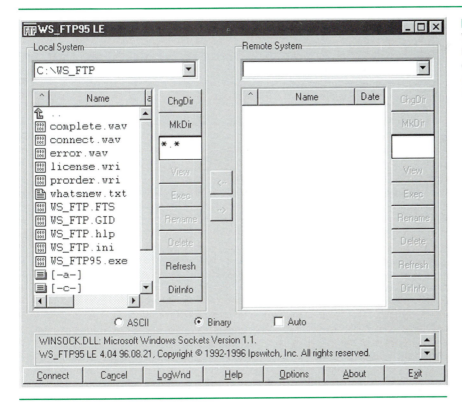

Figure 12-7
WS_FTP Utility Program. *(From Microsoft Internet Explorer 5.0 Textwork Book, 1st edition, © 2000. Reprinted with permission of Course Technology, a division of Thomson Learning. Fax 800-730-2215)*

a difference in terms of what rights you have to use it. For example, **public domain software** is written and made available on the Internet for unrestricted use by anyone. These programs have no copyright. Some commercial software is now also available as public domain software.

Unlike public domain software, **freeware programs** include a copyright and are protected by copyright laws. The authors of these programs grant free, unlimited use to the programs. The only thing that you cannot do is package and resell the programs. With **shareware**, you are able to try the software before you buy it. Sometimes some of the features of the software are not operable until you register and pay for the software. You download the software, install it, and try it for a specified period of time, often 30 days. After the 30-day period, you are expected to send the author or software company the price specified for it. Some software is configured so that it becomes inoperable after the trial period has expired.

Another way to view an anonymous FTP file on the Internet is to use a Web browser. You can do this as long as you know the name of the anonymous FTP server and path (subdirectories). For example, if you happen to know that there are interesting files on the sunsite.unc.edu server with the path /pub/academic/history/marshall/internet, you would key the following URL in Internet Explorer's "Address" box: ftp://sunsite.unc.edu/pub/academic/history/marshall/internet/. After pressing the "Enter" key, the browser will log into the server for you and display the files in this subdirectory as shown in Figure 12-8.

Figure 12-8

FTP Files Displayed in Netscape. *(From Microsoft Internet Explorer 5.0 Textwork Book, 1st edition, © 2000. Reprinted with permission of Course Technology, a division of Thomson Learning. Fax 800-730-2215)*

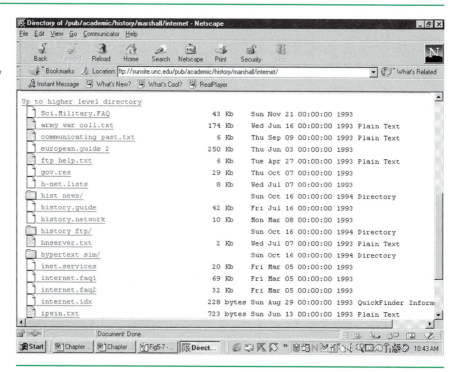

You can then click on the hyperlink to download any file. If it is a text file, the file will be displayed on the screen. If it is a binary file, the "File Download" window will appear to prompt you whether you want to save the file or execute (run) it. If you click on "OK" on the "File Download" window, a "Save As" window will appear. You can indicate the file name, file type, and where you want the file to be saved on your computer. If you also know the server name, subdirectory names, and the file name, you can access the file directly by keying in the full URL: for example, ftp://sunsite.unc.edu/pub/academic/history/marshall/internet/internet.faq2. Sometimes links to files will be placed on Web pages. To download these files, simply click on the hyperlink provided and the "File Download" window should appear.

A **compressed file** is one that has been reduced in size. The reason that this is done is to decrease the amount of time that it takes to download files from an FTP site or Web page. A compressed binary file could also be some type of multimedia file (graphic, audio, or video). Common graphic file extensions are "gif" and "jpg". Common audio file extensions are "wav", "au", and "mid". Common video file extensions are "mov", "avi", and "mpg". Multimedia files do not need to be decompressed to be usable. Another technique that is used to reduce the size of a file considerably without losing any of the original information can be called *regular file compression*.

There are several types of compression techniques, all of which use some type of utility program to compress and decompress a file. Each of these programs uses different algorithms, which are complex mathematical formulas, to make files smaller. Although some programs can decompress in several different styles, it is necessary to download a compression program for each type. Following are some file extensions that identify a few of the more common compression types:

.sit	Stuffit
.cpt	Compact Pro
.zip	Zip
.arc	ARC
.pkg	AppleLink
.gz	GZIP
.tar	TAR
.z	UnizCompress
.uu	Uuencoded
.hqx	BinHex

The most widely used compression/decompression technique for Microsoft Windows is **ZIP**, which produces a zipped file, and the most popular Windows utility is **WinZip**. You will know which files are zipped, because they always have "zip" as the file extension. The WinZip program is an easy way to "unzip" the zipped files that you download from the Internet. It can run independent of a Web browser or will execute the browser automatically when you attempt to link to a zipped file. Figure 12-9 shows the WinZip program.

Figure 12-9
WinZip Program. *(From* Microsoft Internet Explorer 5.0 Textwork Book, 1st edition, *© 2000. Reprinted with permission of Course Technology, a division of Thomson Learning. Fax 800-730-2215)*

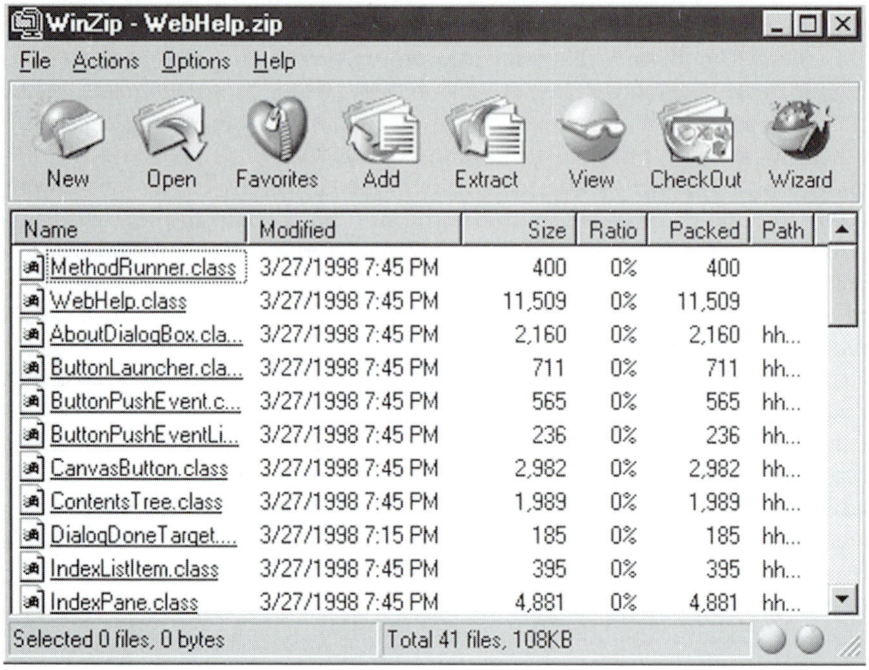
WinZip - WebHelp.zip
File Actions Options Help
New Open Favorites Add Extract View CheckOut Wizard
Name Modified Size Ratio Packed Path
MethodRunner.class 3/27/1998 7:45 PM 400 0% 400
WebHelp.class 3/27/1998 7:45 PM 11,509 0% 11,509
AboutDialogBox.cla... 3/27/1998 7:45 PM 2,160 0% 2,160 hh...
ButtonLauncher.cla... 3/27/1998 7:45 PM 711 0% 711 hh...
ButtonPushEvent.c... 3/27/1998 7:45 PM 565 0% 565 hh...
ButtonPushEventLi... 3/27/1998 7:45 PM 236 0% 236 hh...
CanvasButton.class 3/27/1998 7:45 PM 2,982 0% 2,982 hh...
ContentsTree.class 3/27/1998 7:45 PM 1,989 0% 1,989 hh...
DialogDoneTarget.... 3/27/1998 7:15 PM 185 0% 185 hh...
IndexListItem.class 3/27/1998 7:45 PM 395 0% 395 hh...
IndexPane.class 3/27/1998 7:45 PM 4,881 0% 4,881 hh...
Selected 0 files, 0 bytes
Total 41 files, 108KB

SUMMARY

When you are working on a computer that is connected to the Internet, you are a part of a system of networks composed of millions of computers. Network administrators design networks to allow users on one computer on the network to access another, connected computer. The Internet allows this to happen through a program called telnet. After you use telnet to connect to another computer or subnetwork on the Internet, you are connected directly to the remote site and are able to access files, data, software, and so on. Telnet provides a system of security through login names and passwords, so that the people who have access can be controlled.

Gopher is a UNIX-based, menu-driven program that helps you find files, programs, definitions, and other resources on topics that you specify. It was developed at the University of Minnesota and named after the school's mascot. Gopher is an older Internet tool, which was developed prior to the World Wide Web and considered by some to be obsolete. However, it is still used by those who prefer a quick, text-based information system.

Archie is an Internet tool for finding specific files that are available in publicly accessible archives and that can then be retrieved using file transfer protocol (FTP). Although archie is a useful utility, its one drawback is that to retrieve the file, you must know the precise spelling of some or all of the filenames. Although Archie is no longer widely available, FTP search engines on the Web exist which are similar to Archie. These search engines make it possible to find specific files on the Internet.

A protocol is the set of rules or conventions by which two machines talk to each other. File transfer protocol (FTP) is an Internet standard for the exchange of files between local and remote computers. FTP supports several commands that allow bidirectional transfer of binary and ASCII files between computers. The FTP client is installed with the TCP/IP connectivity utilities. There are several types of FTP servers on the Internet: an anonymous FTP server and a nonanonymous FTP server. The difference is that with an anonymous FTP server, you don't need a special login or password to download files. If you are using a nonanonymous FTP server, you are required to log on with a validated user name and password.

Three types of software can be downloaded from the Internet: public domain software, freeware, and shareware. You need to know that there is a difference in terms of what rights you have to use it. For example, public domain software is written and made available on the Internet for unrestricted use by anyone. These programs have no copyright. Some commercial software is now also available as public domain software. Unlike public domain software, freeware programs include a copyright and are protected by copyright laws. The authors of these programs grant free, unlimited use to the programs. The only thing that you cannot do is package and resell the programs.

With shareware you are able to try the software before you buy it. Sometimes some of the features of the software are not operable until you register and pay for the software. You download the software, install it, and try it for a specified period of time, often 30 days. After the 30-day period, you are expected to send the author or software company the price specified for it.

A compressed file is one that has been reduced in size. The reason that this is done is to decrease the amount of time that it takes to download files from an FTP site or Web page. There are several types of compression techniques, all of which use some type of utility program to compress and decompress a file. Each of these programs uses different algorithms, which are complex mathematical formulas, to make files smaller. Although some programs can decompress in several different styles, it is necessary to download a compression program for each type. The most widely used compression/decompression technique for Microsoft Windows is ZIP, which produces a zipped file, and the most popular Windows utility is WinZip. You will know which files are zipped, because they always have "zip" as the file extension. The WinZip program is an easy way to "unzip" the zipped files that you download from the Internet. It can run independent of a Web browser or will execute the browser automatically when you attempt to link to a zipped file.

QUESTIONS

1. What is telnet?

2. Explain how telnet is used.

3. What is gopher?

4. Explain how gopher is used.

5. What is an FTP search engine?

6. Explain how an FTP search engine is used.

7. What is file transfer protocol (FTP)?

8. How is FTP used?

9. Identify the three types of software that can be downloaded from the Internet.

10. How do the three types of software (public domain, freeware, and shareware) differ in terms of what rights you have to use them?

11. What is a compressed file, and why is it used?

PROJECTS AND PROBLEMS

1. Use a Web browser or telnet utility program to telnet to the U.S. Library of Congress (telnet://locis.loc.gov). No login or password is required for this site. Once you are logged in to this site, choose 3 for "Federal Legislation." Key "browse Internet" to determine the legislation that has been passed that relates to the Internet. Prepare a report that lists the names of the legislation.

2. The Library of Congress also has a Web site (http://www.lcweb.loc.gov). Use a Web browser to link to this site. Click on "Thomas Legislative Information." Do the same search that you conducted in Project 1, keying "Internet" in the search box for the current Congress. Prepare a report that lists the names of the legislation. How did this differ from the search that you conducted in Project 1?

3. Use a Web browser or telnet utility program to connect to Hytelnet (http://www.lights.com/hytelnet). Click on "Search Hytelnet site" and enter "telecommunications." Describe what results.

4. Use a Web browser to link to the gopher at the University of Minnesota (gopher://gopher.tc.umn.edu).* Click on the "Libraries" menu item and then on "Electronic Books." Do a search to determine the number of literary works and their titles that are online for William Shakespeare and display one of his works. [*Note:* There are also electronic books on the Web. One of these sites is at the University of Pennsylvania (http://www.digital.library.upenn.edu/books/).]

5. Use a Web browser to link to the Gopher at the University of Minnesota (gopher://gopher.tc.umn.edu).* Click on the "Other Gopher and Information Servers" and "Search All of the Gopher Servers in the World" menu items. Do a veronica search on the term *telecommunications*. How many

items resulted? Click on one of the links to display the contents. Describe what you were able to display.

6. Use a Web browser to link to the gopher at the University of Minnesota (gopher://gopher.tc.umn.edu).* Click on the "Other Gopher and Information Servers" and the "International Organizations" menu items. Link to two of these organization's gopher servers. How did the menu items differ from the gopher at the University of Minnesota?

7. Use a Web browser to display the Lycos Advanced FTP search form (http://www.download.lycos.com/static/advanced_search.asp). If this link does not work, use one of the other FTP search engines links listed in the chapter. Do a search on "internet.faq." How many hits resulted? Click on one of the links on the right slide of the listing. After the file is displayed on the screen, scroll through it to determine its contents and provide a summary of the contents.

8. Open a Web browser and link to one of the following software archives using FTP. If none of these URLs work, ask your instructor for additional URLs.

    Metalab Software Archive: ftp://metalab.unc.edu/pub
    Garbo Anonymous FTP archive: ftp://garbo.uwasa.fi
    Washington University software archive: ftp://wuarchive.wustl.edu

    Find a software program and click on the filename to download it.

9. If you have a FTP utility program such as WS_FTP available, use the utility to link to one of the software archive sites in Project 8. Find a software program and click on the filename to download it.

Note: If the University of Minnesota gopher is not available, use a search engine to search on "gopher server" to find another gopher site.

Vocabulary

anonymous FTP server

application file

archie

binary file

compressed file

file transfer protocol (FTP)

freeware program

FTP search engine

gopher

gopherspace

hytelnet

jughead

nonanonymous FTP server

protocol

public domain software

shareware

telnet

text file (or ASCII)

veronica

virtual terminal

WinZip

zipped file

References

Ackerman, Ernest, *Learning to Use the World Wide Web*, Franklin, Beedle & Associates, Wilsonville, OR, 1997.

Gehris, Dennis, *Microsoft Internet Explorer 5.0*, South-Western Educational Publishing, Cincinnati, OH, 2000.

PART FOUR

Networking Fundamentals

This section covers three topics: introduction to networks, telecommunication models and network connectivity and telephony. Included are a discussion of data communications, types of networks, network topologies, protocols, transmission media, standards organizations, telecommunication models, and network connectivity. The section concludes with information on telephony technology and a discussion of advances that will allow the Internet to support voice and video as a dedicated telephone connection.

13

Introduction to Networks

In this chapter, an introduction to networks, we discuss types of networks, data transmission, and transmission media. The chapter concludes with a discussion of international and national standard-setting organizations regulating the industry. Common terminology that will help build a foundation is also introduced.

WHAT YOU WILL LEARN

- Definition of a network
- How data are transmitted
- Types of networks
- Types of transmission media
- Roles of standard-setting organizations

ELECTRONIC COMMUNICATIONS TECHNOLOGY

For this discussion on network fundamentals, **electronic communications** refers to the electronic transfer of information from one location to another. Data communications (datacom), telecommunications (telecom), and networking all fall under the communications umbrella.

■ NETWORK DEFINITION

A **network** can be defined as a system that transmits any combination of voice, video, and/or data between users. A network is made up of servers, workstations, a network operating system, and a communications link. It also includes the cables and all supporting hardware, such as bridges, routers, and switches. In wireless systems, antennas and towers are also part of the network. Each component of the network that has a unique address is a **node**. The term **node** includes a workstation, fax, printer, and/or server.

■ ARCHITECTURE

The term *architecture* refers to a design; specifically, it can refer to either hardware or software or a combination of both. When used in discussing a network, it refers to a system and defines its broad outlines or its precise mechanisms. An **open architecture** allows the system to be connected easily to devices made by other manufacturers and software programs developed by other vendors. An open architecture uses off-the-shelf components that conform to approved standards. In contrast, a system with a **closed architecture** is one whose design is proprietary, making it difficult to connect the system to other systems.

Network architecture is described as either client/server or peer/peer (see Figure 13-1). On a **client/server network** each computer is designated as a client or a server. A **server** is a powerful computer dedicated to managing files, printers, or network traffic. **Clients** are personal computers or workstations that run applications; there are two types of clients, **thin clients** and **fat clients**. A *thin client* is a computer on a network designed to access a server for all of its functions. It connects to the server to process applications, access files, and print. In contrast, a *fat client* is a computer on the network designed to operate with or without access to the server. It uses its internal memory and processing power to run applications and store information.

In contrast, a **peer/peer network** also allows any client to be a server. A client/server network has a number of advantages over a peer/peer network. A client/server network is generally more flexible, with more opportunities to upgrade, has more software written for this format, allows administrators better control, is almost infinitely expandable, and is more secure from unauthorized access. However, a client/server network does have its disadvantages; they are more expensive to operate and harder to set up. The decision to configure either client/server or peer/peer depends on the

Figure 13-1
Client/Server versus Peer/Peer Network

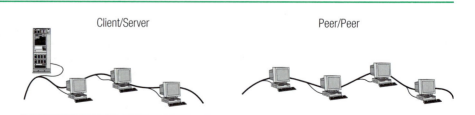

Client/Server   Peer/Peer

number of users, the degree of security desired, the distance separating the users, and the budget available.

■ DATA COMMUNICATIONS AND TELECOMMUNICATIONS DEFINED

The terms *data communications* and *telecommunications* are often used interchangeably; however, they are not synonymous. **Telecommunications** is communications via electronic, electromagnetic, or phontonic means over a distance. The information communicated includes data, text, pictures, voice, and video over long distances using such means as telephone, radio, and television. *Telecommunications* or *telecom* refers to a mix of voice and data, both analog and digital. **Data communications** is actually a specialized subset of telecommunications. It refers to digital transmission of text, voice, and video in binary form from one computer to another and is accomplished through the use of telecommunications technology.

A discussion of electronic transmission of data must include the concepts of **signals**, a pulse or frequency on a wire or fiber that is used to control something in a circuit. Control signals are often carried on dedicated lines that have a singular purpose, such as starting or stopping a function.

A **bit** is short for a binary digit represented by either a 0 or 1 in the binary number system. It is the smallest unit of information handled by a computer. The **bit rate** [bits per second (bps)] refers to the data transfer speed within the computer or between the computer and a peripheral. It also refers to the data transmission speed in a network.

A **baud** is a measure of data-transmission speed named after the French engineer Jean-Maurice-Émile Baudot. It is a measure of the speed of the oscillation of the sound wave on which a bit of data is carried over telephone lines. The **baud rate**, the signaling rate of a line, is the number of signal changes that occur in 1 second. The term has often been used erroneously to specify bits per second; however, only at very low speeds is baud equal to bps.

Frequency refers to the number of vibrations (oscillations) per second and is measured in hertz (Hz), which is the same as oscillations per second or cycles per second.

Bandwidth is the transmission capacity of an electronic line such as a communications network, computer bus, or computer channel. It refers to the amount of data that can be transmitted in a fixed amount of time. It is expressed in bits per second, bytes per second, or in hertz (cycles per second). When expressed in hertz, the frequency may be a greater number than the actual bits per second, because the bandwidth is the difference between the lowest and highest frequencies transmitted.

Baseband is a type of digital data transmission in which each medium (wire) carries only one signal, or channel, at a time. In contrast, **broadband** transmission enables a single wire to carry multiple signals simultaneously. Most communications involving computers uses baseband transmission. This includes communications from the computer to devices such as printers and monitors, communications via modems, and the majority of networks.

Modem is an acronym for modulator–demodulator. A modem is a device or program that enables a computer to transmit data over telephone lines. Computer information is stored digitally, whereas information transmitted over telephone lines is transmitted in the form of analog waves. A modem converts between these two forms. The term may also refer to higher-speed cable or DSL modems or to ISDN terminal adapters, which are all digital and technically not modems. A modem is an analog-to-digital and digital-to-analog converter. It also dials the line, answers the call, and controls transmission speed. Whatever the top speed, some numbers of lower speeds are always supported, so that the modem can accommodate earlier modems or negotiate downward on noisy lines.

For hookup to a personal computer, an internal modem needs a free expansion slot, while an external modem requires a free serial port or USB port. The software required to drive a modem is included in the operating system. Modems have built-in error correction and data compression. They also have automatic feature negotiation, which adjusts to the other modem's speed and hardware protocols.

■ TYPES OF NETWORKS

The different channels of communications, air or cable, available to transport data allow for a variety of network types to be formed. Network types are identified based on the distance of the communications as well as the channel selected. Three types of networks that we will distinguish among include local area networks, metropolitan area networks, and wide area networks.

A **local area network (LAN)** serves users within a confined geographic area, within either a building or a complex. It is composed of computers and peripheral devices linked by cable, either coaxial, twisted pair, or fiber. LANs can vary in size, but the key component of the definition is that all the computers on the network are grouped together in some fashion and connected (see Figure 13-2). Typically, LANs use a bus topology; they can also be connected using ring, star, or a hybrid topology.

Figure 13-2
Local Area Network

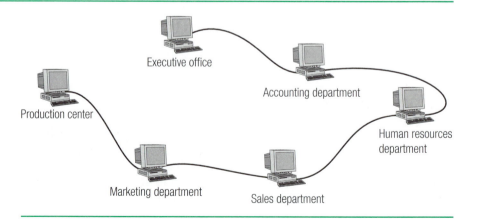

The computers on a LAN are typically PCs or **workstations** linked to each other to share resources, including application software packages, input/output devices, group scheduling, electronic mail, and storage devices. This sharing of resources quickly and efficiently is the main reason that companies are incorporating LANs into the environment.

A "thin processing" client in a client/server environment performs very little data processing. The client processes only keyboard input and screen output, and all application processing is done in the server. A client machine in a client/server environment is one that performs most or all of the application processing with little or none performed in the server.

A LAN may be linked to other LANs or to larger networks using a device called a **network gateway**. This gateway allows one LAN to be connected to the LAN of another office or group.

A **metropolitan area network (MAN)** generally covers a specific geographic area such as a city or suburb. It is considered the next step up from the LAN. A **wide area network (WAN)** is a communications network that covers a wide geographic area, such as state or country. These networks are also worldwide using microwave relays and satellites to reach users over long distances. The most widely used WAN is the Internet.

■ DATA TRANSMISSION MODES

Data transmission is affected by several factors, including speed or bandwidth, serial or parallel transmission, direction of data flow, modes of transmitting data, and protocols. Bandwidth is the transmission capacity of an electronic line such as a communications network, computer bus, or computer channel. It is expressed in bits per second, bytes per second, or in hertz (cycles per second). As discussed earlier, bandwidth is defined either as baseband or broadband, depending on the transmission capability of the channel (see Figure 13-3).

Data flows between devices in one of three ways (see Figure 13-4):

1. **Simplex** is a one-way transmission of data, similar to the movement of traffic on a one-way street. Data travel in one direction only. Consequently, simplex is not often used in data communication systems

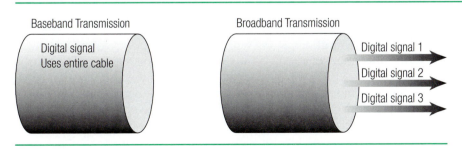

Baseband Transmission

Digital signal
Uses entire cable

Broadband Transmission

Digital signal 1
Digital signal 2
Digital signal 3

Figure 13-3
Baseband versus Broadband
Transmission

Figure 13-4
Data Flow

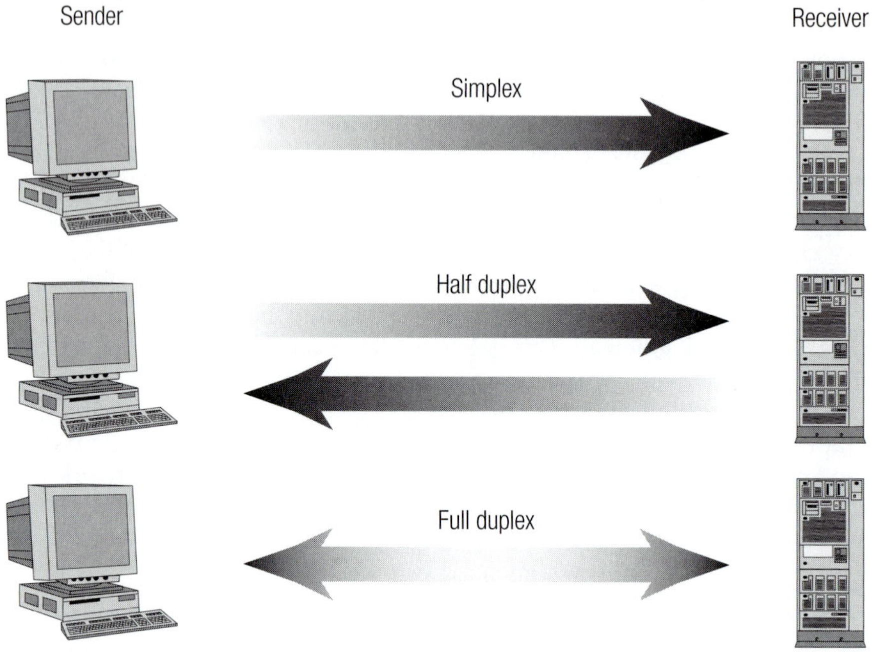

Sender   Receiver

Simplex

Half duplex

Full duplex

today. A typical instance for its use is **point-of-sale (POS) terminals** in which data are only being entered. These systems use personal computers or specialized terminals that are combined with cash registers, bar code readers, optical scanners, and magnetic stripe readers for capturing the transaction instantly and accurately. Point-of-sale systems may be online to a central computer for credit checking and inventory updating, or they may be stand-alone machines that store the daily transactions until they can be delivered or transmitted to the main computer for processing.

2. **Half-duplex** is the transmission of data in both directions, but only one direction at a time. This resembles traffic flow on a one-way bridge. Two-way radio was the first to use half-duplex transmission methods. For example, while one party spoke, the other party listened. Half-duplex is common today and uses telephone lines to link microcomputers with other microcomputers, minicomputers, and mainframes. An example of this type of transmission is the use of an electronic bulletin board through your microcomputer.

3. **Full-duplex** transmission is sending and receiving data simultaneously. It is likened to traffic on a two-way street and is the fastest and most efficient form of two-way communication. In pure digital networks, this is achieved with two pairs of wires. In analog networks or in digital networks using carriers, it is achieved by dividing the bandwidth of the line into two frequencies, one for sending and the other for receiving.

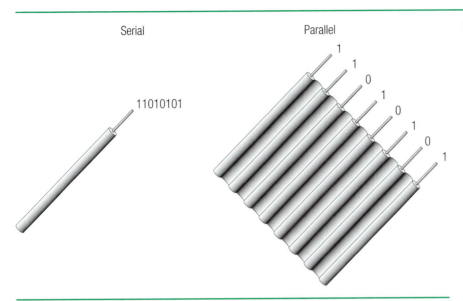

Serial

Parallel

11010101

1
1
0
1
0
1
0
1

Figure 13-5
Serial versus Parallel Transmission

Data travel between devices in one of two ways (see Figure 13-5):

1. In **serial transmission**, data flow in a continuous stream. Each bit travels on its own communication line, much like cars traveling on a one-way street. Phone companies most commonly use this type of transmission. The serial connector on a microcomputer is called a *serial port*; technically, this port is called an RS-232C connector or an asynchronous communications port.

2. In **parallel transmission**, data flow through separate communications lines, much like cars on a multilane highway. Parallel transmission is commonly used to send data from a CPU to a printer. Typically, this type of transmission is limited to short-distance communications.

Data are packaged or arranged for transmission in one of two ways (see Figure 13-6):

1. **Asynchronous transmission** sends data packages of one character or byte at a time. Each character is surrounded by a start and stop bit and includes a parity bit used for error checking. The start and stop bit notifies the receiving device that a character is between them. These bits help identify where each character starts and stops. Asynchronous transmission is often used for terminals with slow speeds. Its advantage is convenient transmission for the sender; its disadvantage is a slow rate of transfer. Because it is less expensive, it is more popular than synchronous transmission.

2. **Synchronous transmission** sends data in packages of more than one character or byte at a time. A header and a trailer byte surround each package of characters. The sending and receiving of the data packages

Figure 13-6
Asynchronous versus Synchronous
Transmission

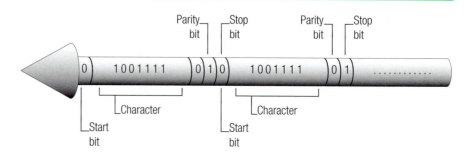

Asynchronous transmission

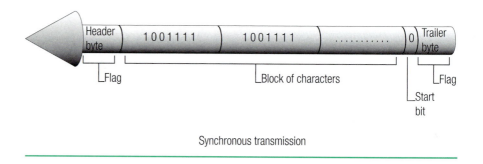

Synchronous transmission

must occur at carefully timed intervals. Its advantage is speed; its disadvantage is the cost of the equipment. Synchronous transmission is best used for high-speed/high-volume data communications.

■ COMMUNICATION MEDIA

Several types of communications media are used for linking microcomputers together for transmitting data. Specifically, this technology includes twisted pair (telephone lines), coaxial cable, fiber optic cable, microwave, and satellite. Each has distinct characteristics, advantages, and disadvantages. The medium selected is determined by such factors as purpose, cost, and expansion potential.

Twisted pair cable has been the standard transmission medium for both voice and data; it is, however, being phased out by more advanced and reliable media. Twisted pair is made of copper, is inexpensive, is easy to install, and is available as either unshielded twisted pair (UTP) or shielded twisted pair (STP). Both UTP and STP use RJ-45 (telephone connectors) to connect to a computer (see Figure 13-7).

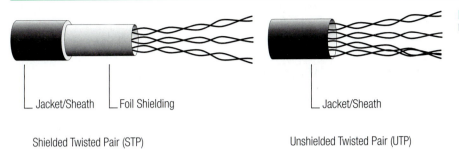

Figure 13-7
UTP and STP Twisted-Pair Cable

Unshielded twisted pair, the most popular type of cable, consists of two unshielded wires twisted around each other. Due to its low cost, UTP cabling is used extensively for local area networks (LANs) and telephone connections. UTP cabling does not offer as high bandwidth or as good protection from interference as do coaxial or fiber optic cables, but it is less expensive and easier to work with. UTP usually refers to unshielded twisted pair cable as specified in the Electronic Industries Association and the Telecommunications Industries Association (EIA/TIA) 568 Commercial Building Telecommunications Wiring Standard. Additionally, EIA/TIA-568 specifies the color coding, cable diameter, and other electrical characteristics, such as:

- **Cross-talk**, which occurs when a signal in one line interferes with the signal in another line. Since this is measured as how many *decibels* (dB) quieter the induced signal is than the original interfering signal, larger numbers are better.
- **Attenuation**, the loss of signal strength that begins to occur as a signal travels farther along a copper cable. Since this is measured as decibels of attenuation, smaller numbers are better.

This standard specifies five categories of twisted pair (see Table 13-1). In addition, the EIA/TIA is developing standards for an addendum to category 5, as well as categories 6 and 7; these specifications are for twisted-pair cabling required for gigabit Ethernet. Category 6 is specified to 155 Mbps and category 7 to 1000 Mbps.

Table 13-1
Twisted-Pair Categories

Category	Characteristics (megabits per second)	Uses
1	None	Analog voice, alarm systems
2	1	Digital voice, low-speed data
3	16	10BASE-T Ethernet, 100BASE-T4, 100 VG-AnyLAN, minimum standard for new installations
4	20	Not widely used
5	100	100BASE-TX, most popular for new installations

Shielded twisted pair uses a woven copper braid jacket and foil wrap between and around the wire pairs, and internal twisting of the pairs. These enhancements give STP excellent insulation to protect the transmitted data from crosstalk. STP is less susceptible to electrical interference and supports higher transmission rates over longer distances than UTP.

Twisted-pair cable is the transmission medium of choice if your LAN is under budget constraints and a relatively easy installation with simple computer connections is desired. Twisted pair should not be used if the transmission integrity of data over long distances at high speed is a necessity.

Coaxial cable (coax) was, at one time, the most widely used network cabling because of its inexpensive cost and ease to work with. This medium supports voice, data, image, and multimedia transmissions. Coax consists of a solid copper core surrounded by insulation, a braided metal shielding, and an outer cover. One layer of foil insulation and one layer of braided metal shielding are referred to as *dual shielded*; two layers of foil insulation and two layers of braided metal shielding are referred to as *quad shielded*. The shielding protects transmitted data by absorbing stray electronic signals so they do not distort the data. Coaxial cable is more resistant to interference and attenuation than is twisted-pair cabling (see Figure 13-8).

There are two types of coaxial cable. Thick coaxial cable (**thicknet**) is made with a single copper wire at the center surrounded by a layer of insulation covered with braided metal shielding. It is a rigid coaxial cable about 0.5 inch in diameter that can carry a signal for approximately 1640 feet (500 meters). Because of its ability to support data transfer over longer distances, it is sometimes used as a backbone to connect several thinnet (thin coaxial cable)-based networks. Its advantages include excellent resistance to interference; its disadvantages include cost and difficulty to work with. **Thinnet**, which looks very similar, has a single copper wire at the center that is covered with less insulation. Thinnet can carry a signal approximately 607 feet (185 meters) before the signal begins to suffer from attenuation. It advantages

Figure 13-8
Coaxial Cable

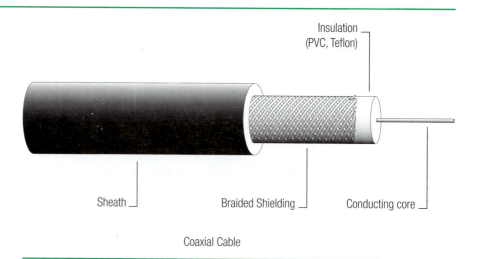

Insulation
(PVC, Teflon)

Sheath   Braided Shielding   Conducting core

Coaxial Cable

include its lower cost and ease of installation; its disadvantages include less resistance to interference.

Both thicknet and thinnet use the BNC (British naval connector) to connect the cable and the computer. The important components in the BNC family include (1) a BNC cable connector, which is crimped to the end of a cable; (2) a BNC T connector, which joins the network interface card to the network cable; (3) a BNC barrel connector, which joins two lengths of thinnet cable to make one longer cable; and (4) a BNC terminator, which closes each end of the cable to absorb stray signals (see Figure 13-9).

Coaxial cable is the transmission medium of choice for transmitting voice, video, and data over longer distances. It is a familiar technology that offers reasonable data security.

Fiber optic cable is constructed from strands of glass or plastic surrounded by protective insulation. The strand of glass at the center, called the **core**, is surrounded by a glass tube called the **cladding**. This cable supports nearly error-free transmission of data encoded as pulses of light traveling at speeds in excess of 100 Mbps. Fiber optic cable can be tapped only with a physical tap, thus making it more difficult for data to be stolen.

Fiber optic cable should be selected if you need to transmit data at very high speeds over long distances in a very secure medium. It is often used for the backbone of a long-distance network, with twisted pair cabling providing the local links. This cable transmission medium should not be selected if you are under a tight budget and do not have expertise available for proper installation (see Figure 13-10).

Microwaves use high-frequency radio waves that travel through the air in straight lines at 1 GHz and above. Microwave transmission is a good

Figure 13-9
BNC Connector Family

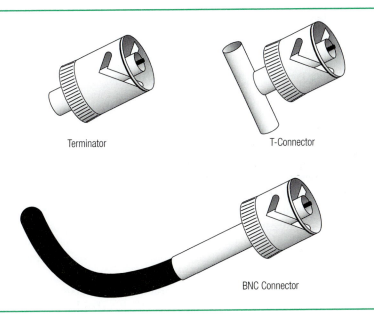

Terminator   T-Connector

BNC Connector

Figure 13-10
Fiber Optic Cable

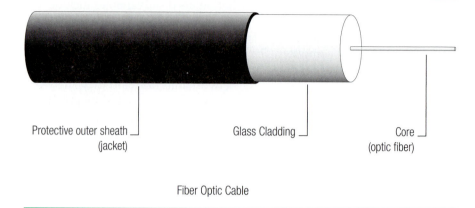

Protective outer sheath   Glass Cladding   Core
(jacket)   (optic fiber)

Fiber Optic Cable

medium for sending data between line-of-sight buildings. For long-distance transmission, "dishes" or antennas must relay the waves. They are commonly used in wireless LANs.

Satellites orbit above Earth and receive, amplify, and redirect analog and digital signals contained within a carrier frequency. There are three kinds of satellites:

1. Geostationary (GEO) satellites, which are in orbit 22,282 miles above the earth and rotate with the earth, thus appearing stationary
2. Low-earth orbit (LEO) satellites, which reside no more than 1000 miles above the earth and revolve around the globe every couple of hours
3. Medium-earth orbit (MEO) satellites, which are in the middle, taking about 6 hours to orbit Earth and remaining in view for a couple of hours

The hundreds of commercial satellites in orbit provide services for both industry and consumers (see Figure 13-11).

■ NETWORK STANDARDS ORGANIZATIONS

Standards are documented agreements that contain technical specifications and/or other precise criteria to be used consistently as rules, guidelines, or definitions. Standards contribute to making life simpler and to increasing the reliability of the goods we use. The networking industry is governed by standards, with several international and national organizations taking the lead; they include the following.

The **International Organization for Standardization (ISO)** is a nongovernmental organization established in 1947. It is composed of national standards bodies from over 130 countries with the mission of promoting the development of standardization and cooperation in the areas of intellectual, scientific, technological, and economic activity.

The **International Telecommunications Union–Telecommunication Organization (ITU)**, headquartered in Geneva, Switzerland, is an international

Figure 13-11
Satellite Communications. *(Courtesy of Johnson Space Center Office of Earth Sciences.)*

organization within which governments and the private sector coordinate global telecom networks and services. This organization, formally the CCITT (Comité Consultatif Internationale de Télégraphie et Téléphonie), recommends telecommunications standards, including audio compression/decompression standards and the V standards for modem speed and compression.

The **American National Standards Institute (ANSI)** is a private, nonprofit organization founded in 1918. Its mission is to administer and coordinate U.S. voluntary standardization and conformity assessment. ANSI does not develop standards; rather, it facilitates standards development by establishing consensus among qualified groups.

The **Electronic Industries Alliance and the Telecommunications Industries Association (EIA/TIA)**, based in Washington, DC, is most active in developing data and voice cabling standards and has the support of all the major vendors of cabling products. EIA, accredited by the ANSI, provides a forum for industry to develop standards and publications in major technical areas of electronic components, consumer electronics, electronic information, and telecommunications. TIA represents providers of communications and information technology products and services for the global marketplace through its core competencies in standards development, domestic and international advocacy, and market development and trade promotion programs.

▓ SUMMARY

When you are working on a computer that is part of a network, you are an integral part of the communications systems of an organization. A network includes servers, workstations, an operating system, a communications link, and transmission media. Antennas and towers are included as components in a wireless network. Networks can be configured as either client/server or peer/peer, depending on the size, needs, and budget of the organization.

In addition, the distance the communications travel and the channel of communications selected further defines a network as a local area network (LAN), metropolitan area network (MAN), or wide area network (WAN). The bandwidth, the type of transmission, and the direction of data flow affect data transmission over the network. A variety of transmission media is available for use in a network; media include twisted-pair cable, coaxial cable, fiber optic cable, microwave, and satellite. The organization selects its transmission media based on purpose, cost, and expansion potential.

The network industry is constantly changing and evolving. This dynamic industry is governed by standards set by several international and national organizations. Leaders in the area of standard setting are the International Organization for Standardization, the International Telecommunications Union–Telecommunication Organization, the American National Standards Institute, the Electronic Industries Alliance, and the Telecommunications Industries Association. Their purpose is to oversee and make recommendations for maintaining quality throughout the network industry.

QUESTIONS

1. What are the major differences between a client/server network and a peer/peer network?

2. Discuss the differences between LAN, WAN, and MAN networks.

3. Give an example of a POS terminal that you have used.

4. Describe the difference between asynchronous transmission and synchronous transmission.

5. What is twisted-pair cable?

6. Name the categories of twisted-pair cable and give one use for each category.

7. What is coaxial cable?

8. How is the coaxial cable connected to the computer?

9. What are the advantages of fiber optic cable?

10. Name two organizations that have developed standards for the networking industry.

PROJECTS AND PROBLEMS

1. A small organization with two departments recently began networking by installing peer/peer networks in each department. Three individuals in one department are working on a project. Each has a different set of responsibilities, but they all produce documentation for their part of the project. Each person has made the hard drive on his or her computer available to the others working on the project. As the project grows, each person produces more documents. There is some question about who has which documents and who was the last person to change the documents. In addition, people who are not directly involved in the project are asking to see the completed material.

(a) Why is there a problem concerning who has which document?
(b) What one thing could you change that would give you centralized control of access to the documents?
(c) Describe one change your solution will bring to the users' environment.

2. The organization you are working for has a 20-user, thinnet, coaxial bus network that has been in use for about a year. Three new client computers were added to the network over the weekend. When you arrived at work on Monday morning, nobody could access the server.

(a) List two things that could cause the network not to function.

(b) What could you do to resolve each of the two possible causes you listed ?

(c) What will be the impact of each of your solutions on network users (assuming that they repair the problem)?

3. This exercise contains the steps for assembling and testing unshielded twisted-pair cable. Before you start, ask your instructor for the following tools and supplies:

- Twisted-pair cable
- Wire cutters
- Crimping tool
- Cable stripper
- Two cable ends (RJ45)
- Twisted-pair cable line tester

Steps:

(a) Using wire cutters, cut off a 6-inch piece of twisted-pair cable. Make certain that the ends are cut squarely, not diagonally.

(b) Following the directions below, use the cable stripper to strip off about 1 inch of the outer cable jacket. Insert the cable until it touches the stop. Squeeze the handles and pull the tool so that the cable stays perpendicular to it. If done correctly, the outer insulation of the cable will be removed without damaging the insulation on the inner connectors.

(c) Fan out the wiring pairs into the following sequence: orange pair, green pair, blue pair, and brown pair.

(d) Untwist the cables, making sure that you have the following sequence from left to right:

(1) White with orange stripes
(2) Solid orange
(3) White with green stripes
(4) Solid green
(5) White with blue stripes
(6) Solid blue
(7) White with brown stripes
(8) Solid brown

All cables should be in a straight line (see Figure 13-12). Grab the cables with one hand and bend north to south and east to west to get cable straighter.

(e) Use the wire cutters and cut across the top of the wires to have a distance of about $\frac{1}{2}$ inch on top. The cable wires need to be exactly the same length as the plastic head.

(f) Hold the plastic head copper side up (there are eight stripes of cable) and gently slide the wire into the plug, making sure that the wires remain in the proper sequence.

(g) Check again to make sure that each pair is in the proper sequence.

(h) With the crimping tool in your hand, notice the well area. You will slide the plastic head pointing down into the crimping tool.

Figure 13-12
Twisted Pair Cable Showing
Untwisted Cables

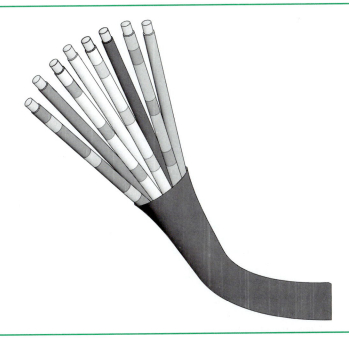

(i) Squeeze the crimping tool until the handles touch and you hear a click (push very hard). Take the cable out and check it visually.

(j) If you are satisfied with the results, repeat steps (b) to (i) for the other side of the cable.

(k) To test the wires, insert one side of the wiring into the adapter of the line tester and the other side into the other adapter. You need to make sure that the twisted-pair wiring fits into the adapters correctly.

(l) To check to determine that the wiring was completed successfully, push the button on the tester repeatedly and red lights should appear alongside all the numbers.

If red lights appear for the numbers in sequence, you have been successful in making an unshielded twisted-pair eight-pin network cable.

4. Use a Web browser and connect to the Web site of the Electronic Industries Alliance and the Telecommunications Industries Association (EIA/TIA) (http://www.eia.org). What organization is the accrediting agency for the EIA/TIA? What is the mission of the EIA/TIA?

5. Use a Web browser and connect to the search engine of your choice. Locate information about the BNC family of connector components. What tools would you need to make your own cables? What is the cost of these tools?

Vocabulary

American National Standards Institute (ANSI)
asynchronous transmission
attenuation
bandwidth
baseband
baud
baud rate
bit (binary digit)
bit rate (bps)
broadband
cladding
client
client/server network
closed architecture
coaxial cable
core
crosstalk
data communications

electronic communications
Electronic Industries Alliance and the Telecommunications Industries Association (EIA/TIA)
fat client
fiber optic cable
full duplex
frequency
half duplex
International Organization for Standardization (ISO)
International Telecommunications Union—Telecommunication Organization (ITU)
local area network (LAN)
metropolitan area network (MAN)
microwave
modem (modulator–demodulator)
network

network gateway
node
open architecture
parallel transmission
peer/peer network
point-of-sale (POS) terminal
satellite
serial transmission
server
signal
simplex
synchronous transmission
telecommunications (telecom)
thinnet cable
thin client
twisted pair cable
wide area network (WAN)
workstation

References

Campbell, P., *Networking the Small Office*, SYBEX, San Francisco, 1996.

Techencyclopedia, http://www.techweb.com/encyclopedia.

Webopedia On-line Dictionary, http://www.webopedia.com.

Williams, J., and D. Johnson, *A Guide to Microsoft Windows NT Server 4.0 in the Enterprise*, Course Technology, Cambridge, MA, 1999.

14

Telecommunication Models and Network Connectivity

This chapter, a discussion of telecommunication models and network connectivity, includes information on communication models, network topologies, and transmission protocols. It concludes with a discussion of various ways of connecting multiple networks. In addition, common terminology is included.

WHAT YOU WILL LEARN

- How the open systems interconnect model (OSI) operates
- How the transmission control protocol/Internet protocol (TCP/IP) model operates
- How transport protocols are used
- Types of network topologies
- How transmission protocols are used
- How to connect multiple networks

■ NETWORK COMMUNICATION MODELS

Communications protocols make communications possible among the nodes of a network. Protocols are defined as a set of rules that govern communication; they are used to facilitate communications between computers. Protocols are to computers what language is to humans. Because computers of different types from different manufacturers need to communicate, using common protocols is important. For successful communication to take place, both computers must understand the same protocols. Many protocols have layers of standards and procedures to allow for sending data from one computer to another.

In 1983, the International Standards Organization (ISO) developed a model to facilitate the sending and receiving of data between two computers. All major computer and telecommunications vendors support the OSI model. This model works on a layer approach, with each layer responsible for performing certain functions. The **open systems interconnect model (OSI model)** contains seven distinct layers, all of which function seamlessly to facilitate data transmission (see Figure 14-1):

- *Application layer* (layer 7): gives applications access to network services. Examples of applications are file transfer and e-mail.
- *Presentation layer* (layer 6): determines the format used to exchange data among networked computers. It sets standards for systems to provide seamless communication from multiple protocol stacks.
- *Session layer* (layer 5): allows two applications to establish, use, and end a connection called a session. It manages who can transmit data at a certain time and the length of the transmission.
- *Transport layer* (layer 4): ensures that data are delivered error-free and in sequence with no loss, duplication, or corruption. This layer repackages data into smaller chunks or packets for transmission and, at the receiving end, reassembles the message from packets.
- *Network layer* (layer 3): responsible for addressing messages so that they are sent to the correct destination and for translating logical addresses and names into physical addresses. It handles network problems such as packet switching, data congestion, and routing.
- *Data-link layer* (layer 2): takes data frames or messages from the network layer and provides for their actual transmission. It also provides for error-free delivery of data between two computers by using the physical layer. This layer defines the methods used to transmit and receive data on the network and consists of the wiring, devices used to connect the network interface card (NIC) to the wiring, and signaling involved to transmit/receive data.
- *Physical layer* (layer 1): transmits the raw bit stream over the physical cable. It defines cables, cards, and NIC attachments to hardware, and cable attachment to the NIC.

Figure 14-1
OSI Model

The Department of Defense developed a set of protocols in the late 1960s for its **Advanced Research Projects Agency network (ARPAnet)**; this set of protocols was the forerunner to **TCP (transmission control protocol)/IP (Internet protocol)**. TCP/IP is designed to connect a number of different networks designed by different vendors into a network of networks—the Internet. Like other communications protocols, TCP/IP is based on a four-layer reference model. Each layer corresponds to one or more layers in the OSI model (see Figure 14-2).

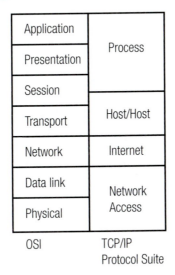

Figure 14-2
Comparison of OSI and TCP/IP Models

- *Application layer:* defines the application protocols and the interface with the transport layer services to use the network.
- *Transport layer:* provides communication session management between host computers. This layer provides either a reliable, flow-controlled connection or an unreliable, faster connection between end nodes.
- *Internet layer:* packages data into IP datagrams that contain source and destination addresses. It discovers how the network segments are interconnected and selects the best path to deliver data from the sending to the receiving computer.
- *Network interface layer:* defines the details of physical sending of data through the network. It includes how hardware devices that interface directly with a network medium signal bits electronically.

The OSI model is the standard for worldwide communications that defines a framework for implementing protocols in seven layers. **Protocols** are rules for transmitting and receiving data over a network; they govern communication and interaction between computers. There are many different protocols, each having a different purpose and accomplishing a different task. Protocols work at various layers in the OSI model, and several may work together in a suite or stack. A **protocol stack** is a combination of protocols each with a specific function working in a different layer. The OSI model defines what protocols should be used at each layer.

■ TRANSPORT PROTOCOLS

Transport protocols provide for communication sessions between computers and ensure that data are able to move reliably between computers. Several popular transport protocols that are used today include:

- *TCP (transmission control protocol):* the TCP/IP protocol for transmitting and translating data between two computers.
- *SPX (sequential packet exchange):* part of Novell's IPX/SPX suite that controls such processes as handling lost packets.
- *NWLink:* the Microsoft version of the IPX/SPX protocol. It enables Windows clients to access NetWare servers and NetWare clients to access Windows NT servers.
- *NetBEUI [NetBIOS (network basic input/output system) extended user interface)]:* developed by IBM to establish communication sessions between computers (NetBIOS) and provide data transport services (NetBEUI). Although a **nonroutable protocol** (messages must be transferred via a bridge), it is one of the fastest protocols.
- *ATP (AppleTalk transaction protocol) and NBP (name binding protocol):* Apple's communication session and data transport protocols.

◼ NETWORK PROTOCOLS

Network protocols handle addressing and routing information, error checking, and retransmission requests. They define the rules for communicating in a particular networking environment such as Ethernet or token ring and ensure that data are transmitted whole, in sequence, and without error. The most popular network protocols today include:

- *IP (Internet protocol):* the TCP/IP protocol for packet forwarding
- *IPX (internetwork packet exchange):* NetWare's protocol for packet forwarding
- *NWLink:* Microsoft's version of the IPX/SPX protocol
- *NetBEUI:* a transport protocol that provides services for NetBIOS sessions
- *DDP (datagram delivery protocol):* an AppleTalk data transport protocol

◼ NETWORK TOPOLOGIES

Networking, connecting multiple nodes to facilitate information sharing, allows one computer to send information to and receive information from another computer. To understand the mechanics of networking, you must first understand the various network *topologies.* Two different and distinct topologies—physical and logical—are part of the network environment. **Physical topology** refers to the physical layout and describes how computers connect to each other. This topology includes cables, connectors, NICs, and hubs. It describes how the network is structured or configured and shows the configuration of the hardware as well as which pair of nodes can communicate. **Logical topology** describes how signals pass between nodes. There are three primary types of topologies: bus, star, and ring.

Physical Topologies

Bus topology is a cable-efficient way of connecting nodes on a network. The cable runs from computer to computer, making each one a line in a chain; it is commonly referred to as *daisy chaining.* Bus topology can be connected in two different ways, **thick Ethernet** (10Base5) and **thinnet** (10Base2), depending on the type of cable connecting the network (see Figures 14-3 and 14-4).

Thick Ethernet, generally yellow, is used as a backbone for the network. A thinner cable called a **drop** runs to the network's nodes. A device called a **transceiver** connects the thinner cable to the thicknet cable. This type of configuration is normally found in mainframe and minicomputer networks. A **terminator** is attached to each end of the LAN to stop the signal from going back in the other direction.

Thinnet cable, on the other hand, connects all network devices directly. Thinnet uses a more flexible coaxial cable and is becoming more popular as a network topology. Adding or removing nodes from the network is easy because devices are daisy-chained along the network bus. At each end of the

Figure 14-3
Physical Thicknet Topology.
T, terminator.

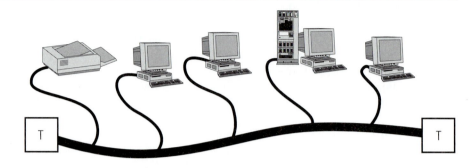

cable is a terminator. This topology is most appropriate when linked devices are physically close to one another.

The physical bus topology has one main advantage—it is cable efficient and thus can save money on one of the most expensive network parts. It is, however, difficult to implement if the network nodes are not lined neatly in a row. Troubleshooting is another disadvantage. If one node is down, the network cannot relay messages and stops. To find the problem, you may need to check every node prior to determining the problem.

Ring topology is not often found in a LAN environment. A ring is a circle with no ends. Since it has no beginning or ending points, it does not use terminators. Because of the circular configuration, it is very difficult to install the cabling. The ring has all the disadvantages of the physical bus (see Figure 14-5).

Star topology uses the server as the center of attention and incorporates a **hub**, a **multistation access unit** (**MAU**), or a **concentrator** to provide a centralized location where all cables in the physical star meet. Each node on the network comes directly to the server through the hub and can talk to any other node that is connected (see Figure 14-6).

The star topology is easy to troubleshoot. If one node does not work, the problem usually lies somewhere between the port on the hub and the node to which it is physically attached. If none of the nodes are working, the problem

Figure 14-4
Physical Thinnet Topology. T, terminator.

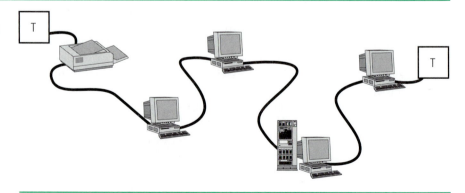

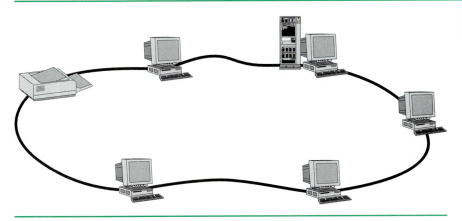

Figure 14-5
Physical Ring Topology

probably is with the server. The biggest disadvantage to the star topology is the cost associated with the amount of cabling needed to join the nodes.

Logical Topologies

Logical, or electrical, topologies describe the way a network transmits information from one node to the next. Bus topology, commonly referred to as **Ethernet**, is the most widely used local area network (LAN) access method, defined by the IEEE in the 802.3 standard; it follows a simple set of rules that govern its operation. Ethernet uses a common pathway between all devices. The pathway that connects the nodes along a common cable is called a **net-**

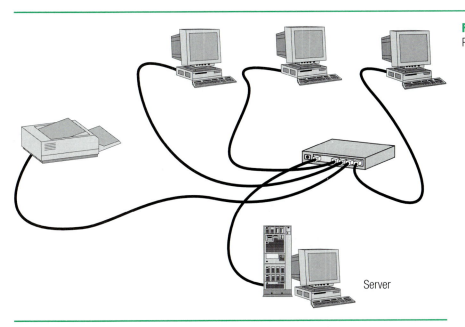

Figure 14-6
Physical Star Topology

Server

work bus. All nodes on the segment share the total bandwidth, which is 10 Mbps (Ethernet), 100 Mbps (fast Ethernet) or 1000 Mbps (gigabit Ethernet). Each node has a unique address that identifies the equipment. No two nodes should ever have the same address.

Every workstation can send out data across the medium in variable-sized chunks called **frames** or **packets**. Any packet or frame transmitted on the network must conform to a strict format, data link layer frame format, which the network type uses for arranging data. Ethernet transmits variable-length frames from 72 to 1518 bytes in length, each containing a header with the addresses of the source and destination stations and a trailer that contains error correction data. Ethernet is a data link protocol and functions at layers 1 and 2 of the OSI model (see Figure 14-7).

A workstation listens to see if another workstation is using the network; if not, the workstation broadcasts. The packet is broadcast to all nodes at the same time. Data are transmitted serially (one bit after the other) over the cable. All nodes will examine the packet to check the destination address. If the packet is not intended for the node, the contents are not examined and the packet is discarded. Only the destination node responds to the signal and accepts the packet.

The biggest problem with the broadcast method is distance between nodes. If the nodes cannot hear each other on the line, they may both send packets at the same time, causing a packet collision. Adhering to the standards for length of cable between nodes on the network helps keep down the number of packet collisions. However, because the logical bus topology works on the broadcast principle, collisions cannot be eliminated.

Twisted-pair Ethernet (10BaseT) uses economical telephone wiring and standard RJ-45 connectors, often taking advantage of wires installed in a building. It is wired in a star configuration and requires a hub. Fast Ethernet (100BaseT) is similar, but uses two different twisted-pair configurations (100BaseT). 10BaseT and 100BaseT are the most popular versions of Ethernet.

Standard Ethernet (10Base5), also called thick Ethernet and thicknet, uses a thick coax cable that can run as far as 1640 feet without using repeaters. Attachment is made by clamping a transceiver onto the thick coax, which contains another cable that is connected to the adapter card via a 15-pin socket (AUI port).

Figure 14-7
Data Link Layer for Ethernet

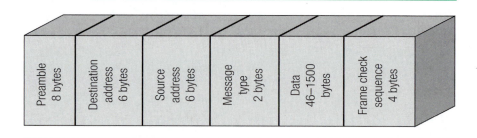

Preamble 8 bytes | Destination address 6 bytes | Source address 6 bytes | Message type 2 bytes | Data 46–1500 bytes | Frame check sequence 4 bytes

Thin Ethernet (10Base2), also called thinnet and cheapernet, uses a thinner, less-expensive coax that is easier to connect but has a limitation of 607 feet per segment. Thinnet uses T-type BNC connectors, and the transceivers are built into the adapter cards.

Fiber optic Ethernet (10BaseF and 100BaseFX) is impervious to external radiation and is often used to extend Ethernet segments up to 1.2 miles. Specifications exist for complete fiber optic networks as well as backbone implementations. FORL (fiber optic repeater link) was an earlier standard that is limited to 0.6 mile distance. All processing takes place at the Ethernet NIC, so all nodes must have Ethernet cards. Ethernet can run on top of a physical bus, physical star, or physical ring.

Token ring topology is the most common local network alternative to Ethernet. It is a local area network (LAN) developed by IBM and identified under IEEE Standard 802.5. It uses a token ring access method and connects up to 255 nodes in a star topology at 4 or 16 Mbps. All stations connect to a central wiring hub called the *multistation access unit* (MAU) using a twisted-wire cable. The central hub makes it easier to troubleshoot failures than in a bus topology. This is a different type of hub than the one used in 10BaseT twisted-pair Ethernet networks.

Token ring is more deterministic than Ethernet. It ensures that all users get regular turns at transmitting their data by implementing a strict, orderly access method. Token ring arranges nodes in a logical ring topology that provides more equal opportunity for each station to gain access to the network than the broadcast method used by Ethernet. The nodes forward packets in one direction around the ring, removing a frame when it has circled the ring once. The ring creates a token, a special type of frame that gives a station permission to transmit data. The token circles the ring like any frame, until it encounters a node that wishes to transmit. This node then captures the token by replacing the token frame with a data-carrying frame. This data-carrying frame then circles the network until it returns to the transmitting node, where it is removed and a new token is created. This new token is then transmitted to the next node in the ring. Because there is only one token for each network, token ring nodes do not listen for collisions. Possession of the token frame provides assurance that the node can transmit without fear of another node interrupting (see Figure 14-8).

There are two types of token ring networks. Type 1 token ring networks allow up to 255 stations per network and use shielded twisted-pair wires with IBM-style type 1 connectors. Type 3 token rings allow up to 72 devices per network and use unshielded twisted pair (category 3, 4 or 5) with RJ-45 connectors (see Figure 14-9). Token ring is a data link protocol (MAC layer protocol) and functions at layers 1 and 2 of the OSI model.

10BaseT is a kind of Ethernet **network** that has a logical bus topology and a physical star topology. It is configured like a set of stars connected by a bus. It behaves like a bus, using broadcast technology to send packets along the network, but it is cabled like a star using unshielded twisted pair (UTP) cable. This configuration is desirable because of its troubleshooting ability (see Figure 14-10).

Figure 14-8
Token Ring Network

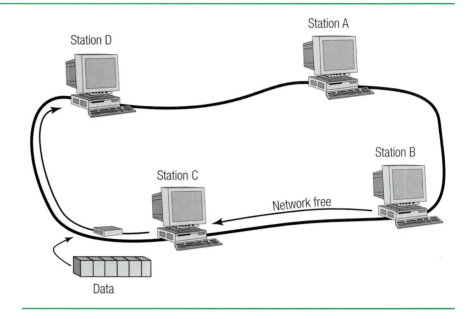

Station D

Station A

Station B

Station C

Network free

Data

Figure 14-9
IBM Type 1 Connector and RJ-45
Connector

RJ-45

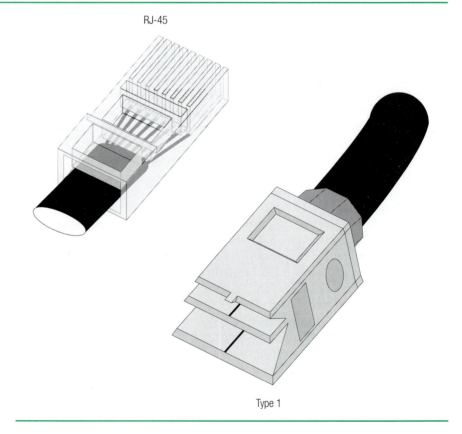

Type 1

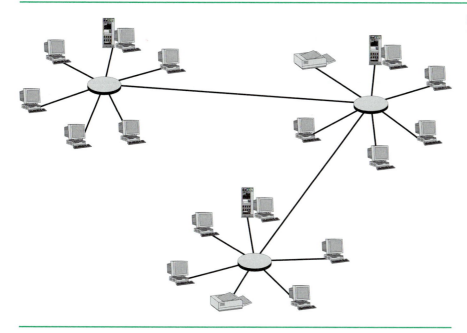

Figure 14-10
10Base T Star Network

▨ NETWORK CONNECTIVITY: INTERNETWORKING

Internetworking is connecting networks together to better use their capabilities. This interconnection is necessary so that various networks can be interconnected and any two devices on any of the networks can communicate. Because each of the interconnected networks retains its identity, special hardware mechanisms are needed for communicating across multiple networks. There are four basic types of connecting hardware—repeaters, bridges, routers, and gateways—that provide a communications path and the necessary logic so that data can be exchanged between networks.

A **repeater** repeats whatever it hears. It will take a packet it receives and send it on to other parts of the network by repeating it. In addition, a repeater will strengthen the signal. Its job is to take the packet signal it receives, add power back to it, and send it on its way.

A repeater operates only at the physical layer of the OSI model. It cannot look into the packet or change it; it just strengthens the signal and repeats it. Because of its limited function, a repeater can connect only network segments that are of the same type; it cannot connect different types of networks. It can connect Ethernet to Ethernet or token ring to token ring; it cannot connect Ethernet to token ring. A repeater performs a very basic function that allows networks to expand very easily (see Figure 14-11).

A **bridge** is a hardware device designed to connect different segments of a network. A bridge can connect networks using different topologies (Ethernet to token ring, Mac segment to PC segment) provided that each segment uses the same high-level protocol, such as IPX or TCP/IP. The function of a

Figure 14-11
Network Connectivity Hardware

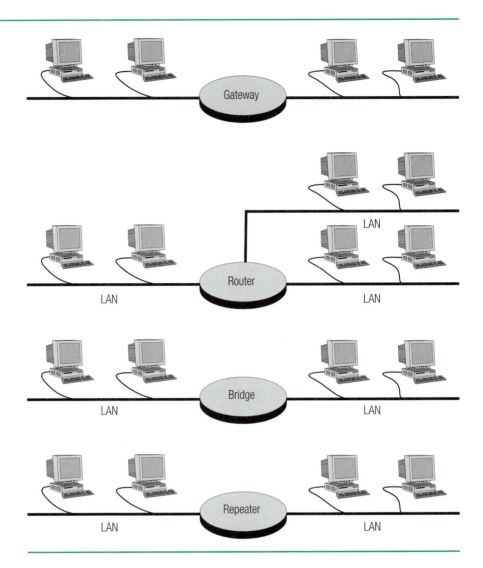

bridge is to improve network performance by segmenting the network and keeping traffic contained within the segments. Bridges have the capability of building and maintaining address tables of the nodes on the network, and by monitoring the node that acknowledged receipt of the address, they learn which nodes belong to which segment.

Bridges work at layer 2 of the OSI model (data link layer) and are faster than routers because they are protocol independent (see Figure 14-11). The communications protocols discussed earlier were established to govern the way that data are transmitted in a network. Because networks use a variety of protocols and operating systems, networks must become compatible so they can talk directly to one another. The primary technology used to establish compatibility between networks is the router.

Routers help bridge the gap between incompatible networks by performing the necessary protocol conversion and then routing the message to its destination. Routers function at two levels of the network. They are used to segment LANs in order to balance traffic and to filter traffic for security purposes, thus serving as an Internet backbone to interconnect all networks in the enterprise. Stringing several routers together and using a high-speed LAN topology such as fast Ethernet or gigabit Ethernet accomplish the interconnection. Routers are also the backbone of the Internet, which spans the planet.

Routers forward data packets from one local area network (LAN) or wide area network (WAN) to another, based on routing protocols. Working in layer 3 of the OSI model (network layer), they read the network address and then decide on the most expedient route. Routers can only route a message that is transmitted by a routable protocol such as IP or IPX. Messages in nonroutable protocols such as NetBIOS cannot be routed but are transferred from LAN to LAN via a bridge (see Figure 14-11).

The last interconnecting device is the gateway. A **gateway** translates information between two different networks or two different data formats. It functions at layer 4 and above in the OSI model and actually performs complete conversions from one protocol to another rather than simply supporting one protocol from within another. A gateway can be used to connect a LAN running TCP/IP to an IBM mainframe. A gateway is very expensive and difficult to install; however, they do allow completely different systems to be connected (see Figure 14-11).

When expansion of a LAN becomes necessary, several factors need to be considered. Each topology has limitations that must be considered. A variety of components can be used to increase both the size and performance of a network. The selection of a repeater, bridge, router, or gateway is dependent on the topology and the expansion needs of the organization.

■ SUMMARY

For a network to function efficiently, the nodes must be able to communicate with one another. Protocols are the rules that govern and facilitate communications between network nodes. Because networks can be composed of a variety of computers from different manufacturers, for communication to occur, standard protocols are necessary. The International Standards Organization developed the OSI model to facilitate communications between computers. Major computer vendors support the OSI model, which sets the worldwide standard for communications and defines a framework for implementing protocols in seven layers. The Department of Defense also developed a set of protocols called TCP/IP that is used to connect a number of networks designed by different vendors into a network, the Internet. A number of protocols, some vendor specific, are used to facilitate communication sessions between computers; the most common include TCP/IP, IPX/SPX, NWLink, AppleTalk, and NetBEUI.

To communicate across a network, computers must be connected through a topology. Topologies are referred to as *physical*, describing the layout of the network, or *logical*, describing how signals pass between computers. The three primary types of topologies are bus, star, and ring; each has inherent advantages and disadvantages. The bus topology, Ethernet, the most widely used LAN access method, uses a common pathway between all nodes. All nodes share the same total bandwidth and send data across the transport medium in packets or frames. The second most popular topology is the token ring topology; it ensures that data are transmitted by a strict, orderly method and provides equal access opportunities to all nodes.

As businesses increase the size and number of networks they are using, it becomes necessary to connect networks for maximum use of capabilities. Each of the networks connected retains its identity; therefore, special hardware is needed to facilitate communication. The four basic connecting hardware devices are the repeater, bridge, router, and gateway. The repeater is used to connect network segments that are of the same type. The bridge connects segments using different topologies if each segment uses the same protocol, such as TCP/IP. Routers convert the protocols and then send the message to its destination; they can, however, only route a message that is transmitted by a routable protocol such as IP or IPX. A gateway translates information between two different networks or two different data formats, thus allowing completely different systems to be connected. The connectivity hardware required to connect networks depends on the type of networks being connected.

QUESTIONS

1. What is the OSI model? Why was it developed?

2. Name the seven layers of the OSI model. What is one function of each layer?

3. Why was TCP/IP developed?

4. What is a transport protocol? Give an example of a commonly configured transport protocol.

5. Distinguish between the terms *"physical" topology* and *"logical" topology*.

6. What are the advantages and disadvantages of a bus topology?

7. Discuss the differences between thick Ethernet and thin Ethernet.

8. Why are businesses interested in connecting multiple networks together?

9. How do you determine if you need a repeater on your network?

10. What is the function of a terminator?

PROJECTS AND PROBLEMS

1. You have been asked by the dean of the college to design a client/server network to be implemented in a new computer lab. The lab will need to be in operation 24 hours a day, 7 days a week. It will contain 30 computer units, one server, and two printers. The network must be reliable and available to meet the needs of students. Prepare a report that answers the following questions:

   (a) What type of network would you install?

   (b) Would you use Ethernet or token ring network?

   (c) What design method would you use?

   (d) What type of cabling would you use?

2. Use a Web browser and connect to the search engine of your choice to research TCP/IP and NetBEUI. What are the strengths of each protocol? What are the weaknesses of each protocol?

3. The organization you are working for has acquired three new offices, located in three different states. Each of the offices currently has its own network, and the company would like to share information among the offices. Because of your excellent reputation, the CIO has contacted you to recommend the parameters for interconnecting the three networks. Write a short report explaining your recommendations in terms of communication protocols and type(s) of connectivity hardware.

4. Use a Web browser and connect to the search engine of your choice to research bus, star, and ring topologies. Develop a chart based on your research that shows the advantages and disadvantages of each topology and the common cable used in each topology.

Vocabulary

Advanced Research Projects Agency network (ARPAnet)

bridge

bus topology

concentrator

drop

Ethernet

frame

gateway

hub

internet telephony

internetworking

logical topology

multistation access unit (MAU)

network bus

network protocol

nonroutable protocol

open systems interconnect model (OSI model)

packet

physical topology

protocol

protocol stack

public switched telephone network

repeater

ring topology

router

star topology

TCP/IP protocol

10BaseT network

terminator

thick Ethernet

thinnet

token ring topology

topology

transceiver

transport protocol

References

Campbell, P., *Networking the Small Office*, SYBEX, San Francisco, 1996.

Techencyclopedia, http://www.techweb.com/encyclopedia.

Webopedia On-line Dictionary, http://www.webopedia.com.

Williams, J., and D. Johnson, *A Guide to Microsoft Windows NT Server 4.0 in the Enterprise*, Course Technology, Cambridge, MA, 1999.

15

Telephony

In this chapter, we discuss telephony, including circuit-based technology, the evolution of this technology, and implementation of IP Telephony. Common terminology, which builds on the fundamentals, is included.

WHAT YOU WILL LEARN

- Fundamentals of the telephone industry
- Operation of circuit-based technology
- Evolution of circuit-based technology
- History of Internet communications
- Basics of Internet communications
- Future of Internet communications

■ TELEPHONE INDUSTRY FUNDAMENTALS

In Chapter 13, electronic communications was discussed and defined as the transfer of information from one location to another. It was further broken into the areas of data communications (datacom), telecommunications (telecom), and networking. In this chapter we focus on voice communications technologies and begin with the definition of telecommunications. **Telecommunications** (telecom) refers to a mix of voice and data communications using both analog and digital technologies.

The telephone network is the world's largest communications system initially transmitting voice using an analog format. This system, based on circuit-based technology, has been the natural choice for implementing voice communications systems. It transmits voice, music, and video in a **continuous** and **synchronous** manner, allowing for uninterrupted, intelligible communication. This technology, known as **telephony**, is the science of converting sound into electric signals, transmitting it within cables or via radio, and reconverting it back into sound. The term *telephony* applies to the telephone industry and is also referred to as the standard **public-switched telephone network (PSTN)**.

◾ CIRCUIT-BASED TECHNOLOGY

A circuit-based system, the foundation of telephone technology, is the pathway over which data are transferred between remote devices. It may refer to the entire physical medium, such as a telephone line, or it may refer to one of several carrier frequencies transmitted simultaneously within the line. Through the use of circuit technology, the telephone system allows for continuous transmission of data represented as voice. Once the connection has been established, there are no breaks or delays in the transmission of sound from the sending to the receiving end. Synchronizing the signal relies on a timing scheme coordinated between the two devices, ensuring that voice is delivered to the receiving end at the same rate that it was transported from the sending end. The continuous, synchronous transmission of data represented allows each party to make a connection and transmit the signal at a given, fixed rate without flaw and without missing a step.

Circuit-Based Technology Evolution

Circuit-based technology, which relies on **multiplexing**, has evolved from **analog circuit switched** (FDM or frequency-division multiplexing) to **digital circuit switched** (TDM or time-division multiplexing) to **digital packet switched (IP telephony)**. The differences in the technologies deal with data transmission. An analog-based telephone transmission uses a dedicated connection made between two people. Multiple voice frequencies are placed on the same line using **frequency-division multiplexing** (FDM). Analog systems are prone to error because the electronic frequencies can get mixed together with unwanted signals (noise) that are nearby. Amplifiers are placed at regular intervals in the line to boost the signal; these amplifiers cannot, however, distinguish between the signal and the noise. Consequently, the noise is amplified along with the signal. In addition, the connections are maintained by all the switches the signals travel through to reach the receiving party (see Figure 15-1).

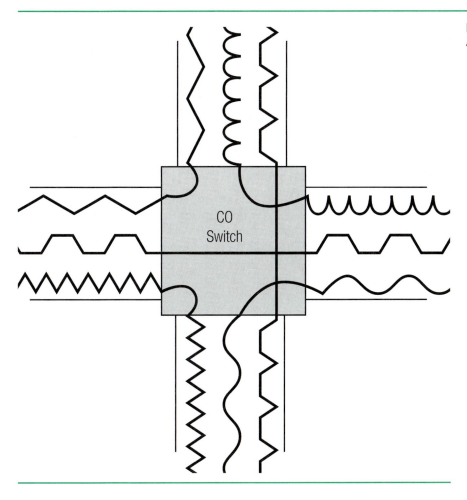

Figure 15-1
Analog Circuit Switched (FDM)

The next enhancement to the circuit-based technology came in the form of digital transmission. The digital circuit-switched technology uses **time division multiplexing** (TDM) as the equivalent of FDM to transport data. Digital technology transmits using only two distinct frequencies or voltages. It uses repeaters rather than amplifiers to analyze the incoming and regenerate a new outgoing signal. Noise on the line is filtered out at the next repeater. By using only two signals (0 and 1), data can be distinguished more easily from noise. In this technology, a digital time slot is reserved for each data stream; the bits and bytes are interleaved one after the other. During a voice conversation, the time slot is reserved even though one-half of the time one person is listening and, therefore, silent. In addition, there are normal pauses in speech (see Figure 15-2).

The latest enhancement to circuit-based technology is the digital packet-switched technology. In the digital packet-switched (IP telephony) technology,

Figure 15-2
Digital Circuit Switched (TDM)

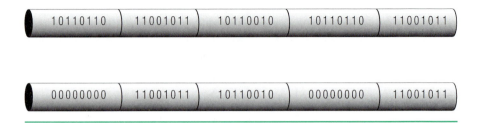

bits and bytes are also interleaved, but a time slot is not dedicated if there is silence on the line and no packets are transmitted. When the conversation resumes, there are codes that accompany the data, indicating the time the conversation was resumed, thus delivering the words in real-time synchronization (see Figure 15-3).

Internet Protocol Packet Technology

As our discussion in Chapter 14 indicated, Internet protocol (IP) is the set of rules used to facilitate transmission of packets of information across the Internet. Standard addresses identifying both the source and the destination are placed on data packets. When an Internet connection is made via a telephone connection, a circuit-based connection through an Internet service provider (ISP) is established. IP data packets originating at the sending computer are handled by the switch and delivered sequentially to the ISP. The ISP moves these packets along another non-circuit-based system and then transfers them to the final destination.

The telephone universally provides a continuous and synchronous connection between the modem and the ISP even though this connection is not used to the fullest. Charges for the connection between the modem and the ISP are levied based on the rate of a full telephone conversation. The data rate of the connection is limited by the rate of the modem—standard of 64,000 bits per second, requiring the purchase of access to a high-speed digital service line. Because the cost of these services can be prohibitive, a new means of connecting to an ISP is necessary. An alternative system, running parallel to the telephone system, to transfer the high-speed data packets over the Internet is necessary to take advantage of the increasing business and communications offering available. The system developed to transfer the high-speed packets over the Internet is IP telephony.

Figure 15-3
Digital Packet Switched (IP telephony)

■ INTERNET PROTOCOL TELEPHONY

Internet protocol (IP) telephony is the two-way transmission of audio over an IP network. When used in a private intranet or WAN, it is generally known as *voice over IP* or VoIP. When the public Internet is the transport vehicle, it is referred to as **Internet telephony**. Both terms can be and are used synonymously. Why are businesses and individuals looking into IP telephony? The benefits of IP telephony sought by users fall into two categories: (1) reduction in cost of voice and fax calls through toll bypass, and (2) development of new applications that use the combination of telephony, computer, and data functions using IP networks as the common communications platform.

History of Internet Communication

Voice communication over the Internet was introduced in 1995 by Vocaltec, Inc. with the introduction of its Internet Phone software. This software allowed two Internet-connected persons to have a live conversation using the Internet and their PCs (see Figure 15-4). Internet Phone software was designed to run on a personal computer equipped with at least a 486/33-MHz processor, sound card, speakers, microphone, and modem. At the sending end, the software compresses the voice signal and translates it into Internet protocol (IP) packets for transmission over the Internet; the process is reversed at the receiving end.

PC-to-PC Internet telephony works only if both parties are using the Internet Phone software, thus replacing the traditional public-switched telephone network (PSTN). The PC-to-PC Internet telephony technology allowed people to communicate cheaply because no per minute charges applied. This technology, however, was neither as convenient nor of the same quality as conventional telephone calls.

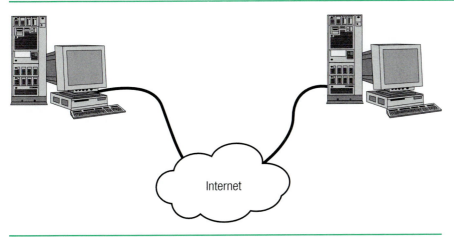

Figure 15-4
PC-to-PC Communications

Internet

Despite continuing limitations in convenience and sound quality, the technology has steadily matured and gained increased support from businesses and individuals. The past few years have seen the rapid evolution of Internet telephony because of the increased number of software developers who now offer PC telephony software and the emergence of gateway servers that act as an interface between the Internet and the PSTN. Communications services now transported via the Internet include voice, facsimile, and/or voice-messaging applications.

PC-to-Telephone Communication

The next advance in communications allowed one person to use a multimedia PC as an IP-based telephone (either connected to a LAN or to an Internet service provider via a modem) to dial a person with a conventional telephone (see Figure 15-5). This involved the use of an **Internet telephony gateway** located in the geographical region of the person with the conventional telephone. This gateway translates the conventional telephone voice transmission to an IP telephony format.

Telephone-to-Telephone Communication

The most recent advancement in the development of IP telephony services is the placement of gateways in multiple geographic areas. This removes the need for a PC on either end of a conversation (see Figure 15-6). The use of private networks instead of the public Internet as well as specialized equipment to reduce some of the sound-quality problems associated with IP telephony

Figure 15-5
PC-to-Telephone Communications

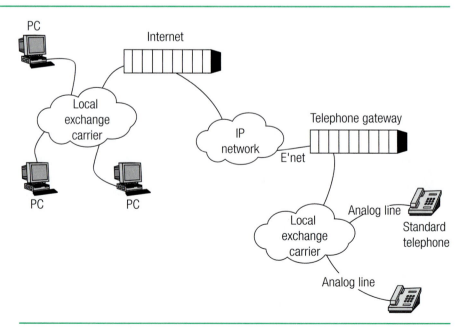

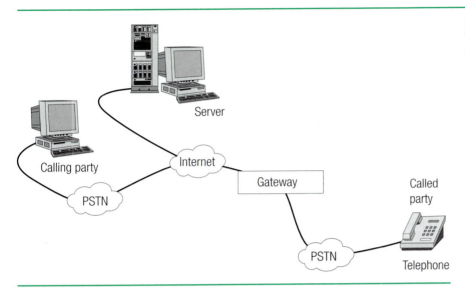

Figure 15-6
Telephone-to-Telephone
Communications

makes telephone-to-telephone communications a feasible alternative to traditional telephone calls.

Limitations of IP Technology

Moving voice over the Internet in packets is subject to distinct types of corruption, including delay and lost packets. The Internet protocol (IP) has a built-in mechanism for some delay in the transmission system. Because the amount of routing involves much more data handling than circuit switching, the delays are generally much larger than those in switched circuits.

Packet loss is generally the result of overloaded routers and/or insufficient cable capacities. The Internet protocol addresses this issue by providing for retransmission of missing data. However, the retransmitted data may arrive too late to be incorporated in the progressive, synchronous reconstruction of the voice. Packet loss can be addressed through packet buffering or streaming technology; unfortunately, the trade-off is an increase in delay in the transmission.

Use of Intranet Telephony

As discussed, Internet telephony has limitations as well as difficulties relating to reliability and sound quality. Enterprises have therefore been confining Internet telephony applications to **intranets** because of more predictable bandwidth available than on the Intranet. With tighter control of their own networks, voice over IP (VoIP) can sound as good as the standard telephone, while flowing over an existing infrastructure that has been upgraded to VoIP. This use of the technology allows for point-to-point calls via gateway servers attached to the LAN; no PC-based telephony software or Internet account is necessary. Enterprises using this technology take advantage of several opportunities for enhanced communications within the enterprise, including teleconferencing and whiteboard technology.

Although not a new technology, teleconferencing, discussed in Chapter 4, has become more widespread because of the use of IP networks. Geographically separate employees can hold online meetings, using voice, data, and video to replicate a face-to-face meeting.

During the teleconferences, employees use a whiteboard to aid and enhance communications. A **whiteboard** is the electronic equivalent of chalk and blackboard, but between remote users. Whiteboard systems allow network participants to view one or more users simultaneously, drawing on an on-screen blackboard or running an application. This is not the same as application sharing where two or more users can interactively work in the application. Only one user is actually running the application from his or her computer. In many desktop systems, the application is not viewable interactively. A copy of the current application window is pasted into the whiteboard, which then becomes a static image for interactive annotation.

IP Telephony Improvements

Software and hardware manufacturers have been working on turning the Internet into one global communications systems since the mid-1990s. Until the Internet's infrastructure can handle **quality of service (QoS)**, which allows traffic to be prioritized, it cannot support voice and video like a dedicated telephone connection. What makes the Internet most attractive is that once upgraded for QoS, all future innovations come at the edge of the network. In contrast to the public-switched telephone network, which must be reprogrammed for each type of new service that is offered, all that is necessary to launch an Internet service is to install the software in the servers, add the client piece to the user's machine, and let it work. If it works, more users purchase and install the new software. If not, the Internet keeps on transporting the bits and bytes, and nobody knows any different. Furthermore, the packet-switching nature of IP maximizes every microsecond of bandwidth. Circuit-switched voice does not. Half the time, only one person is talking, and pauses between speech go wasted on dedicated circuits.

IP has become the new conviction of the telecommunications industry. All the major players, including Quest Communications and AT&T, are expanding and enhancing their infrastructures to make them IP based and looking to determine how IP fits into their future. In light of the development of IP and enhancement to IP, the Internet has become a more powerful influence on all businesses. The way the world communicates is again changing and evolving.

■ SUMMARY

The telephone network remains the world's largest communication system, evolving from analog transmission to digital transmission of voice. Based on circuit technology, it transmits voice and music in a continuous, synchronous manner, allowing each party to make a connection and transmit signals without flaw. Circuit-based technology has progressed from analog circuit switched to digital circuit switched to digital packet switched, allowing data to be transmitted flawlessly in real time.

Digital packet-switched technology, also called IP telephony, was developed as an alternative to the telephone systems. IP telephony is the two-way transmission of high-speed packets over the Internet. Also known as voice over IP or VoIP, it is attractive to business because of its lower cost. Voice communication over the Internet was introduced in 1995 by Vocaltec, Inc. with the debut of Internet Phone software, which allowed two Internet-connected persons to have a live conversation using the Internet and PCs. Voice communication technology using the Internet has advanced to allow communication between a PC and a telephone and a telephone and telephone.

This technology is, however, still being perfected to eliminate potential delay and lost packets. Because of the limitations, many enterprises have confined the use of IP applications to intranets. Using their networks and maintaining tighter control of the bandwidth, voice over IP (VoIP) can sound as good as the standard telephone. Enterprises have taken advantage of this technology to enhance communications among offices by using teleconferencing and whiteboard technology.

Software and hardware manufacturers, as well as companies that are part of the telecommunications industry, have been working on improving the quality of service (QoS) that will allow traffic to be prioritized so that the Internet can support voice and video like a dedicated telephone connection. With the recent developments of and enhancements to IP, the Internet has become an even more powerful influence over all business.

QUESTIONS

1. Name the world's largest communications system.

2. What does the phrase "transmits in a continuous and synchronous manner" mean?

3. What is circuit-based technology? What industry uses this technology?

4. Discuss the evolution of circuit-based technology.

5. What does the term *Internet protocol* (IP) *telephony* mean?

6. Who developed the first voice communications software? When?

7. Discuss the differences among the three types of Internet communication.

8. Name two limitations of IP technology.

9. What is the difference between an intranet and an internet? Give an example of each.

10. How does the quality of service (QoS) affect the future of telephony?

PROJECTS AND PROBLEMS

1. Using a Web browser and the search engine of your choice, access the Web site of any two industries in the telecommunications industry. Research their latest developments relating to Internet Protocol (IP) telephony. Write a brief summary comparing the two organizations' progress in this field.

2. Develop a table that lists the advantages and disadvantages of PC-to-PC communications, PC-to-telephone communications, and telephone-to-telephone communications.

3. Using a Web browser and the search engine of your choice, research the quality of service (QoS) issue as it relates to Internet telephony. Prepare a report that details the advances made toward improving QoS.

4. Interview at least two businesses in your area. Prepare a report that answers these questions.
   (a) Do you schedule meetings using teleconferencing technology?
   (b) If yes, how often do you use the technology? What additional equipment were you required to purchase?
   (c) Has the use of teleconferencing benefited the organization? How?
   (d) If no, why not? Are you discussing the use of teleconferencing in the future?

5. The organization you are working for frequently holds meetings using teleconferencing technology. There has been a great deal of discussion about the need for visual aids to enhance and clarify communications during these conferences. Your supervisor has heard about a whiteboard and asked you to research the technology. Using a Web browser and the search engine of your choice, research whiteboard technology and make a recommendation.

Vocabulary

analog circuit switched
continuous
digital circuit switched (TDM)
digital packet switched (IP telephony)
frequency-division multiplexing
Internet protocol (IP) telephony

Internet telephony
Internet telephony gateway
intranet
multiplexing
public-switched telephone network (PSTN)
quality of service (QoS)

synchronous
telecommunications
telephony
time-division multiplexing
whiteboard

References

Adelson, J. (October, 1998) *Beyond Dial Tone: Opportunities for Value in IP Telephony*, http://www.telephonyworld.com/training.

Campbell, P., *Networking the Small Office*, SYBEX, San Francisco, 1996.

Techencyclopedia, http://www.techweb.com/encyclopedia.

The International Engineering Consortium, *Internet Telephony Tutorial*. http://www.iec.org/tutorials, August 2000.

Webopedia On-line Dictionary, http://www.webopedia.com.

Williams, J., and D. Johnson, *A Guide to Microsoft Windows NT Server 4.0 in the Enterprise*, Course Technology, Cambridge, MA, 1999.

APPENDIX

Professional Associations

Advanced Computing Systems Association (USENIX)   Since 1975, USENIX has brought together the community of engineers, system administrators, scientists, and technicians working on the cutting edge of the computing world. http://www.usenix.org.

Association for Information Systems (AIS)   AIS, founded in 1994, is a professional organization whose purpose is to serve as the premier global organization for academics specializing in information systems. http://www.aisnet.org.

Information Systems Audit and Control Association (ISACA)   Founded in 1969, ISACA sponsors international conferences, administers the globally respected CISA (Certified Information Systems Auditor) designation held by more than 13,000 professionals worldwide, and develops globally applicable information systems auditing and control standards. http://www.isaca.org.

Organizational Systems Research Association (OSRA; Formerly Office Systems Research Association)   OSRA is a professional organization chartered for the purpose of pursuing research and education in the area of information technology and end-user information systems. OSRA provides a platform for dedicated professionals to meet and exchange ideas in the pursuit of excellence. http://www.osra.org.

Urban and Regional Information Systems Association (URISA)   Founded in 1963, URISA is a nonprofit association of professionals using information technology to solve problems in planning, public works, the environment, emergency services, utilities, and throughout state, regional, and local governments. http://www.urisa.org.

Glossary

acoustic processor. In voice recognition software, the filtering out of background noise and conversion of the captured audio into a series of sounds that correspond to the phonemes (units of speech) making up the language selected, such as American English.

acoustical analysis. In voice recognition software, the procedure used to build a list of possible words that contain similar sounds.

Advanced Research Projects Agency network (ARPAnet). A project of the U.S. Department of Defense, forerunner to the TCP/IP protocol suite.

air/ground services. A type of two-way radio that provides two-way communication between airborne telephones and the public-switched telephone network.

alphabetic display pager. A type of pager that displays alphabetic or numeric messages that are entered by the calling party on the telephone or by using a computer with a modem.

American National Standards Institute (ANSI). Private nonprofit organization founded to administer and coordinate U.S. voluntary standardization and conformity assessment.

analog circuit switched. The type of circuit-based technology known as frequency-division multiplexing (FDM).

analog processing method. A method used by group 1 and 2 facsimile machines in which every part of an original (characters, spaces, margins) is scanned.

anonymous FTP server. A server that provides an interactive service allowing any user to transfer documents, files, programs, and other archived data using file transfer protocol. The user logs on using "anonymous" and his e-mail address as the password. He or she then has access to a special directory hierarchy containing the publicly accessible files, typically in a subdirectory called "pub." This is usually a separate area from files used by local users.

application file. A file that was created using a complete, self-contained program that performs a specific function directly for the user, such as word processing, spreadsheet, or database.

Archie. A system to gather, index, and serve information automatically on the Internet. The initial implementation of Archie by the School of Computer Science at McGill University provided an indexed directory of file names from all anonymous FTP archives on the Internet. Later versions provide other collections of information.

asynchronous transmission. Data is sent in packages of one character or byte at a time.

attenuation. Loss of signal strength that begins to occur as a signal travels farther along a cable.

audio conferencing. The simplest and least costly of the four teleconferencing systems. It consists of an audio-only configuration in which two or more groups or three or more individuals at separate locations exchange verbal information with each other using either conference calls and/or amplified telephone speaker devices (speakerphones).

audiovideo interleave (AVI). A video standard designed by the Microsoft Corporation for use with Microsoft Windows.

audio-file format on UNIX machines (SND, AU). An audio standard for use on computers running the UNIX operating system.

bandwidth. The transmission capacity of an electronic line such as a communications network, computer bus, or computer channel; refers to the amount of data that can be transmitted in a fixed amount of time.

baseband. A type of digital data transmission in which each medium (wire) carries only one signal, or channel, at a time.

baud. The measure of data transmission speed over telephone lines, named after the French engineer Jean-Maurice-Émile Baudot.

baud rate. The signaling rate of a line; the number of signal changes that occur in 1 second.

binary file. A file containing arbitrary bytes or words, as opposed to a text file (ASCII) containing only printable characters.

bit (binary digit). The smallest unit of information handled by a computer, represented by either a 0 or 1 in the binary system.

bit rate (bps). The data transfer speed within a computer or between a computer and a peripheral. It also refers to the data transmission speed in a network.

body. The main part of an electronic mail (e-mail) message.

bookmark. A user's reference to a document on the World Wide Web or other hypermedia system, usually in the form of a uniform resource locator (URL) and a title or comment string.

bridge A hardware device designed to connect different segments of a network; it can connect networks using different topologies.

broadband. A type of digital data transmission that enables a single wire to carry multiple signals simultaneously.

bus topology A network configuration in which a cable connecting nodes runs from computer to computer, making each one a line in a chain; it is commonly referred to as *daisy chaining*.

business television. A type of teleconferencing system that involves the transmission of one-way television signals from a central site to one or more sites.

cable connection. A way of connecting to the Internet with the use of a TV cable provided by a TV cable company.

cable modem. A device that connects a computer to the Internet with a TV cable connection and an Ethernet network card.

cache. A small fast memory holding recently accessed data, designed to speed up subsequent access to the same data.

call routing. A voice processing application that acts like an automated phone attendant whereby a recorded message gives instructions for using a touch-tone phone to access menu items.

cellular phone. A type of wireless communication that uses many base stations to divide a service area into multiple cells. Cellular calls are transferred from base station to base station as a user travels from cell to cell. Cellular phones send radio signals to low-power transmitters located within cells of 5 to 12 miles in radius.

character-formatting tag. A type of hypertext markup language (HTML) tag which allows for the application of various styles (such as bold, underline, or italics) to the characters in documents.

citizens' band (CB) radio. A system of two-way radio communication that is used for short distances.

cladding. In a fiber optic cable, the thin glass tube that surrounds the core.

clarity. Communications principle involving the need to choose precise, concrete, and familiar words to construct effective sentences and paragraphs.

client. Personal computers or workstations that have been integrated into the network to access information from the server.

client/server network. A network that uses a dedicated server responsible for storing and distributing data to clients.

closed architecture. An architecture whose design is proprietary, making it difficult to connect the system to other systems.

coaxial cable. Cable consisting of a solid copper core surrounded by insulation, a braided metal shielding, and an outer cover.

codec device. One of the components of a digitized speech system that converts analog voice signals into digital form and then reconverts them back into analog format.

commercial online service connection. One of the ways to connect to the Internet (i.e., America Online, Compuserve, and NetZero).

communications manager. An employee, sometimes called a *distribution services manager*, who supervises the day-to-day operation of all communication technology devices and systems, such as electronic mail, facsimile systems, and teleconferencing equipment.

communications model. A graphical depiction showing the parts of the communication process: a sender (the source), a communications medium and telecommunications channel, and a receiver (the destination).

communications technology. The application and use of technology—computers, software, other electronic devices, and accompanying media and procedures—to make communication more effective than using traditional means of communication that do not utilize technology.

completeness. A communications principle involving the need to provide all necessary information, answer all questions asked, and give something extra when desirable.

compressed file. A file in which the data have been coded to save storage space or transmission time. Although data are already coded in digital form for computer processing, they can often be coded more efficiently (using fewer bits).

computer conferencing. An electronic means of sending, viewing, and sharing real-time communications in areas of common interest by using a computer keyboard.

computer crime and fraud. Occurs when computers are used as a tool to gain access to valuable information and as a means of stealing.

computer fax board. Usually a combination modem/fax board that will allow anything on a computer monitor to be faxed with the proper software.

computer virus. A program that attaches itself to other programs.

computer-related scams. Schemes in which people have lost money when scam artists use the Internet to offer get-rich-quick schemes involving real estate, bank transactions, and lotteries.

concentrator. A star topology device; multiple access unit or hub.

conciseness. The communications principle involving the elimination of wordy expressions, including only relevant material, and avoiding unnecessary repetition.

concreteness. The communications principle involving the use of brief words and sentence structure and as free as possible of elaboration and superfluous detail.

conference bridge. A telecommunications facility or service that permits callers from several diverse locations to be connected together for a conference call.

conference call. A service provided by telephone companies in which three or more people are linked, so that everyone can communicate with everyone else using standard telephones using one telephone connection.

consideration. A communication principle that focuses on "you" instead of "I" or "we," shows audience benefit or interest in the receiver, and emphasizes positive, pleasant facts.

continuous. The throughput of the telephone connection, which contains no breaks or delays in the progression of sounds between the two parties.

continuous speech system. A voice recognition system that allows the originator to speak naturally without pauses between the words.

controlled growth. An electronic mail implementation method in which the e-mail system is implemented in one department of the organization and then management waits for other departments to express an interest in having e-mail.

core. A strand of glass at the center of a fiber optic cable.

correctness. A communications principle that asks us to use the right level of language, verify the accuracy of figures, facts, and words, and maintain acceptable writing mechanics.

coupling. Any means by which energy is transferred from one conductive or dielectric medium to another.

courtesy. A communications principle which states that communication should be tactful, thoughtful, and appreciative. In addition, expressions that show respect should be used and nondiscriminatory expressions should be chosen.

cracker. A computer hobbyist who gains unauthorized access to computer systems by learning passwords or by discovering copy protection schemes of computer software.

critical mass. A theory which claims that a certain number of users can make a system accepted by other employees.

crosstalk. Occurs when the signal in one line interferes with the signal in another line.

CU-SeeMe. A videoconferencing system originally developed by Cornell University and made available as freeware over the Internet. A commercial version of CU-SeeMe is been marketed by 1st Virtual Communications, formerly White Pine software.

data communications. The digital transmission of text, voice, and video in binary form from one computer to another, accomplished through the use of telecommunications technology.

decoder. A component of a voice recognition system which selects the most likely word based on the rankings assigned during word matching and assembles the words in the most likely sentence combinations.

digital circuit switched. A type of circuit-based technology known as time-division multiplexing (TDM).

digital packet switched. A type of circuit-based technology known as Internet packet telephony.

digital processing method. A method used by group 3 and 4 faxes which analyzes the document's actual picture elements and converts these elements into binary codes (1's and 0's).

digital whiteboard. A device that allows you to share images, text, and data simultaneously as you communicate with someone else while utilizing teleconferencing.

digitized speech. Speech that uses a computer to convert human speech into digital signals for storage on a computer disk and then reconverts the signals to human speech for someone to hear on command.

direct (or dedicated) connection. A type of Internet connection through a person's company, educational institution, or other organization.

discrete speech system. A type of voice recognition system which requires that the speaker speak slowly and distinctly and separate each word with a short pause.

discussion group. A communication tool that permits you to read the e-mail messages that others have sent to the group.

distance learning. Learning that takes place via electronic media linking instructors and students who are not together in a classroom.

distribution list. An e-mail program feature that allows the sender to send messages to multiple e-mail addresses.

domain name. The conversion of an IP number into words that identify a computer connected to the Internet.

drop. Thinner cable used with thick Ethernet that runs from the backbone to the network's nodes.

electronic commerce. Using electronic information technologies such as electronic data interchange (EDI) or the Internet to conduct business between trading partners.

electronic communications. The electronic transfer of information from one location to another.

electronic data interchange (EDI). The exchange of standardized document forms between computer systems for business use.

electronic funds transfer (EFT). The transfer of money initiated through an electronic terminal, automated teller machine, computer, telephone, or magnetic tape.

Electronic Industries Alliance and the Telecommunications Industries Association (EIA/TIA). Organization that develops data and voice cabling standards.

electronic mail (e-mail). Messages that are passed automatically from one computer user to another, often through computer networks and/or via modems over telephone lines.

electronic mail connection. A type of Internet connection that limits users to send e-mail outside an organization.

electronic whiteboard. *See* digital whiteboard.

ethernet. A network that uses a bus topology and follows the IEEE 802.3 standard for network connection.

facsimile (fax). A process by which fixed graphic material including pictures, text, or images is scanned and the information converted into electrical signals which are transmitted via a telephone to produce a paper copy of the graphics on a receiving fax machine.

facsimile machines. A device that performs the facsimile (fax) function. *See also* facsimile (fax).

fast implementation. A type of e-mail implementation plan in which users get access to the new system as quickly as possible.

fat client. The client computer on a network designed to operate with or without access to the server. Internal memory and processing power are used to run applications, and to store information.

fax copier. A device that serves as a low-volume copier to preview fax transmissions.

faxphone. A fax with a telephone in one unit.

fiber optic cable. Cable that transmits data through glass fibers encased in a covering.

file transfer. Copying a file from one computer to another over a computer network.

file transfer protocol (FTP). A client/server protocol that allows a user on one computer to transfer files to and from another computer over a TCP/IP network.

frame. A package of information transmitted as a single unit on a network.

freeware program. Software often written by enthusiasts and distributed at no charge by users' groups, the World Wide Web, electronic mail, local bulletin boards, Usenet newsgroups, or other electronic media.

frequency. The number of vibrations (oscillations) per second, measured in hertz (Hz).

frequency-division multiplexing (FDM). During transmission each signal is assigned a different frequency.

FS-232-C interface. A type of connection that makes it possible for facsimile machines to communicate with computers and word processors.

FTP search engine. The utility that replaces Archie. *See also* Archie.

full duplex. Sending and receiving of data simultaneously.

gateway. A device that translates information between two different networks or two different data formats.

geographical spreading. A consideration in the implementation of e-mail within an organization in which the organizational parts are widely dispersed.

global positioning systems (GPS). A system for determining position on earth's surface by comparing radio signals from 24 satellites equipped with radio transmitters and atomic clocks. The GPS receiver samples data from up to six satellites, calculates the time taken for each satellite signal to reach the GPS receiver, and determines a person's location.

Go Chat. A type of computer conferencing on the Internet.

gopher. *See* gopher protocol.

gopher protocol. A popular distributed document retrieval system that provides a menu of documents.

gopherspace. The computer-based "space" that is created by the global dissemination of gopher-accessible resources.

graphical browsers. A program that allows a person to read hypermedia consisting of text and graphics.

graphical interchange format (GIF). A standard for digitized graphic images defined in 1987 by the CompuServe Information Service.

hacker. A computer enthusiast who enjoys learning everything about a computer system and, through clever programming, pushing the system to its highest-possible level of performance.

half duplex. Transmission of data in both directions, but only one direction at a time.

handheld computer. A portable computer that is small enough to be held in one's hand.

handheld phone. A telephone that can be operated comfortably while held in one's hand.

header. The part of an electronic mail message that precedes the body of a message and contains, among other things, the sender's name and e-mail address, receiver's addresses, and the date and time the message was sent.

high-speed train service. A two-way radio service that provides telephone service between a passenger train and the public-switched telephone network.

HTML converter. A utility program that converts an existing file format into hypertext markup language (HTML) coding.

HTML editor. A utility program that assists in the production of hypertext markup language (HTML) coding.

HTML extension. Additional hypertext markup language (HTML) coding which gives Web pages a special appearance.

HTML tag. Hypertext markup language (HTML) coding that is embedded in the HTML file. A tag consists of a "<," a "directive" (case insensitive), zero or more parameters, and a ">." Matched pairs of directives, such as <TITLE> and </TITLE>, are used to delimit text which is to appear in a special place or style.

HTML utility program. A program that assists in the preparation of hypertext markup language (HTML) files.

hub. A component used to provide a common connection among computers in a star topology.

hyperlink tag. A reference (link) from some point in one hypertext document to some point in another document or another place in the same document.

hypermedia. A term coined by Ted Nelson around 1965 for a collection of documents (or *nodes*) containing cross-references or *links*, which with the aid of an interactive browser program, allow the reader to move easily from one document to another.

hypertext markup language (HTML). A hypertext document format used on the World Wide Web.

hypertext transport protocol (HTTP). The Internet standard that supports the exchange of information on the World Wide Web.

hytelnet. A hypertext database of publicly accessible Internet sites created and maintained by Peter Scott. Hytelnet currently lists over 1400 sites, including libraries, campus-wide information systems, and others.

information providing. A voice processing application that consists of a type of voice bulletin board in a listen-only mode. After dialing a publicized number, the caller is directed to hear prerecorded voice files containing messages that the caller seeks.

inline image. A graphic image that appears within a Web page.

installed phone. A type of cellular phone that is permanently installed in a car, airplane, or train.

Integrated Services Digital Network (ISDN) connection. A set of communications standards allowing a single wire or optical fiber to carry voice, digital network services and video. ISDN is intended eventually to replace the plain old telephone system.

interactive television. A two-way cable system from which subscribers can receive and send signals. They will probably do this by punching buttons on their cable TV's remote control, which may look more like a computer keyboard than a tradition cable TV handheld remote signaling device.

International Organization for Standardization (ISO). A non-governmental organization established in 1947 to promote the development of standardization and cooperation in the areas of intellectual, scientific, technological, and economic activity.

International Telecommunications Union—Telecommunication Organization (ITU). An international organization that coordinates global telecom networks and services.

Internet. A system of linked computer networks, worldwide in scope, that facilitates data communication services such as remote login, file transfer, electronic mail, and newsgroups. The Internet is a way of connecting existing computer networks that greatly extends the reach of each participating system.

Internet piracy. Any impersonation, unauthorized browsing, falsification or theft of data, or disruption of service or control information in a network.

Internet protocol (IP) telephony. Two-way transmission of audio over an IP network.

Internet Relay Chat (IRC). A real-time Internet-based chat service in which one can find "live" participants from all over the world.

Internet telephony. A system developed to transfer high-speed packets over the Internet.

Internet telephony gateway. Hardware that enables a person to use the Internet as the transmission medium for telephone calls.

Internet-EDI. A process whereby standardized forms of documents are transferred between systems often run by different companies.

Internetworking. The process of connecting networks together to better use their capabilities.

intranet. A private network that uses Internet software and Internet standards that may or may not be connected to the Internet.

IP address. A unique 32-bit number that identifies the location of a particular computer on the Internet uniquely and precisely. Every computer connected directly to the Internet must have an IP address.

joint photographic experts group format (JPG or JPEG). A graphic image standard designed for compressing either full-color or gray-scale digital images of "natural," real-world scenes.

jughead. A tool that gopher administrators use to get menu information from various gopher servers.

just-in-time (JIT). A manufacturing strategy wherein parts are produced or delivered only as needed.

key. One or more characters or perhaps a field within a data record used to identify the data and perhaps control its use.

laissez-faire. An e-mail implementation strategy in which the e-mail system is implemented in one department of the organization, with management then waiting for other departments to express an interest in having the same service.

language modeling. The likelihood that a given word would appear between those coming before and after it in a voice recognition system.

Listserv. An automated commercial mailing list distribution system or manager.

local area network (LAN). A network that serves users within a confined geographic area and is composed of computers, servers, and peripherals.

logical topology. A topology that describes how signals pass between nodes.

Macintosh audio information file format (AIFF). An audio format developed by Apple Computer, Inc. for storing high-quality sampled audio and musical instrument information.

marine radio telephone. A marine telephone operated on assigned radiotelephone frequencies. Marine telephones can be used to contact other marine telephones or to reach land-based telephones through an operator.

mark. A term that originated with the telegraph. It currently indicates the binary digit "1" in most coding schemes.

metropolitan area network (MAN). A network that covers a specific geographic area; it is considered the next step up from the LAN.

Microsoft Internet Explorer. A World Wide Web browser developed by the Microsoft Corporation.

Microsoft Windows audio format (WAV). An audio format developed by Microsoft Corporation and used extensively in Microsoft Windows.

microwave. Data transmission that uses high-frequency radio waves that travel through the air in straight lines.

microwave radio. A telecommunication device in which signals are transmitted through the air over a line-of-sight path from one station to another.

modem (modulator–demodulator). A device that converts signals produced by one type of device (e.g., computer) to a form compatible with another (e.g., telephone).

Moore's law. An observation made in 1965 by Intel co-founder Gordon Moore that each new memory integrated circuit contained roughly twice as much capacity as its predecessor and that each chip was released within 18 to 24 months of the previous chip. If this trend continued, he reasoned, computing power would rise exponentially with time.

Morse code. A coding system invented by Samuel A. Morse for use in sending character data over extremely low quality pathways such as telegraph and low-quality radio. Morse code expresses characters as pulses of various durations.

Moving Picture Experts Group digital–video standard format (MPG or MPEG). A video format that was developed by the International Organization for Standardization (ISO).

multifunctional fax unit. A type of facsimile machine that combines fax functions with other office technologies, such as fax copier, faxphone, and videofax.

multimedia. Human–computer interaction involving text, graphics, voice, and video, which often includes hypertext. This term has come to be almost synonymous with CD-ROM in the personal computer world because the large amounts of data involved are currently best supplied on CD-ROM.

multimedia (or asset-integration) tag. A type of hypertext markup language (HTML) tag that makes it possible to integrate graphic images, audio, video, and animation into a Web page.

multiplexing. The combining of multiple signals (analog or digital) for transmission over a single line or medium.

multistation access unit (MAU). A token ring wiring concentrator, also called a hub.

musical instrument digital interface format (MID or MIDI). An audio format and hardware specification used to communicate notes and information between synthesizers, computers, music keyboards, controllers, and other electronic music devices.

mutual dependency. A consideration when implementing an e-mail system, which involves the fact that different parts must have a need for communication and coordination.

Netscape Communicator. A World Wide Web browser developed by the Netscape Corporation.

network. A system that transmits any combination of voice, video, and/or data between users.

network bus. A pathway that connects the nodes in a LAN along a common cable.

network gateway. A device that allows one LAN to be connected to the LAN of another office or group.

network manager. A person responsible for maintaining a network and assisting its users.

network protocols. Rules used by computers to communicate on a network to ensure that data are transmitted whole, in sequence, and without error.

newsgroup. A place on the Internet where people can have conversations about a well-defined topic.

newsgroup reader. A program that organizes newsgroup messages in a sensible and presentable manner.

node. A device on a LAN connected to the network and capable of communicating with other network devices. Nodes include workstations, faxes, printers, and/or servers.

nonanonymous FTP server. A server set up to transfer files on a network in which the user must provide a user id and password.

nongraphical browser. A World Wide Web browser that is text-based and does not display graphic images and other multimedia elements.

nonroutable protocol. A communications protocol that contains a device address, but not a network address; NetBIOS is a nonroutable protocol.

numeric pager display. A type of pager that displays numbers, such as phone numbers.

open architecture. A type of architecture that allows the system to be easily connected to devices made by other manufacturers and software programs developed by other vendors.

open systems interconnect model (OSI model). A communications model that contains seven distinct layers, all of which function seamlessly to facilitate data transmission.

Outlook Express. An electronic mail and newsgroup reader produced by the Microsoft Corporation.

packet. A package of information transmitted as a single unit on a network.

pager. A small wireless receiver that, when triggered, will beep, display numeric or alphanumeric messages, or vibrate.

paragraph-formatting tag. A type of hypertext markup language (HTML) tag that specifies the paragraphs and heading levels in a Web document.

parallel transmission. Data that flows through separate communications lines as it flows from sender to receiver.

peer/peer network. A network where there is no dedicated server or hierarchy among the computers. All are equal and function as both a client and a server.

physical topology. The actual physical layout of a network.

pixel. The smallest resolvable rectangular area of an image, either on a screen or stored in memory.

point-to-multipoint conferencing. Delivery of data from a single source to several destinations.

point-of-sale (POS) terminal. A type of one-way data transmission in which data is entered when a sale is made.

polling. The process of checking the status of an input line, sensor, or memory location to see if a particular external event has been registered.

posting. A message sent to a newsgroup or e-mail list (may also be called a *post*) or the act of sending it.

protocol. A set of formal rules for transmitting and receiving data over a network; governs the communication and interaction between computers.

protocol stack. A combination of protocols each with a specific function working in a different layer.

public domain software. The total absence of copyright protection. If something is "in the public domain," anyone can copy it or use it in any way they wish. The author has none of the exclusive rights that apply to a copyrighted work.

public switched telephone network (PSTS). The telephone industry, also called *telephony*.

quality of service (QoS). Used when referring to networking; specifies a guaranteed rate of data transfer from one node to another in a specified amount of time.

Quicktime Cross-Platform Video File Format (MOV). Apple Computer's standard for integrating full-motion video and digitized sound into application programs.

receiver. A device for converting signals (as electromagnetic waves) into audio or visual form.

repeater. A device that repeats signals so they can be sent on to other parts of the network by repeating it.

resource or subject tree. An alternative way of finding resources on the Web. These sites list Web sites by topics.

ring topology. A topology that connects computers on a circle of cable with no terminating ends.

router. A device that connects networks of different types by performing the necessary protocol conversion and then routing the message to its destination.

satellite. Object that orbits above earth and receives, amplifies, and redirects analog and digital signals.

search engine (or spider). A remotely accessible program that lets you do keyword searches to obtain information on the Internet.

sender. Equipment in the originating telephone system that outpulses the routing digits and the called person's number.

serial transmission. Data that flows in a continuous stream from sender to receiver.

server. On a local area network, the computer dedicated to managing files, printers, or network traffic. It stores the software and central resources shared by other computers on the network.

shareware. Software for which the author requests some payment, usually in the accompanying documentation files or in an announcement made by the software itself.

shell or SLIP/PPP connections. A commonly used abbreviation for the two types of dial-up Internet access that integrate a computer directly with the Internet.

signal. Pulse or frequency on a wire used to control something in a circuit.

signature. In electronic mail and newsgroups, a brief listing that contains the message sender's name, organization, address, e-mail address, and telephone numbers.

simplex. A one-way transmission of data.

single-element tag. A type of hypertext markup language (HTML) tag which consists of one tag only rather than two tags (symmetric tag).

smiley. A combination of symbols used to indicate an emotional state in electronic mail messages.

software piracy. The unauthorized duplication and/or use of computer software. This usually means unauthorized copying, either by individuals for use by themselves or their friends or, less commonly, by companies, which then sell the illegal copies to users.

sounder. A device that converts the electrical pulses back into audible dots and dashes in a telegraph circuit.

spamming. The posting of irrelevant or inappropriate messages to one or more Usenet newsgroups or mailing lists in deliberate or accidental violation of netiquette.

speakerphone. A telephone that has a speaker and microphone for hands-free, two-way communication.

speech engine. A mechanism that translates sounds into words and sentences in a voice recognition system.

stand-alone fax unit. A fax unit that performs independent of something else. It is capable of operating without other programs, libraries, computers, hardware, networks, and so on.

star topology. A topology that connects each computer by a cable segment to a centralized component called a hub.

store and retrieve. A system in which each character is transmitted individually using stop bits and the e-mail message is stored on the server until it is retrieved.

store-and-forward conference. A type of message passing system in which a complete message is received before it is passed on to the next node.

structural tag. A type of hypertext markup language (HTML) tag that identifies a file as an HTML document and provides information about the data in the HTML file.

subscribing. The process of requesting to receive messages posted to an e-mail list or newsgroup.

symmetric tag. A type of hypertext markup language (HTML) tag that consists of two tags rather than one tag only (single-element tag).

synchronous. Voice samples are delivered at the receiving end of the connection at the same rate they are formed at the sending end of the connection.

synchronous transmission. Data is sent in packages of more than one character or byte at a time.

synthesized speech. A type of artificial speech that allows a caller with a telephone or computer with sound card and speakers to access an electronic mail message or word-processing document without having to read it from a computer screen or hard-copy printout.

TCP (transmission control protocol)/IP (Internet protocol). The set of protocols developed by the Department of Defense to connect a number of different networks designed by different vendors into a network of networks—the Internet.

technician. A person who installs and maintains electronic equipment and provides technical user support for electronic mail, teleconferences, and other communication technology areas.

telebanking. The use of the Internet to perform banking transactions, such as transfer of funds and payment of bills.

telecommunications (telecom). Communications via electronic, electromagnetic, or photonic means over a distance.

telecommunications network. The public-switched telephone exchange network.

telecommunications manager. A person who manages the planning, installation, and day-to-day operation of telecommunications systems within an organization. This person may also supervise a staff of technicians.

telecommuting. The practice of working at a location other than the normal workplace and communicating with fellow workers through the phone, typically with a computer and modem.

teleconferencing. Holding a conference among people remote from one another by means of telecommunication devices.

telecourse. The delivery of instruction over a television network or over the Internet.

telegraph. An apparatus, system, or process for communication at a distance by electric transmission over wire.

telegraphy. The use or operation of a telegraph apparatus or system for communication.

telephone. A device that changes speech into electrical signals for transmission to someone distant.

telephone answering. A feature of some voice mail systems in which incoming callers are directed immediately to the called party's voice mailbox, where they hear a personal greeting in the called party's voice and are prompted to leave a detailed message.

telephony. The science of converting sound into electric signals, transmitting it within cables or via radio, and re-converting it back into sound.

teleshopping. The purchase of goods and services over the Internet.

telework center. An alternative to working at home while telecommuting, which is designed with equipment and transmission capabilities that would not be available in a home setting.

telnet. The Internet standard protocol for remote login.

10BaseT network. An ethernet network that has a logical bus topology and a physical star topology, configured like a set of stars connected by a bus. It behaves like a bus, using broadcast technology to send packets along the network, but it is cabled like stars using unshielded twisted pair (UTP) cable.

terminator. A device used at each end of an Ethernet cable to ensure that signals do not bounce back and cause errors.

text file (or ASCII). A file type that represents the basis of character sets used in almost all present-day computers.

text-to-speech system (TTS). A system for converting textual information to synthetic speech output.

thick Ethernet (thicknet). A rigid coaxial cable about 0.5 inch in diameter, typically used as a backbone to connect nodes on a network.

thin client. A client device on a network designed to access a server for all its functions.

thinnet (thin-wire Ethernet). A flexible coaxial cable about 0.25 inch in diameter commonly used for short-distance communication on a network.

time-division multiplexing. A process in which each signal, during transmission, is assigned a fixed time slot in a fixed rotation.

thinnet cable. Thin coaxial cable made of a single copper wire covered with insulation at the center.

token ring topology. A topology that configures computers on a continuous loop on which a token is passed from one computer to the next.

tone-only pager. A small wireless receiver that, when triggered, will make the sound of a tone or beep.

topology. The physical and logical relationship of the nodes on a network.

transaction processing. A voice processing application that consists of a telephone interface with an external computer for access to its database or other information.

transceiver. A device used on thick Ethernet to connect the thinner cable to the backbone cable.

transmission control protocol/Internet protocol (TCP/IP). A set of standards for data transmission and error correction that allows the transfer of data from one Internet-linked computer to another.

transmitter. The device in the telephone handset that converts speech into electrical impulses for transmission.

transport protocols. Rules that provide for communication sessions between computers and ensure that data is able to move reliably between computers.

transportable/car phone. A standard 3-watt mobile cellular phone that can be removed from the car and used by itself with an attached battery pack.

twisted pair cable. Cable made of copper and available as either unshielded or shielded.

two-way radio. A type of wireless communication device used for short messages.

uniform resource locator (URL). A standard way of specifying a location or object on the World Wide Web.

unmoderated. A topical discussion group in which postings are not subject to review before distribution.

unsubscribing. The process of removing oneself from an e-mail list or newsgroup.

Usenet. The leading distributed bulletin board, widely available on UNIX-based computer systems, and linked through the Internet and other computer networks.

value-added network (VAN). A data communications network in which some form of processing of a signal takes place, or information is added by the network.

veronica. A search mechanism when using the gopher protocol.

videoconferencing. A discussion between two or more groups of people who are in different places but can see and hear each other using electronic communications. Pictures and sound are carried by the telecommunication network, and such conferences can take place across the world.

videofax. A type of multifunctional fax unit that combines fax and video capabilities.

videophone. A telephone equipped for transmission of video as well as audio signals so that users can see and hear each other.

virtual terminal. A universal terminal that is designed to communicate with any host computer.

voice mail. Any system for sending, storing, and retrieving audio messages, such as a telephone answering machine.

voice processing. A system that recognizes touch tones from remote telephones. It may also recognize spoken words.

voice recognition system. The identification of spoken words by a machine. The spoken words are digitized (turned into a sequence of numbers) and matched against coded dictionaries in order to identify the words.

voice-to-text system. A system that converts spoken words into text.

WATS telephone service. A discounted toll service provided by long-distance and local phone companies.

Web browser. A program that allows a person to read hypermedia.

whiteboard. The electronic equivalent of chalk and blackboard, but between remote users.

wide area network (WAN). A communications network that covers a wide geographic area; the most widely used WAN is the Internet.

WinZip. A Microsoft Windows utility program distributed by Nico Mak Computing, Inc. that compresses and decompresses files or a group of files using the zip compression format.

wireless communications. A communications system in which there is no physical connection (either copper cable or fiber optics) between sender and receiver; instead, they are connected by radio signals.

wireless telegraphy. The forerunner of the modern radio invented by Guglielmo Marconi which transmitted Morse code over the airwaves.

wizard. An interactive help utility that guides the user through a potentially complex task.

workstation. An individual computer connected to a local area network.

World Wide Web (WWW or Web). A part of the Internet designed to allow easier navigation of the network through the use of graphical user interfaces and hypertext links between different addresses.

worm. A program that propagates itself over a network, reproducing itself.

zipped file. A compressed file that was reduced in size using the zip compression format.

Index